THE ASSOCIATION FOR SCOTTISH LITERARY STUDIES
NUMBER THIRTY-SIX

VOICES FROM THEIR AIN COUNTRIE

THE POEMS OF MARION ANGUS
AND VIOLET JACOB

*

EDITORIAL ADVISER: MARGERY PALMER McCULLOCH

THE ASSOCIATION FOR SCOTTISH LITERARY STUDIES

The Association for Scottish Literary Studies aims to promote the study, teaching and writing of Scottish literature, and to further the study of the languages of Scotland.

To these ends, the ASLS publishes works of Scottish literature (of which this volume is an example); literary criticism and in-depth reviews of Scottish books in *Scottish Studies Review*; short articles, features and news in *ScotLit*; and scholarly studies of language in *Scottish Language*. It also publishes *New Writing Scotland*, an annual anthology of new poetry, drama and short fiction, in Scots, English and Gaelic. ASLS has also prepared a range of teaching materials covering Scottish language and literature for use in schools.

All the above publications are available as a single 'package', in return for an annual subscription. Enquiries should be sent to:

> ASLS, Department of Scottish History, 9 University Gardens, University of Glasgow, Glasgow G12 8QH. Telephone/fax +44 (0)141 330 5309 or visit our website at **www.asls.org.uk**

A list of Annual Volumes published by ASLS can be found at the end of this book.

THE ASSOCIATION FOR SCOTTISH LITERARY STUDIES

VOICES FROM THEIR AIN COUNTRIE

THE POEMS OF MARION ANGUS AND VIOLET JACOB

Edited by

KATHERINE GORDON

GLASGOW

2006

*

First published in Great Britain, 2006
by The Association for Scottish Literary Studies
Department of Scottish History
University of Glasgow
9 University Gardens
Glasgow G12 8QH

www.asls.org.uk

Hardback
ISBN: 0 948877 75 8
ISBN-13: 978 0 948877 75 9

Paperback
ISBN: 0 948877 76 6
ISBN-13: 978 0 948877 76 6

All rights reserved. No part of this book may be reproduced, stored in a retrieval system, or transmitted in any form or means, electronic, mechanical, photocopying, recording or otherwise, without the prior permission of the Association for Scottish Literary Studies.

Introduction, Notes and Glossary © Katherine Gordon, 2006

Poems © the Estates of Marion Angus and Violet Jacob

Marion Angus's poetry reproduced by kind permission of
Alan J. Byatt

Violet Jacob's poetry reproduced by kind permission of
Malcolm U. L. Hutton

A catalogue record for this book
is available from the British Library.

The Association for Scottish Literary Studies acknowledges
support from the Scottish Arts Council towards
the publication of this book.

Typeset by AFS Image Setters Ltd, Glasgow
Printed and bound by Bell & Bain Ltd, Glasgow

Contents

Acknowledgements..................................... xii

Introduction 1

The Poems of Marion Angus 53
   From *The Lilt and Other Verses* (1922)
      By Candle Light.......................... 55
      The Drove Road 56
      Remembrance Day........................ 57
      The Fox's Skin.......................... 58
      The Bridge............................. 59
      Treasure Trove 60
      The Turn of the Day 61
      Moonlight 62
      The Lilt 63
      Loneliness 64
      All Souls' Eve 65
      The Graceless Loon...................... 66

   From *The Tinker's Road and Other Verses* (1924)
      The Tinker's Road....................... 67
      The Seaward Toon....................... 69
      Mary's Song............................ 70
      In Ardelot 71
      George Gordon, Lord Byron 72
      In a Mirror 73
      Annie Honey........................... 74
      Patrick 75
      Penchrise 77
      At Candlemas 79
      Most Sad is Sleep 80
      The Fiddler 81
      The Lane Kirkyaird 82
      Alas! Poor Queen 83
      Think Lang 85
      The Ghost 86

   From *Sun and Candlelight* (1927)
      Courtin'............................... 88

The Wife	89
Waater o' Dye	90
Singin' Waater	91
World's Love	92
The Sang	93
The Prood Lass	94
Barbara	95
Wee Jock Todd	96
Jealousy	97
The Blue Boat	98
The Wild Lass	99
'In the Streets Thereof'	100
Memory	101
The Tree	102
The Silver City	103
The Mourners	104
Withy Wands	105
Cowslips Soon Will Dance	106
The Captive	107
Heritage	108
Change	109
Winter	110
Trees	111
Cotton Grasses	112

From *The Singin' Lass* (1929)

The Wee Sma' Glen	113
The Ghaist	114
Heart-Free	115
Winter-Time	116
Hogmanay	117
Ann Gilchrist	118
Welcome	119
The Eerie Hoose	120
The Can'el	121
Invitation	122
This Woman	123
Jean Cam'bell	124
The Singin' Lass	125
Moonlight Meeting	126
Winds of the World	127
A Traveller	128

Huntlie Hill 129
Arrival 130
Evening Walk 131
Among Thorns 132
Cambus Woods 133
Of Sorrowful Things 134
Dawn and Twilight 135
Anemones 136

From *The Turn of the Day* (1931)
Spring 137
A Breton Woman Sings 138
A Small Thing 139
The Broken Brig 140
The Lissome Leddy 141
The Doors of Sleep 142
The Stranger 143
Joan the Maid 144
Lost Things 145
Curios 146
The Blue Jacket 147

From *Lost Country and Other Verses* (1937)
Lost Country 148
Chance Acquaintance 149
When At Familiar Doors 150
Two is Company 151
Corrichie 152
Naomi 153
The Burden 154
The Widow 155
Desires of Youth 156
Gathering Shells 157
The Plaid 158
A Woman Sings 159
The Green Yaird 160
The Musician 161
In a Little Old Town 162
News 163
Nicht o' Nichts 164
The Spae-Wife 165
New Year's Morning 166

Martha's House 167
Foxgloves and Snow 168
Memory's Trick........................... 169
Once Long Ago 170
The Faithful Heart........................ 171
Links o' Lunan........................... 172
At Parting 173
November in Edinburgh 174
On a Birthday 175

Uncollected Poems
Unseen................................... 176
Wizardry................................. 177
The Kiss................................. 178

Uncertain Provenance
The Dove................................. 179
After the Storm........................... 180

The Poems of Violet Jacob 181
From *Verses* (1905)
Half-Way................................. 183
The Shadow............................... 184
An Immortelle............................ 185
Beyond the Walls 186
'Come On, Come Up, Ye Rovers'............ 187
Airlie Kirk................................ 188
In Lower Egypt 189
The Call.................................. 191
The Valley of the Kings................... 192
The Lowland Ploughman................... 194
from Poems of India
   II: Night in the Plains.................... 195
   III: The Resting-Place 196
   IV: Evening in the Opium Fields........... 197
   V: 'God is Great'....................... 197
   VII: Cherry-Blossom at Dagshai............ 199
   IX: The Distant Temple 200

From *Songs of Angus* (1915)
Tam i' the Kirk 201
The Howe o' the Mearns................... 202
The Lang Road 204

The Beadle o' Drumlee	206
The Water-Hen	207
The Heid Horseman	208
The Gean-Trees	210
The Tod	211
The Blind Shepherd	212
The Doo'cot Up the Braes	213
Logie Kirk	215
The Philosophy of the Ditch	216
The Lost Licht	217
The Lad i' the Mune	220
The Gowk	221
The Jacobite Lass	222
Maggie	223
The Whustlin' Lad	224
Craigo Woods	225
The Wild Geese	226

From *More Songs of Angus and Others* (1918)

To A. H. J.	227
Jock, to the First Army	228
The Field by the Lirk o' the Hill	229
Montrose	230
The Road to Marykirk	231
The Brig	232
The Kirk Beside the Sands	233
Glory	234
The Shepherd to His Love	235
A Change o' Deils	236
The Last o' the Tinkler	237
Fringford Brook	238
Prison	240
Presage	241
The Bird in the Valley	242
Back to the Land	243
The Scarlet Lilies	244
Frostbound	246
'The Happy Warrior'	247

From *Bonnie Joann and Other Poems* (1921)

Bonnie Joann	248
The Wind Frae the Baltic	249

The Tramp to the Tattie-Dulie	250
Hallowe'en	252
The Daft Bird	253
'Kirrie'	254
The End O't	255
The Kelpie	256
Baltic Street	258
Bailie Bruce	260
Charlewayn	262
The Gangerel	264
The Tinkler's Baloo	266
The Banks o' the Esk	267
Inverquharity	268
Faur-Ye-Weel	270
The Shadows	272
A Winter Phantasy	273

From *Two New Poems* (1924)

Rohallion	274

From *The Northern Lights and Other Poems* (1927)

The Northern Lichts	275
The Neep-Fields By the Sea	276
The Rowan	277
The Licht Nichts	278
The Jaud	279
The Deil	281
Geordie's Lament	283
The Helpmate	285
Steenhive	286
The Guidwife Speaks	287
The Last Ane	288
Donald Maclane	289
The Cross-Roads	290

From *The Scottish Poems of Violet Jacob* (1944)

The Warld	291
The Poor Suitor	292
The Neebour	293
The Poacher to Orion	294
The Baltic	295
Cairneyside	296

Uncollected Poems
    The Barley 297
    Bindweed 298

Notes for Individual Poems 299

Glossary 372

Bibliography 381

Copyright Acknowledgements 400

Acknowledgements

This volume would not be possible without the efforts of many dedicated people:

Carol Anderson, Margaret Elphinstone, Duncan Jones, Margery Palmer McCulloch, Margaret Renton, Robin Smith, and the board and members of ASLS; Tessa Ransford; Isla Robertson from the National Trust for Scotland; Fiona Scharlau from Angus Archives; my colleagues at St Louis Community College at Florissant Valley; Joyce Dietz, Kirsteen McCue, and other members of the Department of Scottish Literature at the University of Glasgow; the late Nancy Cant; and helpful staff at the following libraries: the National Library of Scotland, the National Archives of Scotland, the British Library, Aberdeen University Special Collections, the University of Stirling Special Collections, the University of Glasgow Library, the University of Edinburgh Library, the Mitchell Library, Montrose Public Library, Arbroath Public Library, Central Library in St Louis, Missouri, the University of Missouri – St Louis Library, and the St Louis Community College libraries.

I am grateful to Alan J. Byatt and Malcolm U. L. Hutton for their support of the project, to Helen Lloyd and Nick Thompson for their research help; to friends and family on both sides of the water for their support, and, most of all, to Tim, for all things.

Dedication

For Margaret Schutz Gordon and Felicity Elphinstone Back, with love.

Introduction

In 1906, an anonymous journalist in the *Glasgow Herald* lamented that 'it is becoming ridiculously evident that the history of Scotland has yet to be written'. Citing the absence of literature depicting the lives of Scottish people, the anonymous writer decries Scotland as a literary 'terra incognita'.[1] One hundred years later, it is clear that Scotland is no longer a 'terra incognita'; in recent times, the expansion of the field of Scottish literary studies has made it possible for contemporary scholars to consider in greater depth the work of Scottish writers of previous centuries and to trace the development of Scottish literature into the present day. Two writers who have benefited from this renewed interest are Marion Angus (1865–1946) and Violet Jacob (1863–1946). Both were already writing poetry in Scots when Hugh MacDiarmid initiated the Scottish Renaissance movement in the early 1920s, and both contributed much to the interwar literary revival. For Angus and Jacob, using Scots was not an overtly political statement as it was for MacDiarmid. Both considered Scots not as a literary or political tool, but as a modern linguistic medium which also drew on a rich Scottish poetry tradition. Their poems of place in particular have given voice to the spirit and tenacity of the North-East of Scotland, where both had roots. Until now, however, their poetry has been difficult to obtain apart from the few poems reprinted in anthologies. In Jacob's case, only her Scots-language poems were collected in the 1944 volume *The Scottish Poems of Violet Jacob*; Angus's volume, *Selected Poems of Marion Angus* (1950), was compiled after her death and does not give a broad enough view of her work. Both of these collections, as well as the earlier individual collections of their poetry, are now out of print.

The purpose of this new edited collection is to make available to students and interested general readers a more extensive selection of the poetry of Marion Angus and Violet Jacob. The volume contains poetry from across the span of each poet's career, including work from six books of poetry by Angus and seven books by Jacob. In addition, the volume reproduces poems previously available only in periodicals. The contents are organised chronologically in the order of their publication to allow readers to follow the development of each poet's writing through time. The volume therefore is designed to introduce readers to the breadth of each poet's work; those readers already familiar with Angus and Jacob's poetry can glean a deeper understanding of individual poems in the context of others in the writer's body of work.

The volume also contains an overview of each poet's life, a short synopsis of major themes in each writer's work, and notes on individual poems. These notes, placed at the end of the edition, offer insights into the poems' production and reception. The notes also include references from the poets' letters or other writings which may shed light upon a given poem's content. When necessary, they also provide information about references to folk culture made in individual poems. The volume is not intended as a variorum; where possible, however, the notes include original publication information and earlier versions of poems are reproduced if they differ significantly from the version published in this volume. A glossary of Scots-language words used in the poems appears at the end of the book. For those wishing to pursue the writers' work more extensively, a bibliography of recommended resources is also included.

Angus and Jacob shared similar birth and death dates; both spent considerable parts of their lives in the North-East of Scotland; both wrote in literary Scots, sometimes using vocabulary and idiom specific to the North-East; and both shared a passionate interest in Scottish literature. Each published poems in Hugh MacDiarmid's literary journals and both had work appear under the imprint of Porpoise Press (Angus published several books with Porpoise Press; Jacob's *Two New Poems* was part of their broadsheet series). They certainly were aware of each other's work, although they did not meet in person until fairly late in life. Angus, in particular, makes reference to Jacob's work in some of her commentary on Scottish literature.[2] It is foolish to assume, however, that because Angus and Jacob share so many characteristics they are indistinguishable from each other. Certainly, some commentators have found it expedient to discuss their work together because they have considered them to be 'minor' poets with similar interests.

However, a consideration of their *individual* poetic careers as well as their biographies makes clear their distinctive identities. Consequently, in this volume their poetry and biographical portraits are presented individually so that readers may follow each writer's progress; the two introductory sections may suggest connections between the writers but allow each to stand independently of the other.

Because neither poet is alive to recommend the definitive version of each poem, the poems appearing in this volume, unless otherwise noted, are reproduced in the same form as they appeared in book format. In the case of a small number of Angus's poems identified in the notes, the earliest book publication is used as Angus, in her tendency to rework poems, occasionally over-revised poems. When the version appearing in this volume differs radically from another published version of the poem, the notes include excerpts from the alternate version for readers to consider. Epigraphs and author's original commentaries upon the text are included in the notes. The spelling has not been standardised; readers can trace the changes in the often phonetic rendering of words into literary Scots made by each poet throughout her career.

2006 is the sixtieth anniversary of the deaths of both Marion Angus and Violet Jacob. It is a good time to celebrate and reassess the work of two poets who have made important contributions to Scotland's rich literary tradition. Their depictions of their beloved North-East, in particular, echo with the voices from their 'ain countrie'.

Marion Angus (1865–1946)

Writing to Alexander Keith about his 1940 anthology *Songs of the North-East*, Marion Angus thanks him for including her poetry and concludes: 'I would rather have a humble place among the poets of the Nor' East than a seat with the Mighty'. Angus here is not being coy; she remained throughout her life committed to the landscape, literature and people of the North-East of Scotland. Her 'humble place' in Scottish poetry, however, has until recently manifested itself as more of an absence than a presence in Scottish letters; although her work has appeared in anthologies

– most recently in Dorothy McMillan and Michel Byrne's *Modern Scottish Women Poets* (2003) – editions of her books have been out of print for years; second-hand copies of her work are even more difficult to find than Violet Jacob's. The only photograph of her normally reproduced in journals is the one taken by Helen Cruickshank when Angus was advanced in years and still recovering from a stroke. In this image, she looks as 'delicate' and unearthly as Maurice Lindsay's introduction to her posthumous *Selected Poems of Marion Angus* implies she was. Moreover, her work, reproduced in small selections and often interpreted only in the context of traditional Scottish ballads, loses a great deal of its dramatic strangeness; those who have read only 'Mary's Song' or 'Alas! Poor Queen' consequently miss her modernist fascination with time and her use of ambiguously gendered voices. In small excerpts, Angus can appear as 'gnomic' and old-fashioned as Cruickshank once described her.[3]

Descriptions of Angus by those who knew her best, however, give a more comprehensive portrait. Nan Shepherd, a fellow North-East writer and friend, produced some of the most illuminating passages about Angus's work and life available. In a 1970 article, she recalls Angus's 'wild gipsy side'.[4] Shepherd indicates that 'she could do disconcerting things' to undercut pomposity or mean-spiritedness in others; she observes that even into her last decade, Angus played 'small, solemn, practical jokes, schoolboy jokes, but much more intelligent. Her jokes had point – they pricked. They pricked where she wanted them to prick – in the quick of dullness and pretentiousness and stupidity'. Angus herself did not mince words when faced with pomposity. In one letter she admits to a friend:

> There are all sorts of people and one type is as precious as another[.] I don't know that I care particularly for what is usually called 'cultivated people'. I found a more delicate and refined sympathy in my charwoman in Aberdeen than I did in any of my educated acquaintances.[5]

Her impatience with self-important 'cultivated people' reappears in many of her letters and often in her short fiction; in a few peppery letters she takes acquaintances to task for false pretensions in a sharp, but not unkind manner.

In another article, Nan Shepherd gives a sense of Angus in her later years. She writes: 'In old age [Angus] did not sit back, serene, with passion spent and desire quieted in her. She was not serene. She still desired'. Later, she adds: 'I have never known anyone so hungry for vicarious experience. She wanted to know all that one did, and saw, all the people one met, the odd things one encountered'.[6] Other accounts of Angus by friends and acquaintances give a similar sense of her unconventional nature. One friend recollected that she disregarded worries about her 'old' body to go bathing when she was in her sixties; another Arbroath resident remembered her as the first woman in town to ride a bicycle and to smoke (although another resident flatly denied the former).[7] A compelling description of her by a long-time friend appeared in the *Arbroath Guide* after her death:

> She was nothing if not original. I feel pretty sure she enjoying shocking correct and conventional people (at times she could say fairly devastating things), but her friends enjoyed her extravaganzas and loved her for them, because they knew that, even when her wit was mordant, she had a capacious and most generous heart [...] She had a keen intellect, and many varied gifts, but she was much more than a merely talented woman. She was a great soul.[8]

A profoundly different image of her life emerges from these vignettes. Her 'mordant' wit and iconoclastic tendencies are a surprising contrast to the image Lindsay offers of her as a mere 'sensitive appreciator' who is 'catapulted' into verse by an unknown stimulus. While these revelations do not answer many of the questions asked by those interested in her work – what kinds of poetry did she write before she published *The Lilt*? what happened to her letters and books not preserved in archives today? – they do offer some insight into the personal influences behind her often enigmatic verse. They also drive home the point that she was hardly the 'home-made Marion' Alan Bold has called her. As she writes to a friend in 1931: 'It's a queer world but you will find someone to laugh at and someone to weep with at every turn.'[9]

Thanks to Nan Shepherd and, more recently, to the work

of a small number of contemporary scholars, one now can acquire a better sense of Angus's life and work.[10] She was born Marion Emily Angus in Sunderland, England, in 1865, the eldest daughter in a family of eight that included her parents Henry and Mary-Jessie (née Watson) and siblings Henry (b.1864), Annie Katharine (b.1869), William Watson (b.1870), Ethel Mary (b.1871) and Amy Margaret (b.1872).[11] They moved to Arbroath when she was eleven. There, she was active in a variety of community groups including the Erskine United Presbyterian Church Young Women's Guild (of which she was president at least once). Known as 'Minnie', she grew up in a household well-acquainted with books. (Her father was a member of the Arbroath Literary Club, among other organisations; this may have given his daughter some exposure to new writers and ideas in writing at a young age, although the club did not admit women as members.) A 1935 article on Angus observes that 'apart from occasional visits to the Continent, her time was occupied chiefly with family and domestic affairs'.[12] She read widely, as her early writing reveals. In a speech given as part of her work for the Scottish Association for the Speaking of Verse, she describes reading 'one poem which, when I was a child, made my flesh creep and filled me with a tearful pity'. The poem, 'The Brownie of Blednoch' by the nineteenth-century Scottish writer William Nicholson, suggests that the interest in the supernatural which informs her work began early in her life.[13]

Unlike her brothers (in particular Henry, who became a doctor), Angus did not continue her education beyond secondary school, although she did well enough in school to win prizes for her writing. As Catriona Burness notes, higher education for women in nineteenth-century Scotland was deemed unnecessary;[14] as the eldest daughter of the manse, Angus would have had ample filial duties. Furthermore, even for women in the generation after her, equal access to education was rare. Margery Palmer McCulloch observes that

> a society organised on patriarchal principles has no means whereby young women can enter into adulthood alongside their brothers as *human beings*; they are instead categorised and constricted by biological

function and by the perception of marriage as their essential goal.[15]

By not marrying or having children, Angus did not fulfil either 'goal'; she did not have the freedom to travel widely, as other members of her family did. She *did* travel – she records one trip to Geneva in 1899, and perhaps managed to reach Algeria, where her father preached in the mid-1880s. If she herself did not travel far, close relatives who did exposed her to a wider world beyond Scotland. Like many Scots, she had relatives, in her case her mother's brothers William and John Watson, who lived in India (John Watson died in the Indian Mutiny before Angus's birth but she recalls visiting William once he had moved back to Scotland). Her brother Henry, too, stayed in the farthest reaches of the British Empire: New Zealand, where he lived for a few years before returning to Britain.[16] As Nan Shepherd remarks, 'her experience is not narrow [...] She has the power – and what is that but creation? – to experience the things that did not happen to her. There is here a consummation of a very rare order'.[17]

While still a young woman, Angus began publishing her writing in Arbroath. Her earliest publications are probably stories which first appeared in 1878 in a magazine started by her brother Henry and his friend William Marwick. Tantalisingly described as 'new and wonderfully written stories', the work is now (as far as is known) no longer extant. William Marwick was also the founder of the Ruskin Reading Guild in Arbroath but whether Angus had involvement with this particular group is unclear.[18] Her first extant publications are the result of newspaper work for the *Arbroath Guide*: a column written under the *nom de plume* Arthur Ogilvie and an accompanying 'journal' written in the voice of a young English woman named Christabel Massingberd who later marries Arthur Ogilvie. Both the column and the journal reveal themes present later in her poetry: an interest in human psychology, a fascination with time, and a delight in the landscape of the North-East. Regrettably she did not pursue fiction as consistently as Jacob did. Stories appear in *Pearson's Magazine*, the *Scots Observer* and other journals, but were not collected during her lifetime. The insightful, often feminist prose she produced in the *fin de siècle* in particular is sharply observant. Writing about tourists in Switzerland, for example, she describes 'Americans being hurried through Europe by their wives and daughters' and laughs at 'the usual boarding-school of young English ladies making an educational tour up the lake, their pleasure sadly spoilt by their being compelled even to exclaim in French'. In *Christabel's Diary* (1899) her eponymous heroine tells her husband that there is 'one lesson no man ever learnt yet, that a woman does not of necessity enjoy all that she endures with patience, nor welcome every ill she tolerates'. In general, her writing reveals a broad knowledge of literature in English and art, and an appreciation of Oscar Wilde's work.[19]

After her father died in 1902, Angus moved with her mother and sister Ethel to Cults, Aberdeen, where they ran a small private school. Their mother died in 1914; both parents are buried in the Western Cemetery in Arbroath. Angus and her sister gave up the school and later volunteered in World War One in various capacities: Ethel worked as a Voluntary Aid Detachment (VAD) nurse in Calais and Angus worked in the dining hall at the base at Stobbs. Their nephew W. S. Angus recalls that Angus was 'much exhausted by this work, with its long hours and harsh conditions, but she spoke after it with the greatest respect and admiration for the ordinary private soldiers, and their simple good sense and kindliness'. Angus's extant letters in archives across Scotland make little or no mention of these aspects of her life; as one of her publishers reveals, 'she knew nothing of self-advertisement'.[20] This tendency makes tracking down information about her life rather difficult. It is interesting, however, that one of her few poems that refers to a discernible historical event discusses Remembrance Day, which was first observed after World War One ended. Titled 'Remembrance Day', it is one of Angus's few war poems; unlike Jacob, who produced nearly an entire volume of war poetry during World War One, Angus did not dwell upon the conflict although she would have had ample opportunity to hear of soldiers' hardships.

After the war, Angus and her sister moved first to Peebles, where their uncle had been a minister, but because they did not consider it an 'abiding city', as their nephew put it, they moved back north to Aberdeen in the early

1920s. There they bought Zoar, the 'old-fashioned cottage' that Helen Cruickshank describes in Octobiography. Angus refers to Zoar as 'a house of happiness' located 'just on the edge of town'.[21] The cottage still stands; one can imagine Angus writing in the spare upstairs rooms or in the dark living room by the hearth. This house – named after the place of refuge occupied by Lot and his daughters after they fled Sodom – is where Angus lived when she wrote her finest poems. During her time there, she published *The Lilt and Other Verses* (1922), *The Tinker's Road and Other Verses* (1924), *Sun and Candlelight* (1927), and *The Singin' Lass* (1929).

One critic notes that 'after the war' Angus 'collected and published the verses she had composed "somewhat aimlessly" over a number of years'. This statement, presumably referring to Angus herself (although the source of the quotation is not identified), fails to acknowledge her abiding interest in poetry by suggesting that her work is the result of a distracted or haphazard approach to writing. Angus's letters give a different view. In a 1930 letter, she admits to a friend: 'my *heart* is always in my verse such as they are. And not in prose'.[22] This is certainly clear when one reads her letters and short essays on poetry. As with Jacob's work, Angus's poetry appeared in Hugh MacDiarmid's *Scottish Chapbook*; she also published poems in newspapers and periodicals such as the *Glasgow Herald*, *Scots Observer* and the *Modern Scot*. Unlike Jacob, however, Angus was adamant about publishing her work in journals and publishers based in Scotland, noting: 'I am no believer in this craze for English publishing houses at all costs'.[23]

Angus's poetry from the 1920s and early 1930s is perhaps her most accomplished writing. The understated lyricism of *The Lilt and Other Verses* becomes, by the late 1920s, distinctly stronger and more emotionally potent in *Sun and Candlelight* and *The Singin' Lass*. Angus revised incessantly, as one can see from earlier drafts of poems published in periodicals, and it appears that the relatively stable existence she lived during this period allowed her the time and space to produce powerful poems such as 'Barbara', 'Waater o' Dye', and 'The Can'el'. During the early 1930s, however, Angus's sister Ethel fell ill and her lingering illness, perhaps as a result of a traumatic wartime experience, forced Angus to sell the house and disperse their possessions. Ethel never recovered from her breakdown and died in 1936.[24] From 1931 onwards, Angus rented rooms (notably in Greenock, near her sister Amy) or stayed in friends' houses; she often stayed at Inchdowrie in Glen Clova, the home of her childhood friend Robert Corstorphine. She did not have a permanent address again thereafter. She found her 'lost and homeless state' difficult, but she managed to write nevertheless. As she explained to a friend in the 1930s, 'I sometimes wonder if people were meant to feel things so deeply, if sensibility to other's suffering is not always desirable. But [...] God keeps us'. During her life she was, as one editor acknowledged, 'very critical of her creative work'; Nan Shepherd mentions that Angus did not even have copies of her own books (although this may have had to do with her peripatetic existence after selling Zoar). Despite this, and despite suffering when her grief for her sister seemed to extinguish her ability to write poetry, she continued to write all her life. Her last book of poetry, *Lost Country and Other Verses* (1937), is perhaps not as accomplished as her two previous volumes, but it still contains haunting lyrics such as 'A Woman Sings' and 'Nicht o' Nichts'.[25]

Angus's work was popular during her lifetime, although her literary output is relatively slim. Like Jacob, she writes in several different genres, including travel writing (*Round About Geneva*), fiction (*Christabel's Diary*), family history (*Sheriff Watson of Aberdeen: The Story of His Life, and His Work for the Young*, about her maternal grandfather), essays and poetry. She too published her poetry in a variety of journals and magazines. She also wrote at least one play – for the 'Children's Hour Scott Centenary'.[26] Nevertheless, her dominant interest remained poetry; she extended her involvement with poetry into other spheres through her work with PEN (of which she was a founding member of the Aberdeen chapter) and other organisations. In 1931, at the behest of Naomi Mitchison and Helen Cruickshank, she met the young W. H. Auden; Helen Cruickshank recalls Angus wrote to her: 'is this the new poetry? It sounds like a voice from another planet'. Although Angus may have found poetry like Auden's baffling, her interest in 'new poetry' did not fade with age or infirmity.[27] Her letters from the 1930s demonstrate her keen interest in new literature – she frequently wrote to fellow writers like Neil Gunn, William Soutar and Nan Shepherd to praise them for new work; she similarly comments upon what contemporary books she was reading in notes to friends.

In addition to her work with PEN, she also was an active member of the Scottish Association for the Speaking of Verse, serving as a member of the General Council in the 1930s.[28] As her correspondence reveals, she gave talks on poetry, often broadcasting them for the BBC during the late 1920s and early 1930s; these topics spanned from eighteenth-century women poets to the 'historic romance of Scottish towns'. In a contemporaneous letter, she explains: 'When I am speaking on Scottish Poetry I am carried away by the beauty of it and the attempt to find if other people will find lovely what I find lovely'. Her nephew W. S. Angus recalled her broadcasts fondly, urging others to preserve them. He notes: 'If she had not had a good broadcasting voice, and a sense of what was suitable for broadcasting, her reputation would have been less wide, and perhaps less well considered.' He continues: '[These] gave her a real satisfaction, and gave pleasure to many who read little that she wrote.'[29]

At the end of her life, Angus moved back to the North-East to the place where she spent her youth. Writing to Helen Cruickshank at this time, Angus remarks: 'I am now very frail and indeed there is little of the original ego left', adding, 'your literary life is of great interest. I have to go to live in Arbroath soon with a kindly competent maid and shall be always glad to hear of or from you.' Angus, like Jacob, died in 1946; her ashes were scattered on Elliot Links outside Arbroath by her friend W. S. Matthew and her nephew W. S. Angus.[30] According to one source, W. S. Matthew had teased Angus that she would 'take [the ashes] there in the basket of her bicycle' and Angus replied: 'Good. That's a promise'. Silvie Taylor notes that 'her ashes were taken by taxi', prompting Matthew to quip: 'Miss Angus would have preferred the bicycle basket'. Clearly, she was, in the words of Nan Shepherd, 'impish as well as elfin [...] Whiles, one would think, she was inhabited by the very Mischief'.[31]

In a talk she gave for the Scottish Association for the

Speaking of Verse at the height of her writing powers, Angus reflected upon the state of contemporary poetry and concluded:

> I myself would like to be the one (unfortunately I am not) to write a great poem on the spirit of place, producing something born of myself and of the place, which would be neither the one nor the other, but something very strange and beautiful. I should like to write of fairies, not the identical fairies of the old days, but the elusive glamour of the universe; and, above all, I would fain give voice to Scotland's great adventure of the soul. I never shall; some one may, perhaps.[32]

Angus was too modest. Looking over the work she produced during her life, one can find ample proof of 'strange and beautiful' poetry that illuminated the 'elusive glamour of the universe'; her writing in many ways provides glimpses of the timeless 'great adventure of the soul'.

Technique and Themes in Angus's Poetry

One of Angus's primary interests, as her letters and poetry reveal, was lyric poetry. According to Nan Shepherd, when Angus was asked to name some of the best Scottish poems, she 'chose exclusively lyrics, and lyrics where the haunted and yearning note predominates: "The Flowers o' the Forest", "Aye Waukin' O'", "Proud Maisie", "Waly, Waly", "Gone were but the Winter Cauld", "O Wert Thou in the Cauld Blast".' Nan Shepherd is quick to note 'how wide and varied' Angus's reading habits were, but adds: 'it would seem that for her the heart of the mystery lay in pure lyric'. Angus confirms this suspicion in a letter she wrote critiquing the work of another poet whose verse she felt lacked 'rhymes and music'; she adds with some modesty: 'I may be too fastidious as regards the lilt and croon of a poem'.[33]

Angus's interest in lyric poetry – and a related fascination with the ballads – informs her work at the most essential level. As Leslie W. Wheeler has remarked: 'we can recognise all the hallmarks of the ballad in her work: the simplicity of the form opening up a complex world – a world where man and woman are at the mercy of incomprehensible forces'.[34] Angus's poem 'Singin' Waater' from *Sun and Candlelight* gives one a good sense of her dual interests in lyric poetry and the Scottish ballad tradition and her fascination with depictions of raw, often mysterious emotional states. In the poem, the speaker attempts to 'mak' her 'hert clean' of past sins in the purifying water of a stream. Angus alternates lines of four and three stressed syllables in the poem to capture the inexorable movement of the 'singin' waater' over the speaker's body; she uses assonance, particularly on short vowel sounds, to create a soft, musical quality in the poem. In the first stanza alone, for example, one finds the repeated short *i* sound in 'singin'', 'rin', 'mist', 'siller', 'kist', 'smellin'', 'till', 'bricht', 'linen' and 'licht'. This quiet lyricism underscores the turbulence of the speaker's 'tanglet' emotions. In the poem Angus also integrates balladic language to heighten the poem's eerie subtext. The poem alludes to several ballads, including 'Sir Patrick Spens' in which the women mourning for their drowned lovers 'tore their hair, / a' for the sake of their true loves'. The poem recalls 'Edom of Gordon', too, in which Edom, in remorse, turns a woman he has killed 'owr and owr again / O gin hir face was wan'.[35] The unspecified cause of the woman's grief in 'Singin' Waater' similarly echoes the unsettling, inexplicable narrative of many romantic relationships in the ballads. 'Singin' Waater' is just one example of many poems throughout Angus's work that blend an interest in lyric with a lifelong involvement with the ballads.

Time

Reading through her poetry, one can trace her enduring interest in depicting facets of the individual's experience with time, place, faith and love. These four themes are explored in brief here and related resources are included in the bibliography for those interested in pursuing individual themes more extensively.

It is helpful to begin by considering her interest in time; poems grappling with age and the passage of time recur in her poetry. 'Hogmanay', 'At Candlemas', 'Once Long Ago' and others explore what can be called *dual time narratives* in which the present moment of the poem splits into two: one in which the self moves forward in time and another in which a moment in time is forever frozen, allowing the speakers to witness younger or older versions of themselves. By splitting the poem into more than one moment in time, Angus explores how age affects the speaker's perception of herself and the world around her. Dorothy McMillan argues that Angus's use of 'shifts in person and tense' in her poetry can 'confuse present and past' and 'fragment experience'.[36] Many of her poems explore the fragmented psyche in ways that suggest a shared bond with other proto-modernist and modernist poets of the time.

While Angus did not formally codify her theories about time, she does discuss her understanding of time in her letters and essays. In a letter to Nan Shepherd, she gives an insight into how she perceives time. She writes:

> I am engrossed by two other books at present. *An Experiment with Time* and *The New Immortality* by J. W. Dunne. I took a while to grasp the theory and even yet have only got it partially clear; yet it, I mean the idea, seems to have got an almost uncanny grasp on my mind and along with this a queer instinctive feeling that half consciously I knew all this in a vague way before.[37]

Angus's fascination with J. W. Dunne's theories post-date almost all her books; her belief that 'I knew all this in a vague way before', however, suggests that although she did not read his work until the late 1930s, her poetry shares some degree of correspondence with his principles. In *An Experiment with Time* (1927) and *The New Immortality* (1938), J. W. Dunne 'elaborated a whole theory of the existence of a fourth dimension, free from the ordinary passage of time'. His works were tremendously popular; *An Experiment with Time* 'remain[ed] in print almost sixty years after its first publication'. Angus was not the only writer who found J. W. Dunne's work interesting. Other contemporaneous writers in Scotland and beyond – ranging from Lewis Grassic Gibbon and Neil Gunn to Jorge Luis Borges – responded to his theories on time.[38] Angus's engagement with his work reflects a wider societal interest in his work at the time; significantly, it encourages one to read her poetry with reference to contemporaneous philosophical works on time – not in a prescriptive way, but as an introit into her complex portrayal of what I refer to elsewhere as the self-in-time.[39]

In many poems, Angus presents moments in which the speaker meets an earlier version of herself, often at a moment of crisis. The two contrasting selves found in poems such as 'At Candlemas', 'Graceless Loon', 'The Fox's Skin' and 'Huntlie Hill', among others, witness the evidence of time and change in their lives against a static, continually looping moment of time preserved in memory. The shock of recognising that change is inevitable is balanced by the constant reminder that time is cyclical in nature; as the seasons progress in order and then return to their starting point, so too do the speakers in many of Angus's poems move through time only to discover that time is both non-linear and cyclical. In 'The Fox's Skin', for example, she presents a spectral Pict who watches a young girl, noting 'a thoosand years o' clood and flame, / an' a'thing's the same an' aye the same'. In poems such as 'At Candlemas', the speaker meets a younger version of herself and, for a brief moment, forgets which she is: the 'lassie' or the 'auld witch'. The ambiguity of the present moment in poems such as these is interesting for it both dramatises the way memory allows one to replay past events and it expresses the human desire to control the passage of time.

Place

As in Jacob's poetry, a sense of place is vital to Angus's work. Unlike Jacob's, however, her poems do not focus primarily upon the lives of the exile far from home; instead, her speakers often speak from a familiar landscape but are isolated from others around them by their sorrow, loneliness or haunting memories. She contends that 'poetry of dear places, individual places' contains within it the lyric 'yearning for the unobtainable'; certainly, one finds this to be the case in poems such as 'Penchrise', 'Memory' and 'The Wee Sma' Glen'. In Angus's poems, the landscape portrayed is often in the North-East of Scotland. As Nan Shepherd notes: 'the landscape [in Angus's work] is nor'-

eastern, and so is the weather'.[40] A survey of Angus's poetry uncovers many North-East place references in her work: Hill of Fare, Castleton, Dye, the braes of Dee, Huntlie Hill, Cambus Woods, Tarland and others. One commentator claims: 'Angus glens and Angus woods and Angus roads' are 'the inspiration of Marion Angus, and the Scots in which she expresses herself is Angus Scots'. Nan Shepherd concurs, observing that 'the north names make singing tunes in her verse – Culblean and Cambus; Tarland and Inverey; the Water o' Dye and the Corby Burn and the Braid Hill o' Fare. She had a strong feeling for the potency in names'. Angus's letters also make frequent reference to beloved places in the North-East. Writing to Nan Shepherd after a long illness, she remarks: 'I have been housebound so long that I have forgotten the "feel" of sun and wind and "werena my hairt licht I wad dee" for longing for the old places'. Certainly, having spent part of her childhood tramping in the hills of Angus, she had an acute understanding of the places she describes in her poetry.[41]

In Angus's poetry, landscape is both associated with real places – Glen Doll, Tarland, Penchrise, Aberdeen – and a psychological landscape existing within the speaker's mind. Charles Graves, her publisher at Porpoise Press, recognises that the 'landscape behind her poetry' is 'essentially Scottish', but argues that the places referred to in her work – often imbued with supernatural presences – are 'an attitude of mind'. Another reviewer considers that the 'most idiosyncratic quality' of Angus's poetry is 'her gift of blending the real and the unreal' so that some of her poems are able to 'awaken in the reader that feeling of apprehensive expectancy which is sometimes experienced when one is alone in a solitary place'.[42] Janet Caird adds:

> The flowers, trees, burns are not in her verse for their own sake, as is often the case in the verse of, say, Violet Jacob. They are used more like pigment, to express, to enhance, a mood, an atmosphere. Her lily-flowers, roses, marigolds are not rooted in common earth, any more than the thorn-trees that loom in so many of her poems.[43]

Elements of the natural world in Angus's poems thus stand in for psychological states. Poems such as 'The Seaward

Toon' have both a real-world correlate (in the case of 'The Seaward Toon', probably Arbroath) and depict a psychologised place; the poem's actual geography is layered over with the internal, symbol-rich landscape of the speaker's mind. In 'Cambus Woods', the speaker calls upon a dead friend to return to the beloved woods, but readers understand that the woods the speaker invokes exist within memory. Similarly, in 'The Eerie Hoose', the 'hoose / wi' chaumers braid and blue' both suggests an actual location while pointing dramatically to itself as a mental construct.[44] 'Lost Country', one of her late poems, both describes a real place and, more evocatively, a region constructed out of memory and lost landscapes.

Angus's interest in the internalisation of space manifests itself in her letters and essays as well as in her poetry. In a 1930 essay she describes how one may 'read' the landscape in terms of the literary events that have occurred there; she describes visiting the home of Scottish writer George MacDonald and reflects upon how his presence is stamped indelibly upon the place.[45] For her, the haunting is twofold: the speaker is surrounded by the spectral presence of events or people in the landscape; the author herself marks the landscape with her words. Nan Shepherd confirms this years after Angus's essay on landscape by suggesting that Angus's 'landscape is recognisibly [sic] our own, but [it] is suffused with her presence'. Similarly, one reviewer suggests that even in her last poems, she 'calls up figures of the past [...] as if they were projections of her personality'. Visiting Arbroath now one can see in its streets the 'crooked' and 'cranky' town and its surroundings she lovingly described in her writing.[46]

Faith

Angus's poetry also exhibits an interest in the Christian faith so strongly associated with her family. Coming from a 'line of seceding ministers in the North East', as she once described herself, Angus was immersed in biblical language from childhood.[47] This is evident in many of her poems such as 'Naomi' and 'Martha's House' that discuss Christian figures; often, she considers the stories and lives of biblical women. The biblical figures in her poetry inhabit thoroughly Scottish landscapes and domestic interiors; even in a poem such as 'Arrival', the visitation of 'One' occurs not in a biblical landscape but in the speaker's simple 'darkened house'.

Angus's interest in faith in her poetry is not straightforward, however. Often, her poetry blends Christian references with pre-Christian supernatural elements. This practice may stem from her interest in ballads and folk tales, many of which include references to Christian and pre-Christian cosmologies. Nan Shepherd reveals that 'one of [Angus's] own favourite books was *Primitive Beliefs in the North-East of Scotland*'. This book, a survey of folk practices, gives one a sense of the intermingling of Christian and pre-Christian beliefs in North-Eastern folk culture; it is particularly interesting to read it in conjunction with Angus's poetry for one can find resonances between it and her work.[48] Colin Milton gives another reason for the mixture of Christian and pre-Christian references in her poetry. In his *Oxford Dictionary of National Biography* entry on Angus, he contends that she 'synthesises elements of the folk tradition with powerfully suggestive religious images to convey kinds of experience beyond the rational and explicable'. In his helpful overview of her work, he indicates that poems such as 'The Seaward Toon' use this blend of references to articulate experiences and emotions otherwise inexpressible.

Are the Christian references in Angus's poetry made to express the inexplicable, as Colin Milton suggests? Or is it possible to see her poetry as exploring the mysteries of Christian belief outwith the confines of doctrine? She certainly was aware of religious tensions in her work. In a 1929 letter, she admits: 'I am sometimes told my poetry is [...] pagan with no religious message in it and this I believe is true somehow, I cannot tackle big ideas altho' I am *not a heathen*.'[49] Her assertion that she is 'not a heathen' is an interesting one because it draws attention to her awareness of how poems such as 'The Stranger' may be perceived. In 'The Stranger', she describes an encounter with a woman with 'e'en maist like a bairnie's e'en'. By the poem's conclusion, 'the stranger' remains unidentified but it is clear that the encounter is charged with spiritual significance. Dye Water, associated with supernatural presences in

'Waater o' Dye', here becomes 'a gowden burn, / frae Hills o' Paradise' when the woman appears. The 'wild rose' she holds becomes 'like cup o' Sacrament'. Angus suggests that the speaker appropriates the role of priest offering the sacrament of Communion. The woman could be seen as a holy Christian presence, but she also recalls the supernatural fairy presences in Angus's work. Angus makes a connection in several poems between shining eyes and supernatural figures. In 'The Stranger', she plays upon the idea of 'communion' to suggest a spiritual union with nature, embodied as a woman. That the leading figure is female is not accidental. In poems such as 'Waater o' Dye', 'The Singin' Lass', 'Penchrise' and 'The Spae-Wife', she describes a female presence with power that is often from a mysterious source. In 'The Stranger', she reminds her readers that the poem's subject may be an enigma, but she is, nevertheless, tangible; she concludes the poem with a reference to the 'flittin' o' her feet'. The focus in Christian doctrine with Jesus as the incarnation of the deity in human form is shifted in some of her poems to look instead at a *female* mediator. It is no wonder that she was so diffident about the response to her poems about belief. The women in her poems who appear to be allied both with Christian and older pre-Christian traditions remain, ultimately, mysterious.

Love

While issues of time, place and faith are dominant in Angus's work, one cannot overlook perhaps the most central focus in her poetry: the difficulties of love. During her life and after her death, critics have argued about the content and meaning of the love poems, speculating aloud about possible episodes in her life that may have inspired the longing expressed in poems such as 'Anemones'. John MacRitchie wonders whether her love poems emerge out of the loss of a lover in World War One; others have pondered, warily, her female speakers' 'covert narratives', wondering about the poems' elusive meanings. In *Christabel's Diary*, the protagonist quotes from *The Rubaiyat of Omar Khayyam* ('a book of verses [...], / a jug of wine, a loaf of bread – and Thou!') and then quips:

> There is an art of doing without, which is better than the duty of contentment; and make me sure of the first three, or their equivalents to an ordinary domesticated, tea-loving woman, and I will very cheerfully admit that the 'Thou' is not a necessary adjunct to a day at Lunan Bay.[50]

In many of Angus's love poems, love is often 'an art of doing without'; love frequently in her poetry is unrequited and destructive. In 'Mary's Song', for example, the speaker offers herself to her lover in a disturbing evocation of Eucharist rites. Desire transubstantiates Mary from body into a balladic wedding feast, eerily like Communion wine and wafers.

Dorothy McMillan suggests that Angus 'makes us feel that women have secret stories that cannot be simply brought to the surface without falsifying their distinctive lives'.[51] The 'secret stories' to which Dorothy McMillan refers appear throughout Angus's poetry. In Angus's poetry, however, what is unusual is the insistence upon ambiguity. Her exploration of love relationships recalls the ballads, but, perhaps more challengingly, her poetry frequently elides any gender references so that the lover's gender is often obscured. Isolated incidents do not seem significant, but when one notices how carefully Angus's love lyrics avoid specifying gender, it becomes more compelling. Those poems in which Angus does define the gender of speaker and beloved specifically are almost entirely male–female pairings; these often are her least successful poems ('Mary's Song', 'A Woman Sings' and 'Heart-Free' are notable exceptions). Her most daring poems do not specify gender; in their ambiguity lies their strength and their subversive power.

There are several possible reasons for Angus's tendency to omit gender references in her poetry. Janet Caird considers as 'daughter of a Victorian U[nited] P[resbyterian] manse' for Angus 'reticence is in order'; she also believes that Angus's reticence in part stems from her age, claiming that 'if at the age of fifty you begin to write love poetry, it will be nostalgic, sad, wistful, secretive, wrapped round in imagery'.[52] This conclusion is interesting, but limited by its ageist assumptions – poets who write about desire in their fifties and beyond (in contemporary times Adrienne Rich and Denise Levertov spring to mind) need not produce solely 'wistful' poems. Another possibility is that Angus deliberately avoids gender references. She was remarkably elusive about the meaning of her poems. She once refused to elucidate her work for a critical male reader: 'I see you think my poems [...] are incomprehensible', she writes, retorting, not entirely in jest: *'I shall never explain them to you'*. In a letter to Neil Gunn thanking him for a review of her poems, Angus describes her happiness at finding 'one reviewer who is not puzzled by something *"obscure"* in my efforts', adding, 'I always think whatever my efforts are they are *not* obscure'.[53] Nevertheless, her love poems are often not immediately clear to the reader. Her use of coded language may relate to a need to conceal the fact that some of her poems may chronicle a woman's love for another woman. In poems such as 'Waater o' Dye' or 'The Blue Jacket', the female–female bond is made absolutely clear; whether one chooses to read these relationships vis-à-vis the speaker's sexual orientation depends upon one's willingness to consider Angus's poetry outside of the heterosexual context in which critics tend to place her writing.[54] Certainly, as Diana Collecott emphasises, one can examine a poet's work 'beyond the biography of the writer' – that is, without forcing a direct correspondence between textual emotions and the poet's personal orientation; one fruitfully can consider Angus's work within a broad spectrum of literature that includes 'any writing by women that gets its energy from erotic attraction between women' regardless of the poet's own sexual orientation.[55]

However one chooses to read Angus's love lyrics, her love poetry is fascinating in its depiction of different responses to desire. In 'The Kiss', an uncollected love poem, she describes a lover as 'half enemy, half friend'; this ambivalence towards love illuminates many of her finest poems. Although critics have lamented that her 'range is not wide', one can see that she explores depictions of desire in careful detail, noting the effect of 'Time's strange Alchemy' upon her speakers. Janet Caird claims that 'the charge of narrowness may be due to the restricted range of her imagery. The same images recur again and again [...] One begins to feel she is writing in a kind of code'.[56] It is impossible to 'crack' Angus's poetic 'code'; nevertheless, it is interesting to observe how she returns repeatedly to the subject of love from a variety of angles, remapping its emotional contours in the process.

Reception of Angus's Work

During Angus's lifetime, critics praised her work for its lyricism and grace. The *Scotsman* claimed that 'she is probably the most individual poet writing [...] in Scots' in the 1920s. Many noted the connection between her poetry and the Scottish ballads. Angus's interest in traditional forms, particularly the ballad form, is immediately evident when reading through her work; similarly, her fascination with what one critic has called 'unknown modes of being' or the 'region where the partitions between seen and unseen, present and past, melt away' characterises many of her finest poems.[57] Margaret Sackville, writing in the *Scots Observer*, claims that Angus 'has taken, as it were, the ancient precious stones of the ballads and given them a new setting, not imitatively in any sense – rather the deathless ballad spirit has found, through her, reincarnation in a new body'. Perhaps most potently, Charles Graves suggests that Angus's poetry is responsible for returning to Scottish letters what he calls the 'magic of the ballads'. He continues: 'she did not write ballads in imitation of the old models, and indeed none of her poems could be strictly placed in the ballad category'. Indeed, as Nan Shepherd reveals in her reminiscence of Angus, 'her reading' of the ballads out loud 'was astonishing, an incantation of power. She was aware always of the mystery and terror of living'.[58] Critics also recognised the careful evocation of the natural world and human emotions in Angus's work. Charles Graves reflects upon how her poetry examines the 'splendour and beauty of life in its fullness and tragedy and to the wild things of nature'. One reviewer observes that in her poems 'beyond time's treason and the weakness and pathos of men she has a vision of the abiding hills of the North, and it is their staunchness and mystery which sound as an undertone even in her lightest and gayest verses'.[59]

After her death, demand grew for a volume of her selected poetry as her original books were out of print.

W. Hamilton wrote a letter claiming the need for a collected volume of her work, concluding:

> Let some younger poet make it a pious duty to recover the whole [of Angus's poetry] for Scotland and mankind forthwith, and enlist the very widest co-operation to secure the success and permanence of the publication by a house of adequate repute and resources which will maintain them in print and publicity.[60]

By the time her posthumous *Selected Poems of Marion Angus* finally appeared in 1950, however, the tide in critical studies was beginning to turn. The 'younger poet' Hamilton requested appeared in the person of Maurice Lindsay, who edited the volume. In his introduction, Maurice Lindsay admits that 'it is never easy to assess the poetry of the generation or two immediately before one's own'. This perhaps may be the reason behind the often disdainful approach scholars in the mid-twentieth century took towards Angus's work. Maurice Lindsay, clearly uncomfortable with the task of selecting Angus's work for the *Selected Poems*, claims that 'however much her subject may vary [...] her theme is almost always the same. For that reason it is inevitable that she should often have written the same poem several times over'. Alastair Mackie dismisses both Angus and Jacob as 'minor' in his survey of modern Scots poetry for *Akros* in the 1970s.[61] Some have seen Angus and Jacob merely as precursors to Hugh MacDiarmid.

In the past thirty years, however, scholars have begun to embrace Angus's work – as they have Jacob's poetry – for its contributions to the development of literature in Scots. Articles published throughout the 1980s and 1990s made pleas for the reissue of her poems. More recently, J. Derrick McClure in *The Edinburgh Companion to Scots* calls Angus 'one of the greatest lyric poets of the twentieth century'. Recent anthologies have made a selection of her poems available but to do her work justice one needs to see a wider variety of her poems. As Janet Caird reminds readers, Angus is 'a true poet, who merits and requires careful reading. Surely the time has come for a collected edition. It would be a friendly slim volume, but "guid gear gangs in sma' bouk"'.[62]

This edition of Angus and Jacob's poetry comes nearly twenty years after Janet Caird's plea; the intention of this volume is to make their poems available for the 'careful reading' Caird's article recommended and to provide a starting point for those interested in reading more widely in each poet's body of work.

For More Information

Because Angus has no gravestone, there is no permanent marker to her life. However, the intrepid reader can find ample other memorials, however unofficial, to her life and work in the places where she once lived. A visit to Arbroath can introduce the reader to places that appear in her writing; in particular, Arbroath's library offers a good selection of Angus's books – including the wonderful *Christabel's Diary* – and an array of archival material about Angus. The library occupies the building that was once the Arbroath High School, which Angus attended. The homes where Angus lived are in private hands but the haunts mentioned in her writing are, for the most part, in public domain. For those interested in seeing the landscapes described in Angus's poetry, Ordnance Survey maps of Angus and Aberdeen allow one to explore Cambus Woods, the Braid Hill o' Fare, and other locations mentioned in her work. The National Library of Scotland holds some of Angus's letters, including her correspondence with Mairi Campbell Ireland. Aberdeen University Special Collections holds perhaps the most useful collection of Angus's papers, including selections from her correspondence with Nan Shepherd. Aberdeen also provides Angus's readers with the opportunity to visit sites mentioned in her work.

A more extensive list of archival material related to Angus's life and work appears in the bibliography.

Violet Jacob (1863–1946)

A striking feature of Violet Jacob's writing is its sheer variety. Not content to write in one genre, Jacob published books in many – poetry, memoir, family history, and fiction for children and adults; restless in language and form, she produced insightful work in both English and Scots, ever aware of the nuances of each. In her fiction and poetry, one finds a kaleidoscope of voices: there are Jacobites, travellers, village worthies, sailors, the old and young, exiles and those who long to leave but, because of poverty or circumstance, cannot. Until recently, most of Jacob's work was out of print. Fortunately, with the republication of her 1911 novel *Flemington*, some of her short fiction, her India diaries and letters – and now this volume of her poetry – her writing is more widely available.

While still a young woman, Jacob scribbled down an entry in her journal that gives a useful glimpse into the optimism and adventurous spirit underlying her writing throughout her life. She admits:

> Before getting to sleep I lay looking at the stars that seemed entangled in the boughs above my head and thinking of the good fortune of my life that had brought me into places the like of which many people have never even dreamed of, places that would convey nothing to so many I have met; but I did not forget to remember those who would give anything to see what I was seeing and would never get the chance.[63]

This passage highlights many of the themes in the poetry she wrote in the decades after this was originally penned: an appreciation for the natural world, the exile's exhilaration and loneliness, and a sensitivity towards those who lacked the opportunities that she had. Her dual fascination with place and people echoes through her writing. Her poetry, a vital part of her *oeuvre*, gives her readers the chance to 'see' what she saw: the people and landscapes of both her 'own country' and places far from her home.[64]

Jacob was born Violet Augusta Frederica Kennedy-Erskine at the House of Dun in Angus on 1 September 1863.[65] The eldest daughter of Catherine Kennedy-Erskine (née Jones) and William Henry Kennedy-Erskine, the eighteenth laird of Dun, Jacob came from a landed family whose history she later recorded in *The Lairds of Dun* (1931). The House of Dun, now owned by the National Trust for Scotland, is located outside Montrose where, as Jacob describes it in her poem 'Montrose', one finds 'the Esk ae side, ae side the sea'. Educated at the House of Dun, Jacob had access to its extensive library, and it is clear from her personal writing that she read widely. Although it is not clear at what point she first began writing, from an early age she was a careful observer of the world around her. Part of her education at the Dun estate was the exposure it provided to people from a wide cross-section of the socio-economic spectrum, from her aristocratic relatives to the farm labourers on the estate. Jacob's grandmother, Lady Augusta Fitzclarence, was a daughter of the Duke of Clarence (later King William IV) and Dorothea Bland (known by her stage name, Dorothy Jordan). This connection, among other familial bonds, involved Jacob in the small social circle of landed families. Members of the Kennedy-Erskine household seemed to have had a sense of humour about their social distinction; a 'family tradition, arising out of numerous feuds between the Erskines and the inhabitants of Montrose' was kept up by Jacob's father and her brother Augustus who would 'blow their horns when going through the north part' of Montrose to warn town residents of their presence as they would drive 'into the High Street in their four-in-hand'.[66]

Jacob also had insight into the lives of those at the other end of the economic spectrum: the hired labourers working on the estate and the many servants managing the household. As Helen Cruickshank notes, Jacob spent her childhood 'aye in and oot amo' the ploomen's feet at the Mains o' Dun';[67] Jacob's work is influenced by folk-song and the Scottish poetry tradition, but her ability to capture the voices of farm labourers in her poetry and fiction no doubt also owes a debt to her exposure to the lives of the men and women on the Dun estate. In 'Charlewayn', for example, she describes the long hours of a 'warkin' lass' for whom 'the wark seems niver past'; in 'Bonnie Joann', her speaker prepares to 'gaither' the harvest in after hours of labour. Throughout her poetry, one can find numerous compassionate portraits of farm workers, revealing the conflicting pressures placed upon them by their labour and their love. Her ability to negotiate between the wealth and position of her landed family and her interest in the lives of others outside that social sphere informs her best poetry; more often than not the people appearing in her writing are not the landed gentry or army officers of her own social circle but the travellers, ploughmen and rural people of her childhood.

An intensely private woman, Jacob did not write openly about herself very often; her reminiscences are even more valuable for their rarity. When pressed for details about her life, she responded in a letter that 'all the personal details' she 'wish[ed] to give' are:

> born at House of Dun, Montrose, Angus. Daughter of Capt. W. H. Kennedy-Erskine of Dun, late of the 17th Lancers. Married Lieut. Arthur Otway Jacob, 20th Hussars. Had one son who died of wounds received at the Battle of the Somme, 1916. Address: Ladies' Empire Club, 69 Grosvenor Street W.[68]

The careful placement of herself within a frame of reference bracketed by men is not unusual for the period. Carol Anderson comments that Jacob 'is of her time and of her class in her personal reticence'.[69] One can see this distance throughout her work – both in her rare personal writing and in her poetry and fiction. In her poetry one finds the frequent use of personae to distance herself from the sentiments expressed by the poems' speakers; in her personal life, she achieved the same distancing with the use of titles (wife, mother).

Her reticence perhaps contributes to the general lack of available images of her. Photographs of her are rare; few photographs from her youth, and only a handful of her in later life, appear in print. She resolutely avoided using photographs for publicity purposes. Once, when asked for one, she gently but firmly replied:

> As for a photograph, I do not possess one and in any case I am bound to admit that I could not let you have one. I have stood out permanently for declining to join the throng of writers who advertise their books by their countenances; and as I have refused so many applications for mine, I can never make an exception, no matter how anxious to connect, without giving offence to people whom I should regret in any way to offend. I hope you will forgive me for this.[70]

The extant images of Jacob – including a bronze bust by Scottish artist William Lamb, and an oil painting – suggest a regal, slightly distant woman of considerable beauty. One can understand why a maharajah once told her: 'You are a most aristocratic person; I have seen people like you in Buckingham Palace'. This elusiveness makes finding out more about Jacob's life both a challenge and a frustration. One exasperated reader wondered aloud in the arts journal *Cencrastus* about the 'enigma' of Jacob's personality. Her letter concludes: 'Surely there is someone who could supply the [...] answers we will never get from that tight-lipped woman in the portrait'.[71] The 'answers', if there are definitive ones, may be found in Jacob's own writing and in the work of commentators such as Carol Anderson who have looked at her writing in depth. A close consideration of Jacob's own personal writing, letters and journals reveal a rich – although still incomplete – portrait of her life.

What little Jacob did write about her childhood is illuminating in the glimpses it gives of the writer as a young woman. What Carol Anderson calls Jacob's 'irreverent sense of humour' is evident in Jacob's occasional vignettes of her younger self. In one letter to a friend, she recalls having *The History of the Fairchild Family*, a nineteenth-century instructive book for children, read to her. She writes:

> I am so glad you know it – so many of my contemporaries *don't* that it makes me feel more like Methuselah then ever. The book had belonged to my mother as a child [...] We *loved* having it read to us, and used to groan with hypocrisy and emotion at all the parts where the Fairchild children erred. But the little beasts erred seldom.[72]

Occasional references to her childhood such as this give one a sense of her early life and of her relationships with her siblings. In an essay from 1920, similarly, she describes another incident that illustrates her impatience with the 'suffocating respectability' she and her siblings were meant to maintain. She recalls that when they were on holiday in Brittany, they raced 'decorous little French girls' down the road to the beach in a donkey cart.[73] Her glee in reporting this is evident. Certainly, in excerpts such as these she reveals her impatience with sentimental portrayals of morality and inflexible social structures; this same desire for honesty in portrayals of moral choice is evident in her finest poetry.

Jacob's descriptions of the manor home rented by her family in Brittany one summer when she was young reveal as much about her own nature as they do about the place:

> There were corners dark enough for mystery, windows high enough in the roof for us to look out over the boundaries of its domain and see snatches of the foreign world of which we knew so little. On the roof, the bell was there in its iron pagoda, suggestive of everything romantic – of curfews, alarms, dangers, the summons to desperate deeds.[74]

The yearning for the 'foreign world of which we knew so little' reappears in her poetry, spoken through the voices of both women and men who long for something beyond their own proscribed lives. In 'The Deil', for example, she imagines a woman's response to meeting the devil; the woman discovers that the devil's life is far from the 'puir an' cauld' life she leads and she longs to embrace that freedom for herself. Often in Jacob's poetry one finds moments such as these when the speaker must weigh an opportunity 'suggestive of everything romantic' against societal expectations.

The chance to see 'snatches of the foreign world' came in Jacob's own life with her marriage and the extensive travel that that marriage brought with it. In 1894, aged 31, she married Arthur Otway Jacob, an Irish soldier, at St John's Episcopal Church in Edinburgh. Although there is little information available about how the two met, they shared a happy marriage. In an unpublished occasional poem, she calls Cupid 'no guest, because a lodger' in a couple's home; what she called her 'forty years of such happiness' with her husband suggest that portraits of marriage in poems such as 'The Helpmate' or 'Kirsty's Opinion' – where marriage brings with it 'argy-bargyin'' – are not based on her own experience.[75] In 1895, she and Arthur had their only child, Arthur Henry ('Harry'). Thereafter they lived a peripatetic life because of her husband's military career: first settling in India (1895–1900), then South Africa (1901–2) and Egypt (1903–4) before returning to Britain. As Marion Lochhead observes, Jacob had 'known the military fate of having no settled home'. Jacob herself admitted that despite the demands of living abroad, she liked being a 'nomad'.[76]

By the time Jacob married, she was already a published author. Her first book, a whimsical Scots poem she co-authored with William Douglas Campbell, appeared when she was still in her twenties. Entitled *The Bailie MacPhee* (1891), the book showcases her carefully observed, humorously detailed portraits of Scottish villagers.[77] The poem is good-natured doggerel, but it is valuable because of the contrast it provides for her later forays into poetry. It also marks the beginning of her public writing career. This public aspect of her writing, and her reputation as a 'literary' woman, were at times problematic for her in her role as military wife. She recalls in her India journal a surprising visit from a high-ranking army official who, she recalls, 'announced plainly that he had heard I like books and as hardly anybody in the place did, or ever spoke of them, he had come to see if it was true. I was a little taken aback and rather pleased'. Unlike Angus, Jacob apparently was not involved in writers' organisations and, consequently, one imagines that such gestures of support would have been invaluable. Susan Tweedsmuir, a fellow writer and acquaintance from Jacob's time in Egypt, notes sympathetically that Jacob's writing 'made her a little suspect to the military society of Cairo. But her charm and beauty and aptitude for getting on with people helped her to live down even poetry'.[78] Susan Tweedsmuir's comments give one a better sense of why so little appears in Jacob's public and private writing on her own development as a poet. One gets very little sense in her personal writing of a self-conscious crafting of a poet's (or novelist's) role. Instead, the reticence about her personal life extends to include expressions of her personal attitudes about poetic craft.

By the time Jacob's first full-length volume of poetry appeared in 1905, she and her family were living back in Britain. Titled *Verses*, the volume is interesting more for its suggestion of how Jacob's poetic taste evolves over time than for its specific contents. In general, the poems in *Verses* recall the poetry of Algernon Swinburne and the Pre-Raphaelites in their evocation of lush, haunted landscapes. Some representative poems from *Verses* appear in this volume to give readers a sense of Jacob's earliest published poetry. While the poems in this volume are often quite derivative, they do provide one with a glimpse of some of the issues that reappear in later poems: the disparity between freedoms allowed men and women, the complicated and conflicting power of love to transform a person, and the exile's keen yearning for home. In 'Come On, Come Up, Ye Rovers', she asks, 'shall small men's limits bind you / whose milestones are the stars?' In 'Airlie Kirk', it is the 'curlew-haunted braes' and the 'tangled ground' of home that draws one back again – if only in death or dreams. The volume also includes poems about Egypt and India, some of which are included in this volume to give readers an insight into Jacob's perceptions of both countries. Read in conjunction with her diaries and correspondence from her time in India, these poems give a valuable portrait of how she translated into verse experiences originally recorded in prose.

The period from the publication of *Verses* to the appearance of *Songs of Angus* (1915) is not vast and yet the change in style and poetic approach revealed during that period is tremendous. One example can be found in 'Tam i' the Kirk', one of her most popular poems. This poem first appeared in *Country Life* in 1910 and, unlike the poems in *Verses*, it is in literary Scots. As her obituary in *The Times* notes, 'Tam i' the Kirk', one of her most famous poems, 'has attained a wide celebrity and an almost classical standing'.[79] The poem, spoken by a young man, captures his desire for his lover Jean; his erotic longing has so consumed him that everything – even the church bell – reminds him of her. The poem is frank, earthy and confident in tone, a world away from the love poetry in *Verses*. In the five-year period between the publication of *Verses* and the appearance of 'Tam i' the Kirk', then, something happened which changed Jacob's writing style noticeably. The poems in *Songs of Angus* are, for the most part, simple in their language and imagery and, unlike the poems of *Verses*, spoken almost exclusively by poor rural people, some of whom are exiles. Most significantly, the poems in *Songs of Angus* are in literary Scots and associated chiefly with the North-East. What brought about these linguistic and thematic changes? The move back to Britain? A desire to explore issues and voices in verse that she was addressing already in her fiction? A sense of national pride?

One clear explanation for the shift in quality between

Verses and the poetry that follows is difficult to discover; Jacob's own extant writing does not offer much in the way of commetary and, as such, pinning down the definitive reason for this change is fraught with risk. In a letter to Helen Cruickshank, Jacob reveals that *Songs of Angus* took

> ten years to put together because I never allowed myself to write unless it was at top-pressure – which doesn't come often – nor to keep a line I did not feel entirely satisfied with. So it was a long process. But I am glad now.[80]

Jacob's suggestion that *Songs of Angus* is the product of 'top-pressure' writing is useful because it indicates how emotionally intensive her writing process was. This certainly is evident in the resulting poems. Besides this emotional intensity, another change in the poems in *Songs of Angus* is the increased use of the dramatic monologue form, a recurrent form in the Scottish literary tradition. In *Songs of Angus* and later volumes, Jacob includes many poems in the voices of personae; Joy Hendry explains that Jacob 'rarely' uses her own voice to 'speak directly to her readers' but instead 'assumes the persona of a recognisable, rural type, through which a particular situation, or feeling, or attitude is explored'.[81] By making her speakers poor rural men and women often on the margins of society, Jacob created characters as far from her own aristocratic background as possible. By writing many of these monologues in Scots, Jacob acquired a second level of distancing between her voice and that of her poem's speakers. It is worth remembering that Jacob also published several novels and collections of short fiction during the early years of the twentieth century, many of which feature rural characters speaking in Scots. Clearly, her desire to craft believable characters in fiction informs her explorations of the emotions and conditions of her poetic speakers. The distance provided by the personae and the use of Scots, combined with the 'top-pressure' approach to writing, markedly strengthened her poetry from 1910 and after.

Because Jacob did not leave an extensive account of her technique and influences, one must glean what one can from what little she did write about the ways she observed and recorded the world around her. One clue to explain her greater use of dramatic personae in her poems after 1905 can be traced, however obliquely, to a passage in her journal. In one key entry from her time in India, Jacob reflects upon the nature of *purdah*, the practice of screening women from the view of men. Her description gives the reader a useful insight into the use of personae in her poetry. She observes:

> A *purdah* has an advantage that never occurred to me till I got behind one, though it is obvious enough; it doesn't matter how untidy and dishevelled you may be, or how frightful, for your guest will never know it. You may laugh at him, shake your fist in his face, allow everything you may think, however uncomplimentary, to appear on your own and he will be none the wiser.[82]

Although Jacob clearly enjoyed the freedoms of life outside *purdah*, this passage suggests she can imagine the surprising freedom such unfamiliar restrictions provided. From her discussion of this, one can see that to some extent her use of poetic masks similarly allowed her to protect her emotions and ideas from view while simultaneously expressing them through the voice of the poem's speaker. The freedom to 'allow everything you may think' to remain hidden must have been tremendously appealing to her, especially when one takes into consideration her personal reticence and desire for privacy.

Another possible reason for Jacob's use of personae may relate to a desire to control intense personal emotions by expressing them in the voices of others. In an essay about Hans Christian Andersen's autobiography, an often sentimental self-portrait by the Danish children's author, she describes him in a way that is perhaps more revealing about her own character than about his; in assessing what she perceived as his overly emotional response to negative experiences, she contends that he was 'unequipped [...] with the serviceable hide that becomes many of us so well'. One can see in Jacob's work how this 'serviceable hide' both protects the bearer and mutes her emotional responses. As Sarah Bing claims, Jacob's 'desire to communicate her individual experience' expresses itself in the 'disguises offered by fiction' – and, one could add, her poetry;

she is perhaps 'more comfortable communicating deeper emotions behind the mask of a fictional persona'.[83] Jacob's use of the dramatic monologue in many poems allowed her to speak indirectly of great personal emotion. This becomes more significant when one considers the weight of personal tragedy she carried with her throughout her adult life. As a young woman, she faced the death of her younger sister Millicent (b.1866) and her brother John (b.1864) when he was just an infant. Their father died when she was a child as well, leaving her brother Augustus (b.1866) to become the nineteenth laird. Tragedy followed her later in her life, too. Augustus died while away at sea on holiday in 1908. Her niece, who was also named Violet, took her own life, perhaps as a result of depression.[84]

Most traumatic of all, however, was the death of her son during World War One at the Battle of the Somme. They had been close, as their correspondence preserved in the National Library of Scotland reveals. Susan Tweedsmuir claims that 'a spring' in Jacob 'broke' when Harry died. Jacob admitted to a friend: 'I believe so much in the "communion of saints" that I am certain that he is never far from me'. In the letter, Jacob adds that she knows that her grief will 'cloud' Harry's joy, so she tries 'harder than ever to conquer [grief] and to wait in hope and patience'.[85] Perhaps part of the attempt to 'conquer' grief, particularly after Harry's death, manifested itself in the cultivation of personae in her poetry. Whether it was her grief at the loss of her son or feelings of frustration at limited roles for rural women, she contained these emotions in verse. One imagines that the *purdah* screen Jacob describes in the passage above could serve as a physical embodiment of the same poetic screen she employs in her dramatic monologues; the reader cannot see the poet's *personal* thoughts because they are hidden from view by the text. As readers can discover, some of her war-era poems from *More Songs of Angus and Others* are often not entirely successful at balancing emotional content with poetic form. Her work in this period frequently falters; perhaps her son's recent death meant that her material was too raw to be formed into enduring poetry.[86] Poems such as 'Glory', in which the speaker sees a vision of her dead son, or 'Jock, to the First Army', in which the speaker warns his troops that 'deith comes skirling through the sky', make for uncomfortable reading because the emotion bursts through into verse that is less mediated than in her usual poetry. Nevertheless, in much of her writing, and her later poetry in particular, she powerfully constructs poetic voices in both dramatic monologues and ballad dialogue form that capture her speakers' characters much as she does in her novels. Marion Lochhead explains that Jacob's poems in a 'few words [...] indicate emotion all the more effectively for being restrained'.[87]

Jacob's poetry volumes appeared at regular intervals after 1915 and she frequently published her poems in journals before they were collected in book form. Most often, her poems first appeared in *Country Life*, the glossy weekly magazine of essays, poetry and stories that also includes photographs of aristocratic Britons. (Unlike Angus, who preferred to publish her poetry in Scottish publications, Jacob was more likely to have her work appear in publications geared towards readers in England.) During these years, she and her husband lived nomadically, settling briefly in Shropshire and, when able, spending winters in mainland Europe because Arthur's asthma was aggravated by the British weather. They returned to India in the early 1920s for a short trip, although the trip was marked with memories of what Jacob had called her 'Four Good Years' in India and her son's presence where 'he began his life [...] among soldiers'.[88] During this period, as well, Jacob published her work in *Scottish Chapbook* and *Northern Numbers*, two publications associated with the Scottish Renaissance, and her work continued to be popular in Scotland and overseas. *Bonnie Joann and Other Poems* (1921) and *The Northern Lights and Other Poems* (1927) both met with success. As in *Songs of Angus*, many of the poems in these later books examine the lives of poor rural Scots, but her later work often investigates the lives of women more extensively. Poems such as 'The End O't' and 'The Jaud', in particular, use the dramatic monologue and dialogue forms to explore the limited opportunities available to poor rural women. Her best work from this later period captures quite effectively the frustration of knowing 'the price' to be 'paid' for sexual expression for many women was pregnancy, social ostracism, or complete rejection by family and community.[89]

In 1936, Arthur Jacob died and soon after Violet moved back to Scotland after many years living outside the country. In a letter written not long after Arthur's death, she describes for a friend her sorrow, noting: 'I am getting on all right but no words can express how I miss him. But it is not everyone who can look back for over forty years of such happiness. There never was anyone like him.' She moved to Kirriemuir, to live in a 'good solid stone [house] about ninety years old' that she described as 'stand[ing] on the top of the brae looking down on Kirrie Station'. Writing to a friend, she explained: 'I always knew that, should I be left alone, the only thing that would keep me from breaking my heart would be to live in Angus.'[90] Her poem 'Kirrie' from *Bonnie Joann and Other Poems* praises the 'braw, braw toon o' Kirrie' that later became her home.

Ten years later when Jacob died, she was buried next to her husband in the cemetery at Dun Church under a simple headstone. Carol Anderson observes, 'Jacob might have claimed a place in the Erskine private family graveyard. She chose instead to share a modest grave with her husband, marked by a small stone in the public churchyard, beside the tiny church at Dun.' Sarah Bing describes the memorial stone Jacob had made for her husband and notes that her

> vision of the afterlife is best expressed by the quotation [...] she had carved on her husband's memorial stone: 'And life is eternal and love is immortal and death is only an horizon and an horizon is nothing save the limit of our sight'.

In the late 1950s, a communion table was placed in the Dun Church in memory of Violet Jacob. Her work, for many, is the best memorial available for in it, her insights and humour live on.[91]

Technique and Themes in Jacob's Poetry

In addition to her concern with death and loss, Jacob, like Angus, found inspiration in the language and narratives of the ballads. The facet in Jacob's poetry that is more overlooked, however, is her use of traditional poetic forms, including folk-song. Although one reviewer suggests her verse is 'entirely lacking in experiment', a survey of her poetry reveals that while she did not embrace the interest in fragmentation favoured by Modernist poets, she did make deft use of poetic forms to echo the content of her verse. Hugh MacDiarmid, who took Jacob to task for what he perceived as her lack of interest in national concerns, begrudgingly agreed that she was making a 'distinct contribution to vernacular verse' with what he called 'a new consciousness of technique'.[92] Throughout her work one often can find poems written in standard ballad form (a four-line stanza alternating eight- and six-syllable lines) but she is also experimental in her form; she adapts rhyme schemes and rhythmic structures to accentuate a poem's narrative. One useful illustration of her technical skill can be seen in her poem 'The End O't'. In this poem, she mimics the urgency of the pregnant speaker with the diction and rhythm: the internal rhymes speed up the poem's rhythm and the two short lines concluding each stanza suggest the truncated youth of the speaker as she confronts what will happen to her and her child. In stanza two, for example, Jacob reminds her readers of the 'end' of the speaker's freedom with aggressive consonance. In just eight lines there are numerous words with hard *d*'s and *t*'s that sound as negative and limited as the speaker's future. The careful way she constructs this and the other stanzas in the poem reveals her acute sensitivity to the sound and structure of the poem. Reading her poems with an awareness of Jacob's interest in prosody reveals another layer of richness in her work.

Women's Voices

There is a noticeable engagement in Jacob's poetry of women's voices, the depiction of place, and the experience of love. Her recurrent interest in exploring the characters and lives of women manifests itself even in her earliest published poems. While the male voices in her poems tend to be pompous and self-important, it is clear that in her later poetry, especially, the voices of women are the most powerful and most convincing. Many have observed her interest in using speakers from outwith her socio-economic class: 'ploughmen, shepherds, country lasses, [and] hardworked women'. Poems such as 'The Jaud', 'The End O't' and

'Donald Maclane', among many others, reveal her fascination with exploring the limited choices available to rural women 'within grey vanished walls / who bore and loved and died'.[93] Some are conventional women who seem to uphold traditional roles – for example, those women's voices in 'The Jacobite Lass' or 'The Guidwife Speaks'. Others, however, are women whose lives are characterised by what Carol Anderson reads as 'loss, frustration, or ill treatment'. Jacob's 'frank exposure' of the power structures underlying rural society – particularly its treatment of women, who were often left voiceless and unrepresented – characterises her best work.[94] In 'The Jaud', one of her later poems, for example, she explores one woman's growing respect for another woman who, because of her unrepressed sexuality during her lifetime, was ostracised by her community. The poem records the speaker's recognition that the dead 'jaud' in fact had far more freedom and – one suspects – satisfaction in her life than the morally upright speaker ever could have experienced. In 'Donald Maclane', Jacob compassionately portrays the life of a woman who has brought 'black disgrace' upon herself for running away with a traveller. The speaker's acknowledgement of her father's 'broken pride' is tempered with her hope that 'the love o' mithers is deep an' wide'; she longs to find some forgiveness from her parents but cannot leave 'Donald Maclane' to do so. Voices such as these are not sentimental or patronising; they alternate between a fierce desire for independence and a deep recognition of the price such independence demands.

Readers will find it interesting to consider Jacob's fiction in conjunction with her poetry in the depiction of women's lives, as many of her stories focus upon the narrow range of opportunities afforded to women in rural Scotland, showing both the ingenuity of women who forge new roles for themselves and the crushing inability of others to resist social pressures. As she describes in 'Back to the Land', the voices of women – and men – 'call' from the 'bare bones of the country'; one gets the sense that her poems are a way to capture these insistent voices.

Place

In addition to a focus on the lives of women in Jacob's poems, one can see a recurrent interest in landscape and place, particularly the North-East of Scotland, and the exile's longing for these familiar spaces: a longing often linked to a sense of mystery and mortality. As Marion Lochhead has noted, in Jacob's work, 'two elements meet': the 'love of home with all its intimate appeal, and the thirst for space and voyaging'. The elements of place Jacob describes and names in her poetry – the Esk, Craigo Woods, the Vale of Strathmore, the Mearns, among many others – will be familiar to readers who know what she called her 'own country' well. J. Derrick McClure notes that 'even in poems where no specific place is named, a strong sense of locality pervades the writing, suggested by frequent references to landscape features, landmarks, and directions'.[95] Certainly this incorporation of the landscape contributed to her popularity during her lifetime among Scots living abroad. Her focus upon place stems from her own longing for the North-East. At the end of her life, her 'own country' offered her the solace she needed after her husband died; after years as an exile, Jacob was able to return to the familiar landscapes of her childhood.

The exile's longing for home is a theme that appears in the work of numerous Scots-language writers of the period: notably Jacob; Charles Murray, who lived in South Africa; and Robert Louis Stevenson, who died in the South Pacific after a brief lifetime of travels. The simple reason for the popularity of the theme is that the Scottish diaspora, which was extensive due to the continual waves of emigration in the nineteenth and early twentieth centuries, formed a large population of readers eager to hear about their homeland. Many of the speakers in Jacob's poems find themselves far from Scotland for economic reasons, a reality both then and now; others, in particular the war poems, express the soldier's longing for the familiar braes of home while in a threatening or dangerous environment. Poems such as 'The Howe o' the Mearns', 'The Gean-Trees' and 'The Wild Geese' depict, often poignantly, the exile's yearning for a familiar landscape far out of reach. As Marion Lochhead argues, poems such as these 'haunt us with their cry for the shores of Forth, wave-beat and wind-blown; the sadness of that wind and water is in them'. An article in *The Scottish Bookman* suggests that 'in Mrs. Jacob the deep understanding of the native is intensified by the yearning of the exile, yet, in spite of an occasional sentimentality, she can qualify this yearning with the freshness of vision of the returned exile'.[96]

Jacob's own experience of living far from home certainly influenced her writing about the North-East. The detailed glimpses of the landscape appearing in her poetry remind us that she was a skilful painter as well as a literary artist. In 'The Howe o' the Mearns', for example, she describes the point between seasons when 'the burnin' yellow's awa' that was aince a-lowe / On the braes o' whin' with such detail it captures that transitional moment keenly. Even a minor poem such as 'The Doo'cot Up the Braes' offers a closely observed image of a marine landscape: 'And fine's the glint on blawin' days / O' the bonnie plains o' sea'. The specificity of her imagery of home, particularly in the exile poems, suggests that she was acutely aware of the exile's longing not just for the familiar landscape but also for the beloved details of the place: the 'cauld, sweet taste' of the water or the 'flame o' the gean-trees burnin' / roond the white house door'.[97] As she concludes in her poem 'The Shadows': 'the heart may break for lands unseen, / for woods wherein its life has been, / but not return'.

Concomitant with her poems about the North-East, one finds poems – particularly in her earlier work – that express an intense desire to travel far from home. Some of these poems date from her travels overseas. 'The Distant Temple', for example, describes the landscape of India 'calling, at sundown, from the temple gate / to me, who cannot come'. The way in which these poems capture the distant landscape give a sense of the interest Jacob took in unfamiliar cultures made most evident in her *Diaries and Letters from India, 1895–1900* and in her unpublished journals from her return trip to India in the 1920s.[98]

In other poems, the desired destination is not far away geographically, but often represents a longed-for opportunity to leave restrictive family and social mores behind. In poems such as 'The Gowk', for example, she describes the speaker's desire to be 'far awa' from the control of her family. In 'Charlewayn' and 'The Deil', among others, she describes the deep-rooted wish for freedom to live and love without societal restrictions. In 'The Deil', the speaker's admiration for the 'deil' who boasts 'the polestar kens ma bed' is weighed against her recognition that her 'feyther's hoose is puir an' cauld' and she is also destined to marry a man whose household will be very like her own father's. Jacob's compassionate portraits of the yearning for a new landscape make her poetry appealing to those readers who either are far from home and wish to remember that desire, or those who, like her speakers, wish to escape their too-confining home. Poems such as 'The Lad i' the Mune' serve as a counterweight for poems such as 'Come On, Come Up, Ye Rovers' in which the speaker proclaims, the 'world was built for you' to explore.

Love

In addition to discussing the importance of place in her poetry, Jacob returns repeatedly to the subject of love, investigating it from numerous angles. The relationships between men and women in her poetry, often fraught with frustration and disappointment, also reveal flashes of joy. Her use of both male and female voices in her poems allows her the chance to explore a similar situation from two different perspectives. Dorothy McMillan usefully suggests that one can read within love poems in male voices such as 'Tam i' the Kirk' 'covert' women's voices; she pairs 'Tam i' the Kirk' with 'The End O't' to illustrate what she finds as 'other poems encoded' within the male-voice poems.[99] With this pairing, one can see that the jubilation of early love expressed by the male speaker in 'Tam i' the Kirk' is tempered by the female speaker's revelation in 'The End O't' that 'there's little love for a lass to seek / when the coortin's through'.

Jacob's love poems vary in quality: some of her least successful appear to be written quickly and do not appear here; by contrast, however, her most successful poems, such as 'The Guidwife Speaks', 'Maggie' and 'The Wind Frae the Baltic', exhibit powerfully evocative depictions of a person's feelings for a beloved. Looking at 'Maggie' and 'The Wind Frae the Baltic' side by side, for example, one can see two versions of how lovers handle loss. In 'Maggie', the speaker addresses his dead beloved, telling her how much he misses her and begging her 'dinna look an' see yer lad that's sittin' / his lane aside the fire'. By contrast, in 'The Wind Frae the Baltic', the speaker, grief-stricken and alone, tells herself her 'tears wad be a sin' as others waiting for the arrival of a new ship would be discouraged by her public grief. She reassures herself that she may go 'hame to greet' in private where others will not see her.

The tension between public and private proclamations of love appears in many of Jacob's love poems. In 'The Guidwife Speaks', for example, she contrasts the 'dandy lad' the speaker's husband once was with the 'soor auld deil' he has become by showing the shift from the public side of their relationship – the courtship where he 'dance[d] curcuddoch tae the pipes' and their marriage – with the grinding monotony of their private relationship. She explores the same theme in 'The Jaud'; the 'auld wife' who speaks part of the poem compares her publicly acceptable but perhaps emotionally unfulfilling love with the private loves she imagines for the 'prood an' lichtsome an' fine' woman the other speaker dismisses as a 'jaud'.

Reading Jacob's poetry in chronological order helps give one a sense of the development of her treatment of love in verse, from the earliest love poems from *Verses* (1905) such as 'Airlie Kirk' to the late poems such as 'The Warld'. For many readers, her most successful love poems are among her most lasting and powerful work. As L. M. Cumming suggests, 'it is in her love songs that most of all we find an individual note that will surely give one or two of them at least their place among the great songs of our country'.[100]

Reception of Jacob's Work

Violet Jacob received numerous honours for her writing throughout her life. Initially praised as a short fiction and novel writer, she later was lauded for being what a contemporary writer has called 'that rare thing: a prose writer gifted with the clear, uncluttered eye of a poet'. Her use of the Scots language brought her great acclaim; one reviewer encourages 'readers who appreciate the lilt of the vernacular' to read her poetry while another reviewer argues that her volumes contain the 'spirit of true poetry'.[101] Praise for her poetry was not limited to its use of the Scots language. Her 'graceful, dreamy' poems in English also received recognition. Most strikingly, her work was appreciated for its depiction of 'the straths and the braes of Angus' and her ability to make 'both the ordinary and the fantastic' both believable and 'real'.[102] In 1924, in the early years of the Scottish Renaissance, the *Glasgow Herald* called her 'one of the most genuine of living Scottish creative writers'. By 1936, she was so established as a prominent writer that she was recognised by the University of Edinburgh with an honorary degree. Photographs of the event show her regal and serious, dressed in the honorary robes for the ceremony.[103]

Jacob was also identified as part of a long line of Scottish women poets and song-writers, many of whom hailed from aristocratic families as she did, and who wrote in Scots. Marion Lochhead refers to her 'lang pedigree' and claims she is in 'true descent from the singers and story-tellers who sat by the fire and held both bairns and grownups enthralled'. In another article, she compares Jacob to earlier women poets such as Joanna Baillie and observes that

> the soul of the ballad-makers is in her, with all that wealth of pathos and humour, passion and irony, strangeness and homeliness that makes their song so glorious a heritage; and, like them, she has a fine simplicity of form, removed from common speech only by the imperceptible touch of art that the born poet alone can attain.[104]

But as Leslie W. Wheeler reminds readers, Jacob's 'poetic voice' is 'wholly natural' and 'no mere aristocratic nod in the direction of "quaint" underlings. Clearly visible in all her verse was a deep respect for the countryside and the people of Angus.' It is a testament to the popularity of Jacob's final book, *The Scottish Poetry of Violet Jacob*, that despite wartime paper rations, the book was reprinted several times. In the year of her death, one reviewer referred to her as the 'doyen [sic] of Scottish poets'.[105]

Jacob's acclaim during her lifetime was not restricted to Britain. Her fiction and her poetry received strong reviews in American newspapers, in particular. One reviewer in the

Saturday Review of Literature claims her poetry 'lives, breathes, entertains the mind, and moves the heart', qualities the reviewer suggests are indicative of 'real poetry'. A feature on her work in the American journal *Current Literature* declares that 'she has rare distinction of style, and her whole work has literary quality of a high order [...] The English critics agree that Mrs. Jacob's place in literature is secure.'[106]

In recent years, Jacob's writing has been acknowledged by the inclusion of an excerpt from her poem 'The Wild Geese' in Makar's Court in Edinburgh. Located outside the Writers' Museum, Makar's Court includes flagstones engraved with quotations from the work of prominent Scottish writers; Jacob was one of the first twelve writers to have her writing represented. Isobel Murray, in a review of *The Lum Hat and Other Stories: Last Tales of Violet Jacob*, argues that 'it is time we looked again' at Jacob's work.[107] The present volume contributes to the recent interest in Jacob's writing, making available for the first time a substantial edition of her poems, many of which have not appeared in other collections and many which were not acknowledged by her earlier selected edition of 1944. It is hoped that her poetry once again will receive the critical attention it deserves and that readers will be able to follow her development as a poet from her earliest to her most accomplished poems.

For More Information

Jacob's childhood home, the House of Dun, is owned by the National Trust for Scotland. A tour of the house and grounds gives one a sense of what Jacob's upbringing must have been like: surrounded on all sides by land, the property gave the young poet access to a wide range of people and places that appear in her poetry and prose. One also may visit her grave while at the House of Dun. In addition, a visit to Montrose and the surrounding countryside also gives the interested reader an insight into places such as Craigo Woods that appear in her poetry. The Montrose Public Library, itself greatly loved by Jacob, offers the interested reader the opportunity to see archival material related to Jacob's life and work, including her own copies of some of her novels (complete with pasted-in newspaper clippings and related commentary). Other archival materials include the journal and correspondence of her son Harry along with some of her correspondence in the National Library of Scotland. The bibliography includes a list of specific archival material related to Jacob's life and work for those interested in pursuing her work more extensively.

Endnotes

[1] 'Scotland as a Terra Incognita', *Glasgow Herald*, 14 July 1906, p. 9.
[2] Colin Gibson, 'They Sang of Angus', in *Arbroath Herald Christmas Number* (Arbroath: Arbroath Herald, 1984), n/p; Marion Angus, 'Scottish Poetry Old and New', in *The Scottish Association for the Speaking of Verse: Its Work for the Year 1927–1928* (Edinburgh: Constable, 1928), pp. 18–29 (p. 28); the late Nancy Cant, who met Angus when Angus was in her sixties and she was a teenager, insists that Angus was antagonistic towards Jacob and her work, although there is little written by either writer to support this (personal interview c.1999).
[3] Aberdeen University Special Collections (hereafter abbreviated as AUSC), MS 3017, folder 8/1/1, c. 2 May, no year; Maurice Lindsay, 'Introduction', in *Selected Poems of Marion Angus*, ed. Maurice Lindsay (Edinburgh: Serif, 1950), pp. ix–xiv (p. xiv); Helen Cruickshank, *Octobiography* (Montrose: Standard Press, 1976), p. 76.
[4] Nan Shepherd, 'Marion Angus as a Poet of Deeside', *Deeside Field Club*, 2 (1970), 8–16 (p. 10).
[5] Nan Shepherd, 'Marion Angus', *Scots Magazine*, October 1946, pp. 37–42 (p. 37); papers of Mairi Campbell Ireland, National Library of Scotland (hereafter abbreviated NLS), MS 19328, folio 71 [c.1930].
[6] Shepherd, 'Marion Angus', p. 38.
[7] Personal interview with the late Nancy Cant, Arbroath, 1999; Private papers of the editor. Angus's *Christabel's Diary* (Arbroath: Buncle, 1899) meditates upon bicycling and smoking.
[8] P. W. L., 'Miss Marion Angus: An Appreciation', *Arbroath Guide*, 31 August 1946, p. 6.
[9] Lindsay, p. xi; Alan Bold, *Modern Scottish Literature* (London: Longman, 1983), p. 25; NLS, MS 19328, folio 133, c. 13 April 1931.
[10] The bibliography includes a list of selected secondary sources on Angus writing and life.
[11] 1865 is her birth year, not 1866 as commonly recorded. Census returns for 1871, Sunderland; 1891, Arbroath. I can find no information about Annie after 1902 but 'Annie' recurs in Angus's work in 'The Blue Jacket', 'Annie Honey', 'Links o' Lunan', 'Ann Gilchrist' and 'Green Beads'.
[12] *Sketch of Arbroath Literary Club* (Arbroath: Brodie and Salmond, 1896); *Arbroath Herald Annual 1889* (Arbroath: Buncle, 1889), passim. Angus's father and grandfather are authors of numerous religious tracts

available in the NLS; N. K. W., 'Modern Scotswomen III: Marion Angus', *Scottish Standard*, April 1935, p. 29.

[13] Angus, 'Scottish Poetry Old and New', p. 25.

[14] 'English Department Prizes for 1880', *Arbroath Herald*, 3 July 1880, p. 1. The paper reports that Angus won a special prize for composition on the subject of 'The Sea'. The following year, the paper reports a prize for Angus for her essay 'The Power of Kindness Over Lower Animals' in the *Arbroath Herald*, 2 July 1881, p. 1; Catriona Burness, ' "Kept Some Steps Behind Him": Women in Scotland 1780–1920' in *A History of Scottish Women's Writing*, ed. Douglas Gifford and Dorothy McMillan (Edinburgh: Edinburgh University Press, 1997), pp. 103–18 (p. 111); John MacRitchie, 'Arbroath's Singin' Lass', in *Arbroath Herald Annual 1996* (Arbroath: Arbroath Herald, 1996), n/p, passim.

[15] Margery Palmer McCulloch, 'Fictions of Development 1920–1970' in *A History of Scottish Women's Writing*, ed. Douglas Gifford and Dorothy McMillan (Edinburgh: Edinburgh University Press, 1997), pp. 360–72 (p. 366), her emphasis.

[16] 'Death of Rev. Henry Angus, D.D.', *Arbroath Herald*, 22 May 1902, p. 5; AUSC, MS 2737, folio 49; NLS, MS 10551, folio 163, c. 25 May 1930; *Roll of Graduates of the University of Aberdeen, 1860–1900* (Aberdeen: Aberdeen University Press, 1906), p. 188. Henry Angus was in Palmerston, Otago, New Zealand for two and a half years. I have no proof of letters between Angus and Henry, who also spent time in Vienna, where he enrolled in a postgraduate course in medicine; obituary of Henry Angus, *Aberdeen University Review*, 25 (1937–8), p. 188.

[17] Shepherd, 'Marion Angus', p. 40.

[18] J. M. McBain, *Bibliography of Arbroath Periodical Literature and Political Broadsides* (Arbroath: Brodie and Salmond, 1889), p. 52; William Marwick, *Handbook Containing Rules, Programme, etc. of The Reading Guild (Late Ruskin Reading Guild)* (London: Mathews, n/d; Arbroath: Brodie and Salmond, n/d), passim.

[19] *Round About Geneva* (Arbroath: Buncle, 1899), n/p; *Christabel's Diary*, p. 30. In *Christabel's Diary*, Angus alludes to Wilde's contemporaneous *The Critic as Artist* when Christabel notes, 'indiscretion is the better part of valour' (p. 38).

[20] Shepherd, 'Marion Angus as a Poet of Deeside', pp. 8–16; AUSC, MS 2737, folio 47, c. 7 November 1968; Ethel is buried beside her parents in the Western Cemetery; J. B. S[almond], 'An Appreciation', *Arbroath Guide*, 24 August 1946, p. 6.

[21] Colin Milton, 'Angus, Marion Emily (1865–1946), in *Oxford Dictionary of National Biography*, ed. H. C. G. Matthew and Brian Harrison (Oxford: Oxford University Press, 2004), **http://www.oxforddnb.com/view/article/59069** [accessed 17 August 2005]; AUSC, MS 2737, folio 47, c. 7 November 1968; Cruickshank, *Octobiography*, p. 76; NLS, MS 19328, folios 94, 20, c.1930.

[22] W., N. K., 'Modern Scotswomen III: Marion Angus', p. 29; NLS, MS 19328, folio 20, c. January [1930], her emphasis.

[23] NLS, Dep. 209, box 17, folder 1, no date.

[24] Genesis, 19.20–22; writing to a friend, Angus laments: 'Alas and alas!

I clung to the hope until yesterday that I would still have a roof of my own under which to receive you next Sunday but it is not to be. My lawyer insisted on me taking the offer of a lady who wanted to buy my house [...] So you see I am writing this in the midst of a confusion and worry which is like to drive me distracted. It breaks my heart to leave this nice little house where my sister and I have been so happy but one has to go where one is led (or driven) and I feel like a leaf before the wind only a leaf has no business worries nor sleepless nights nor human feelings of anxiety or grief (NLS, MS 19326, folio 48, c. May [1930]).

[25] NLS, MS 19328, folio 109, folios 87–8; S[almond], p. 6; Shepherd, 'Marion Angus', p. 37; NLS, MS 19328, passim.

[26] Gibson, n/p. Gibson quotes Matthew as saying that Angus's play was 'accepted by the BBC, but they had already accepted a play for the Centenary, and said they would broadcast her's [sic] at a later date. She asked for it to be returned, and burned it in the furnace! The Centenary or nothing!' (n/p); AUSC, MS 3036, folio 8; in one letter Angus asks Nan Shepherd for advice about historical plays for children for the BBC.

[27] Cruickshank, 'A Personal Note', p. xvi; Shepherd usefully counters this story with the observation that 'the generosity of her judgments, in one whose tongue could be so caustic, was fabulous'; Auden, Shepherd suggests, 'was seeking not advice, but what we in the North-East call "addisens"; and as an audience she was perfect. If she sighed a little because the subsequent discussion was all about him and never about her, she never, one imagines, made him aware of it' ('Marion Angus', p. 38); 'In Memoriam: Marion Angus', Glasgow Herald, 23 August 1946, p. 3.

[28] 'Report of the Annual Meeting 1932', in The Scottish Association for the Speaking of Verse: 1931–33 (Glasgow: Davidson, n/d), p. 33.

[29] 'Radio Programmes', Scotsman, 18 September 1930, p. 14, in Scotsman Digital Archive, **http://archive.scotsman.com/article.cfm?id=TSC/1930/09/18/Ar01405** [accessed 31 December 2005]; NLS, MS 19328, folios 82–3, c. 16 September 1930 and folio 35, c. 30 March 1930; AUSC, MS 2737, folio 35, c. 15 September 1950. Her talks spanned several years.

[30] AUSC, MS 2737, folio 7, c. 13 February, no year; Gibson, n/p.

[31] Silvie Taylor, 'A Passion for the Splendour of Life', Scots Magazine, March 2001, pp. 304–8 (p. 308); Shepherd, 'Marion Angus', p. 37.

[32] Angus, 'Scottish Poetry Old and New', p. 29.

[33] Shepherd, 'Marion Angus', p. 41; NLS, MS 19328, folio 32, c. 9 March [1930].

[34] Leslie W. Wheeler, 'Marion Angus (1866–1946)', in Ten Northeast Poets: An Anthology, ed. Leslie W. Wheeler (Aberdeen: Aberdeen University Press, 1985), p. 1.

[35] Scottish Ballads, ed. Emily Lyle (Edinburgh: Canongate, 1994), p. 53, 58.

[36] For a more extensive analysis of time in Angus's work, please see my doctoral dissertation 'Voices from the "Cauld, East Countra": Representations of the Self in the Poetry of Violet Jacob and Marion Angus' (University of Glasgow, 2000) and 'Women "Wha' Lauched and

Lo'ed and Sinned": Women's Voices in the Work of Violet Jacob and Marion Angus', *Études Écossaises*, 9 (2003–4), 77–89; Dorothy Porter [McMillan], 'Scotland's Songstresses', *Cencrastus*, 25 (1987), 48–52 (p. 49).
[37] AUSC, MS 3036, folio 3, no date.
[38] Randall Stevenson, *Modernist Fiction: An Introduction* (London: Longman, 1998), p. 114; Borges engages with Dunne's ideas in several essays, but rather pointedly claims Dunne is 'a famous victim of that bad intellectual habit denounced by [Henri] Bergson: to conceive of time as a fourth dimension of space' in 'Time and J. W. Dunne', in *Other Inquisitions: 1937–1952*, trans. Ruth L. C. Simms (New York: Clarion, 1965), pp. 18–21 (p. 20).
[39] See my 'Voices from the "Cauld, East Countra": Representations of the Self in the Poetry of Violet Jacob and Marion Angus'.
[40] Angus, 'Scottish Poetry Old and New', p. 28; Shepherd, 'Marion Angus', p. 42.
[41] S[almond], p. 6; Shepherd, 'Marion Angus', p. 42; AUSC, MS 3036, folio 3, no date; Marion Angus, 'Robert H. Corstorphine: 1874–1942' in *Robert H. Corstorphine: 1874–1942* (Arbroath: Buncle, c.1942), pp. 3–5.
[42] Charles Graves, 'The Poetry of Marion Angus', *Chapbook*, 6 (1946), 97, 107 (p. 107, p. 97); W. S., 'The Poetry of Marion Angus', *The Free Man*, 7 (1934), 10.
[43] Janet Caird, 'The Poetry of Marion Angus', *Cencrastus*, 25 (1987), 45–7 (p. 47).
[44] For more extensive commentary on 'The Eerie Hoose', please see my article 'Liltin' in the "Eerie Hoose": Aspects of Self in the Poetry of Marion Angus' in *Terranglian Territories*, ed. Susanne Hagemann (Berlin: Lang, 2000), pp. 379–88.
[45] Marion Angus, 'The Little Grey Town', *Scots Observer*, 2 January 1930, p. 9.
[46] Shepherd, 'Marion Angus as a Poet of Deeside', p. 12; Review of *Lost Country and Other Verses* by Marion Angus, *Scotsman*, 6 December 1937, p. 13, in Scotsman Digital Archive, **http://archive.scotsman.com/article.cfm?id=TSC/1937/12/06/Ar01306** [accessed 31 December 2005]; Arthur Ogilvie [Marion Angus], 'Diary', *Arbroath Guide*, 5 February 1898, p. 2.
[47] Letters of Charles Graves, NLS, MS 27477, folio 71, c. 22 July, no year. Many of Angus's male relatives were ministers and at least one of her sisters also married a minister.
[48] Shepherd, 'Marion Angus as a Poet of Deeside', p. 15; J. M. McPherson, *Primitive Beliefs in the North-East of Scotland* (London: Longmans, 1929; New York: Arno, 1977).
[49] NLS, MS 19328 folio 16, c.1929, her emphasis.
[50] MacRitchie, 'Arbroath's Singin' Lass', n/p; Porter [McMillan], p. 49; Angus, *Christabel's Diary*, p. 31.
[51] Porter [McMillan], p. 50.
[52] Caird, 'The Poetry of Marion Angus', p. 45.
[53] NLS, MS 19328, folio 120, c. 6 March 1931, her emphasis; NLS, Dep. 209, box 17, folder 1, her emphasis.
[54] Lindsay, p. xii; Porter [McMillan], passim; Caird, 'The Poetry of Marion Angus', passim; Helen Cruickshank, 'A Personal Note', in

INTRODUCTION   49

Selected Poems of Marion Angus, ed. Maurice Lindsay (Edinburgh: Serif, 1950), pp. xv–xxi (passim); Christopher Whyte obliquely considers, and brushes aside, a lesbian reading of Angus's poetry in 'Marion Angus and the Borders of Self', in *A History of Scottish Women's Writing*, ed. Douglas Gifford and Dorothy McMillan (Edinburgh: Edinburgh University Press, 1997), pp. 373–88.
[55] Diana Collecott, 'What is Not Said: A Study in Textual Inversion', in *Sexual Sameness: Textual Differences in Lesbian and Gay Writing*, ed. Joseph Bristow (London: Routledge, 1992), pp. 91–110 (p. 102).
[56] Review of *The Singin' Lass* by Marion Angus, *Times Literary Supplement*, 10 October 1929, pp. 798–9 (p. 798–9); Caird, 'The Poetry of Marion Angus', p. 47.
[57] Review of *The Singin' Lass* by Marion Angus, *Scotsman*, 15 July 1929, p. 2, in Scotsman Digital Archive, **http://archive.scotsman.com/article.cfm?id=TSC/1929/07/15/Ar00201** [accessed 31 December 2005]; Review of *The Singin' Lass* by Marion Angus, *Times Literary Supplement*, p. 798.
[58] Margaret Sackville, 'Scottish Poets', *Scots Observer*, 3 October 1929, p. 21; Graves, 'The Poetry of Marion Angus', p. 97; Shepherd, 'Marion Angus as a Poet of Deeside', p. 16.
[59] Graves, 'The Poetry of Marion Angus', p. 107; review of *The Turn of the Day*, *Times Literary Supplement*, 20 August 1931, p. 635.
[60] [W.] H[amilton], letter to the editor, *Scotsman*, 22 August 1946, p. 4, in Scotsman Digital Archive, **http://archive.scotsman.com/article.cfm?id=TSC/1946/08/22/Ar00404** [accessed 31 December 2005].
[61] Lindsay, p. ix, p. xiii; Alastair Mackie, 'Change and Continuity in Modern Scots Poetry', *Akros*, 11 (1977), 13–40 (p. 13).
[62] J. Derrick McClure, 'The Language of Modern Scots Poetry', in *The Edinburgh Companion to Scots*, ed. John Corbett, J. Derrick McClure and Jane Stuart-Smith (Edinburgh: Edinburgh University Press, 2003), pp. 210–32 (p. 219); Caird, 'The Poetry of Marion Angus', p. 47.
[63] Violet Jacob, *Diaries and Letters from India, 1895–1900*, ed. Carol Anderson (Edinburgh: Canongate, 1990), pp. 66–7. Hereafter abbreviated DLI.
[64] Violet Jacob, *Tales of My Own Country* (London: Murray, 1922).
[65] I am indebted to Carol Anderson's writings on Jacob for much of the information on events in Jacob's life. See in particular: Carol Anderson, 'Jacob, Violet Augusta Mary Frederica (1863–1946)', in *Oxford Dictionary of National Biography*, ed. H. C. G. Matthew and Brian Harrison (Oxford: Oxford University Press, 2004), **http://www.oxforddnb.com/view/article/58422** [accessed 15 December 2005].
[66] 'The Late Mr Kennedy-Erskine of Dun', *Scotsman*, 27 February 1908, p. 7, in Scotsman Digital Archive, **http://archive.scotsman.com/article.cfm?id=TSC/1908/02/27/Ar00707** [accessed 15 December 2005].
[67] Cruickshank, *Octobiography*, p. 135.
[68] Papers of Robert Macleod, NLS, MS 9997.
[69] Carol Anderson, 'Tales of Her Own Countries: Violet Jacob', in *A History of Scottish Women's Writing*, ed. Douglas Gifford and Dorothy McMillan (Edinburgh: Edinburgh University Press, 1997), pp. 347–59 (p. 347).

[70] Letters of Marion Cleland Lochhead, NLS, MS 26109, folio 245.
[71] DLI, p. 31; Charlotte Reid, letter to the editor, *Cencrastus*, 21 (1985), 59.
[72] Carol Anderson, 'Tales of Her Own Countries: Violet Jacob', p. 349; Papers of James Christison, c. April 1918, Montrose Library Archives. Mary Sherwood's *The History of the Fairchild Family* is, as Jacob's letter indicates, a morally instructive children's book that reveals its intentions in its subtitle: *The History of the Fairchild Family: Or, the Child's Manual: Being a Collection of Stories (the Importance and Effects of a Religious Education)* (London: Hatchard, 1818; Roehampton: University of Surrey Roehampton Digital Library). **http://wordsworth.roehampton.ac.uk/digital/chlit/shehis/ind.asp** [accessed 15 December 2005].
[73] Violet Jacob, 'A Manor House in Brittany', *Country Life*, 22 May 1920, pp. 685–6 (p. 686).
[74] Jacob, 'A Manor House in Brittany', p. 686.
[75] NLS, MS 27413, folio 57, 'To Cupid, In Sugar on a Wedding Cake'; Papers of James Christison, Montrose Library Archives, c. 1 March 1937; Violet Jacob, 'Kirsty's Opinion'.
[76] Marion Lochhead, 'Violet Jacob', *Scots Magazine*, November 1925, pp. 130–4 (p. 130); Jacob quoted in Sarah Bing, 'Autobiography in the Work of Violet Jacob', *Chapman*, 74–5 (1993), 99–109 (p. 106).
[77] Violet Kennedy-Erskine and William Douglas Campbell, *The Bailie MacPhee* (Edinburgh: Blackwood, 1891).
[78] DLI, p. 74; Susan Tweedsmuir, *The Lilac and the Rose* (London: Duckworth, 1952), pp. 54–5.
[79] Violet Jacob, 'Tam i' the Kirk', *Country Life*, 12 November 1910, p. 668. A brief discussion of Scots in Jacob and Angus's poetry appears in the notes; 'Death of Violet Jacob: A Notable Scottish Poet', *Scotsman*, 11 September 1946, p. 4, in Scotsman Digital Archive, **http://archive.scotsman.com/article.cfm?id=TSC/1946/09/11/Ar00407** [accessed 21 January 2006].
[80] Papers of Helen Cruickshank, Stirling University Library, c.1915.
[81] Joy Hendry, 'Twentieth-Century Women's Writing: The Nest of Singing Birds', in *The History of Scottish Literature*, IV, ed. Cairns Craig (Aberdeen: Aberdeen University Press, 1987), pp. 291–310 (p. 293).
[82] DLI, p. 140.
[83] Violet Jacob, 'Preface', in *The True Story of My Life* by Hans Christian Andersen, trans. Mary Howitt (London: Longman, 1847; London: Routledge, 1926), pp. vii–x (p. viii); Bing, p. 101.
[84] Carol Anderson, 'Introduction', in *Diaries and Letters from India, 1895–1900*, ed. Carol Anderson (Edinburgh: Canongate, 1990), pp. 1–17 (p. 2); 'The Late Mr Kennedy-Erskine of Dun'; 'Scotswoman's Death: Suicide Verdict at Inquest', *Scotsman*, 28 December 1934, p. 6, in Scotsman Digital Archive, **http://archive.scotsman.com/article.cfm?id=TSC/1934/12/28/Ar00600** [accessed 21 January 2006].
[85] Papers and Journal of Harry Jacob, NLS, Acc. 11110, folios 1–5 (microfilm); Tweedsmuir, p. 55; Jacob quoted in Bing, p. 109.
[86] Porter [McMillan], p. 48; Janet Caird, 'The Poetry of Violet Jacob and Helen B. Cruickshank', *Cencrastus*, 19 (1984), 32–4 (p. 33).
[87] Marion Lochhead, 'Feminine Quartet', *Chapman*, 27–8 (1980), 21–31 (p. 22).

[88] Ronald Garden, 'Violet Jacob in India', *Scottish Literary Journal*, 13 (1986), 48–64 (p. 48); Violet Jacob, quoted in Anderson, 'Introduction', in *Diaries and Letters from India, 1895–1900*, p. 15.
[89] Violet Jacob, 'The End O't'.
[90] Papers of James Christison, Montrose Library Archives, c. 1 March 1937.
[91] Carol Anderson, 'Spirited Teller of Tales from a Beloved Country', *Glasgow Herald*, 9 May 1998, p. 12; Bing, p. 109; D. B. M. Mellis and W. J. Sinclair, 'The Parish of Dun', in *The Third Statistical Account of Scotland: The County of Angus*, ed. William Allen Illsley (Arbroath: Arbroath Herald Press, 1977), pp. 257–63 (p. 258).
[92] 'Death of Violet Jacob: A Notable Scottish Poet'; Hugh MacDiarmid, 'Violet Jacob', in *Contemporary Scottish Studies* (London: Parsons, 1926; Edinburgh: Scottish Educational Journal, 1976), p. 8.
[93] My article 'Women "Wha' Lauched and Lo'ed and Sinned": Women's Voices in the Work of Violet Jacob and Marion Angus' addresses the treatment of women's voices in Jacob's poetry; C. M. B., 'A Glance at the Field of New Literature – What Authors are Saying and Doing', review of *The Sheep Stealers* by Violet Jacob, *Los Angeles Times*, 5 October 1902, p. D10, in ProQuest Historical Newspapers, **http://hngraphical.proquest.com** [accessed 7 July 2005]; Caird, 'The Poetry of Violet Jacob and Helen B. Cruickshank', p. 33; Violet Jacob, 'Back to the Land'.
[94] Anderson, 'Tales of Her Own Countries: Violet Jacob', p. 351, p. 350.
[95] Lochhead, 'Violet Jacob', p. 130; J. Derrick McClure, *Language, Poetry, and Nationhood: Scots as a Poetic Language from 1878 to the Present* (East Lothian: Tuckwell, 2000), p. 73.
[96] Lochhead, 'Violet Jacob', p. 133; L. M. Cumming, 'A Singer of Angus', *Scottish Bookman*, December 1935, pp. 35–45 (p. 35).
[97] 'Cairneyside'; 'The Gean-Trees'.
[98] Garden, 'Violet Jacob in India', pp. 57–64.
[99] Porter [McMillan], p. 49.
[100] Cumming, p. 40.
[101] Angela Cran, 'Forgotten Spy Story Comes In From the Cold', review of *Flemington* by Violet Jacob, *Scotland on Sunday*, 11 December 1994, p. 13, in Lexis-Nexis, **http://www.lexisnexis.com** [accessed 21 January 2006]; review of *More Songs of Angus* by Violet Jacob, *Scotsman*, 18 November 1918, p. 2, in Scotsman Digital Archive, **http://archive.scotsman.com/article.cfm?id=TSC/1918/11/18/Ar00215** [accessed 15 December 2005]; review of *Bonnie Joann and Other Poems* by Violet Jacob, *Scots Pictorial*, 3 December 1921, p. 521.
[102] Review of *More Songs of Angus* by Violet Jacob, *Scotsman*; review of *Songs of Angus* by Violet Jacob, *Scotsman*, 18 February 1915, p. 2, in Scotsman Digital Archive, **http://archive.scotsman.com/article.cfm?id=TSC/1915/02/18/Ar00201** [accessed 31 December 2005]; obituary of Violet Jacob, *Times*, 11 September 1946, p. 7.
[103] Review of *Two New Poems* by Violet Jacob, *Glasgow Herald*, 18 December 1924, p. 4; 'Edinburgh Graduation', *Scotsman*, 4 July 1936, p. 20, in Scotsman Digital Archive, **http://archive.scotsman.com/**

article.cfm?id=TSC/1946/07/04/Pc02003/ [accessed 21 January 2006].
[104] Lochhead, 'Feminine Quartet', p. 23; Lochhead, 'Violet Jacob', p. 134.
[105] Leslie W. Wheeler, 'Violet Jacob (1863–1946)', in *Ten Northeast Poets: An Anthology*, ed. Leslie W. Wheeler (Aberdeen: Aberdeen University Press, 1985), pp. 73–4 (p. 73); Scotland's Muse in Modern Dress', review of *Modern Scottish Poetry: An Anthology of the Scottish Renaissance, 1920–1945*, ed. Maurice Lindsay, *Scotsman*, 22 August 1946, p. 7, in Scotsman Digital Archive, **http://archive.scotsman.com/article.cfm?id=TSC/1946/08/22/Ar00703** [accessed 31 December 2005].
[106] W. R. B. 'Cursive/Discursive', *Saturday Review of Literature*, 17 October 1925, p. 224; 'People in the Foreground: Violet Jacob', *Current Literature*, 37 (1904), p. 417.
[107] Isobel Murray, 'The Forgotten Violet Jacob', review of *The Lum Hat and Other Stories: Last Tales of Violet Jacob*, *Cencrastus*, 13 (1984), p. 54 (p. 54)

THE POEMS OF MARION ANGUS

Marion Angus (*left*)
Marion Angus in an undated photograph

Zoar (*below*)
Zoar, the home in Aberdeen where Marion Angus lived in the 1920s

From *The Lilt and Other Verses (1922)*

BY CANDLE LIGHT

Mary Forbes weaves in the candle light
When the straw is stacked in the barn.
Round and about her fingers slim
She twists the fleecy yarn—
    The candle light—the candle light— 5
And the shadows on the floor
And the wrinkled leaves of the rowan bush
    A'-rustling beyond the door—

'Now what is't you think on
My yellow-haired lad, 10
With your fiddle upon your knee?'
'On the days when I counted the lambs, mother
By the bonnie green links o' Dee'—
    The candle light—the candle light—
And a wind that sparks the peat 15
And a sleety rain, on the window pane,
    Like the patter o' birdies' feet.

'Come play me—"Whaur Gowdie Rins" my son,
Or a reel with a heartsome tune.'
But he minds how he how danced at the Castleton 20
In the long clear gloamings o' June—
    The candle light—the candle light—
And the lass with the tawny shoon,
That danced with him at the Castleton
    In the silver shine of the moon. 25

Mary Forbes weaves in the candle light—
Her fiddler plays in the gloom
The dowiest airs in all the world
Trail round and about the room,
And Mary blesses the candle light— 30
    The witchin', watchin' Flame—
The eerie night and the candle light
    That keeps her bairn at hame.

THE DROVE ROAD

It's a dark hill track over grey Culblean
    Though light on the rocks may glisten
The lonesomest road that ever was seen
    But the old folks say—if you listen—

You may hear the tread and the march of the dead—
    (The young folks know the story)
Of the wild hill men that came out of the glen—
    Fierce for battle and glory.

And they tell how at dawning on dark Culblean
    You may hear the slogan ringing
Where clansmen and foe in the moss below
    Sleep sound—to the brown burn's singing.

I hear no tread of the wild hill men
    Nor slogan at dawning pealing,
Only the tune of the brown burn's croon
    And a breeze on the bracken stealing.

I wish I were hearing Wat Gordon cry
On his collie 'Jock', as the herd goes by
On the lonesome track above dark Culblean.
The blithest days are the days that have been.

The laugh and the cry
    And the blue eyes glisten—
Never more, never more, and the years go by
    Yet . . . listen!

REMEMBRANCE DAY

Some one was singing
    Up a twisty stair,
  A fragment of a song,
  One sweet, spring day,
When twelve o'clock was ringing,
    Through the sunny square—

'There was a lad baith frank and free,
Cam' doon the bonnie banks o' Dee
Wi' tartan plaid and buckled shoon,
An' he'll come nae mair to oor toon.—

'He dwells within a far countree,
Where great ones do him courtesie,
They've gien him a golden croon,
An' he'll come nae mair to oor toon.'—

No one is singing
    Up the twisty stair.
Quiet as a sacrament
    The November day.

Can't you hear it swinging,
    The little ghostly air?—
  Hear it sadly stray
  Through the misty square,
In and out a doorway,
    Up a twisty stair—
Tartan plaid and buckled shoon,
He'll come nae mair to oor toon.

THE FOX'S SKIN

When the wark's a' dune and the world's a' still,
And whaups are swoopin' across the hill,
And mither stands cryin' 'Bairns, come ben,'
It's the time for the Hame o' the Pictish Men.

A sorrowfu' wind gaes up and doon,　　　　　　　　　5
An' me my lane in the licht o' the moon,
Gatherin' a bunch o' the floorin' whin,
Wi' my auld fur collar happed roond ma chin.

A star is shinin' on Morven Glen—
It shines on the Hame o' the Pictish Men.　　　　　　10
Hither and yont their dust is blown,
But there's ane o' them keekin' ahint yon stone.

His queer auld face is wrinkled and riven,
Like a raggedy leaf, sae drookit and driven.
There's nocht to be feared at his ancient ways.　　　15
For this is a' that iver he says—

The same auld wind at its weary cry:
The blin' faced moon in the misty sky;
A thoosand years o' clood and flame,
An' a'thing's the same an' aye the same—　　　　　　20
The lass is the same in the fox's skin,
Gatherin' the bloom o' the floorin' whin.

THE BRIDGE

She loves not this dark street of stone,
   Nor loves she windows high;
She loves the wind's wild trumpet blown
   Across the moorland sky,
     And the three wild cherry trees at Little Invereye.

She for herself a bridge has weft,
   All wan and silvery;
She for herself a road has cleft
   To take her soundlessly
     To the three tall cherry trees growing up so high.

With slender hands a branch she breaks
   Between the moor and sky;
Of blossoms white a crown she makes,
   On her pale hair to lie,
     From the tallest wild cherry tree at Little Invereye.

She for herself a bridge has weft
   Of strands of memory;
She for herself a road has cleft
   To take her soundlessly
     To the green, green waters that flow by Invereye.

Her slender hands she smoothes and laves
   In floods of ivory;
Her slender feet beneath the waves
   Move pale and shadowy
     In the green, green waters that flow so sweetly by.

Could I her feet in fetters hold
   Behind those windows high,
Her mocking heart so light and cold
   Would pass me heedless by,
     Haunting the green waters at Little Invereye,
     Where three tall cherry trees are growing up so high.

TREASURE TROVE

Do you mind rinnin' barefit
In the saft, summer mist
Liltin' and linkin' on the steep hill heids?
In below your tartan shawl, your hand wad aye twist
Your bonnie green beads. 5

Do you mind traivellin', traivellin'
Ower and ower the braes,
Reistlin' the heather, and keekin' 'naith the weeds,
Seekin' and greetin' in the cauld weet days
For yer tint green beads. 10

Whist! Dinna rouse him,
The auld sleepin' man—
Steek, the door; the mune-licht's on the lone hill heids—
Wee elfin craturs is delvin' in the sand,
They canna' miss the glimmer 15
O' yer auld green beads.

Here they come, the wee folk,
Speedin' fast and fleet—
There's a queer, low lauchin' on the grey hill heids—
An' the bricht drops, glancin', followin' at their feet— 20
It's green, green beads—
The last ye'll ever see o' yer bonnie green beads.

THE TURN OF THE DAY

Under the cauld, green grass
   I hear the waukenin' burn.
   The day's at the turn—
Oh, winter, dinna pass!

Your snaw was white for a bride,
   Your winds were merriage wine.
   Love is fine, fine,
But it doesna bide.

The saft, warm April rain
   An' the clear June day,
   An' floors o' the May—
I'll see them a' my lane.

Under the cauld, green grass,
   Wee waukenin', wanderin' burn,
Sing your ain sang.
   The day's at the turn,
But simmer's lang, lang.

MOONLIGHT

When the sweet moon has come,
Her slender pattern thrown
   Along the silent sands, the empty shore,
One, hearing with delight,
The whisper of the night,   5
   Softly behind her shuts her cottage door.

The wild thyme's fragrance shed
Upon its dying bed—
   Red wine all spilt upon the moon-stained bent—
To her unfaded is,   10
For she persuaded is,
   Of beauty triumphing in beauty spent.

When from a moon-lit mist,
Silver and amethyst,
   The spendthrift waves   15
Fly far in broken gleams,
   She in sweet folly sees
   Enchanted treasuries,
With glittering fabrics stored for endless dreams.

When the moontide is full,   20
Across the rocky pool,
   The salty pool, where weeds grow bitterly,
Only her own heart knows
Why she so tranquil goes
   Alone, yet in such friendly company.   25

When the sweet moonbeams wane
Up the lone path again
   Like a grey, flitting moth she homeward hies.
How hardly do the rich,
How hardly do the rich,   30
   How easily the poor in heart find Paradise.

THE LILT

Jean Gordon is weaving a' her lane
Twinin' the threid wi' a thocht o' her ain,
Hearin' the tune o' the bairns at play
That they're singin' amang them ilka day
And saftly, saftly, ower the hill 5
Comes the sma, sma rain.

Aye, she minds o' a simmer's nicht
Afore the waning o' the licht—
Bairnies chantin' in Lover's lane
The sang that comes ower an' ower again, 10
And a young lass stealin' awa' to the hill,
In the sma, sma rain.

Oh! lass, your lips were flamin' reid,
An' cauld, mist drops lay on yer heid,
Ye didna gaither yon rose yer lane 15
And yer hert was singin' a sang o' its ain,
As ye slippit hameward, ower the hill,
In the sma, sma rain.

Jean Gordon, she minds as she sits her lane
O' a' the years that's bye and gane, 20
And naething gi'en and a'thing ta'en
But yon nicht or nichts on the smoory hill
In the sma, sma rain—
And the bairns are singin' at their play
The lilt that they're liltin' ilka day— 25

LONELINESS

Green were the bents to-day,
    Clear shone the skies above,
But many a mile away
    Are the bents I love.

The wind and waves they sang
    All the sweet day long,
But never above them rang
    The dearest song.

The long shore glistened fair,
    All laid with silver fine,
But no footprint was there
    Along with mine.

The wild thyme's purple-grey
    Was soft as crooning dove
Where I sighed my heart away
    For the bents I love.

ALL SOULS' EVE

At the darkening of the west
   O'er the night-bewildered sea,
Wind-borne strains my heart arrest,
   Luting loveliest litany.

Sister, does a dream of me
   Dim the glory in your eyes,
Fluting your wild melody
   On the hills of Paradise?

With the falling of the night
   At the ebbing of the tide,
Bearing chalice of delight
   Comes the bridegroom to the bride.

Brother, would you comfort me,
   All with grief foredone and spent;
From the deep tranquillity
   Bid me drink content.

While the night grows dark and late,
   See the shadows weave and weave
Garments for the guests who wait,
   And pass, on All Souls' Eve.

THE GRACELESS LOON

As I gaed east by Tarland toun
I heard a singin' neath the müne
A lass sang in a milk-white goon
    Aneath a ha'thorn tree.
The sma' green trees bowed doon till her;   5
The blooms they made a croon till her;
I was a graceless loon till her,
    She frooned and scorned at me.

As I gaed east thro' Tarland toun
There came an auld wife, bent and dune,   10
Speirin' at me to sit me doon
    In her wee hoose up the Wynd
And wile awa' the nicht wi' her,
The weary candle licht wi' her;
A bairn's een was a sicht till her,   15
    An' auld folks herts is kind.

Fu' mony a year o' sun and rain,
An' I'm for Tarland toun again,
Wi' drift upon a cauld hearth stane
    An' a wind gaen thro' the Wynd.   20
Oh, lass, tho' a' yer sangs be dune,
Ower leafless thorn aye hangs the müne;
Turn ye until yer graceless loon
    Gin ye've grown auld and kind.

From *The Tinker's Road and Other Verses (1924)*

THE TINKER'S ROAD

The broon burn's speerin',
Frettin' a' the wye,
'What gars ye gang
Auld Tinker's Road,
Whaur there's naither fouk nor kye,   5

Kirk nor croft nor mill,
A' thing lane and still?'
But it's aye 'Haud on'
Wi' the Tinker's Road
Fur the far side o' the hill.   10

Stannin' stanes gloomin',
Grim an' straucht an' dour—
'An unco place for a Tinker's Road
On sic a ghaist-rid moor!'

Ghaist or witch or deil,   15
Stanes o' dule an' ill,
It's aye 'Hing in'
Wi' the Tinker's Road
Fur the far side o' the hill.

The black thorn's maenin',   20
'O rauch winds, let me be!
Atween ye a'
Ye've brak ma he'rt,
An' syne I canna dee!'

Weerin' til a threid,   25
Smoored wi' mosses reid,
The soople road wins ower the tap
An' tak's nor tent nor heed.

The muir-cock's crawin',
'I ken a dowie bed   30
Far ben in a nameless glen
Wi' lady breckan spread.'

Whaur dreepin' watters fill
The bonnie green mools intil,
The Tinker's Road maun sough awa'   35
At the far side o' the hill.

THE SEAWARD TOON

Gin ye hadna barred yer painted door
Fur dreid o' the dreepin' mists,
Ye micht hae h'ard the news gang by
That blaws as the wind lists.

Better hae spun wi' a gowden threid   5
By the grey ash o' the peat,
Than woven yer sorra's weary web,
Cauld as a shroodin' sheet,

Moornin' aye for the seaward toon,
Lapt roond wi' the hungry wave,   10
Wi' ilka ruint stane a wound,
An ilka yaird a grave.

Gin ye hadna steekit sae fast yer door
Wi' heid and he'rt fu' hie,
A lily bud for a fair breist-knot   15
An' a sprig o' the rosemarie,

Ower the bent, an' ower the bent
Ayont the blawing sand,
Yer fit wad hae fint a seaward toon
Ne'er biggit by mortal hand,   20

Wi' a glimmer an' lowe fae shinin' panes,
An' the stir o' eident feet,
A'thing hapt in a droosy air
That's naither cauld nor heat.

Thir's ane that cries sae clear and sweet   25
Three names baith kin an' kind,
Marget, Maud'lin, Lizabeth,
Far ben a quaiet wynd.

Gin ye hadna steekit yer painted door
Ere the licht o' day was dune,   30
Ye micht hae h'ard the Host gang by
Ower this braw Seaward Toon.

MARY'S SONG

I wad ha'e gi'en him my lips tae kiss,
Had I been his, had I been his;
Barley breid and elder wine,
Had I been his as he is mine.

The wanderin' bee it seeks the rose; 5
Tae the lochan's bosom the burnie goes;
The grey bird cries at evenin's fa',
'My luve, my fair one, come awa'.'

My beloved sall ha'e this he'rt tae break,
Reid, reid wine and the barley cake, 10
A he'rt tae break, and a mou' tae kiss,
Tho' he be nae mine, as I am his.

IN ARDELOT

In Ardelot
Nine years ago,
'Twas you who sang
In Ardelot.

Of doves that to 5
Their ark repair,
And find a constant
Refuge there,
All gentle souls
My heart enthrall, 10
And you most gentle
Were of all.

In little houses
Warm and lit,
When with the country 15
Folk you sit,
Dream of your altars
Still, my dove,
The resting-places
Of your love. 20

Yet hear in winds' call
My heart's call,
For you the dearest
Were of all

In Ardelot, 25
In Ardelot,
By rocking pines
Of Ardelot.

GEORGE GORDON, LORD BYRON
Aberdeen, 1924

This ae nicht, this ae nicht
By the saut sea faem,
The auld grey wife
O' the auld grey toon,
She's biddin' her bairns hame
Fae the far roads
An' the lang roads
An' the land that's ayont them a',
She's cryin' them hame
Till her ain toon
Atween the rivers twa.

This ae nicht, this ae nicht
Fan the win' dra's fae the sea,
Thir's a laddie's step
On the cobbled steens—
Fatna laddie can it be?
Is't him that sang
Wi' the stars o' morn,
An' brak his he'rt
On a bleedin' thorn
An' thocht nae mair o' me?

This ae nicht, this ae nicht,
The mirk an' the dawn atween,
Yon bairn he weers the Gordon plaid
An' his een's the eagle's een.
He sings as he gangs
By the Collidge Croon,
He fustles it ower the faem,
A queer auld rune
Til a gey auld tune,
I'm thinkin' my bairn's won hame.

For it's: 'Brig o' Balgownie,
            Black's yer wa',
            Wi' a mither's ae son
            An' a mare's ae foal
              Doon ye sall fa'.'

IN A MIRROR

My mirror is a starlit lake
Where three tall candles flare and shake.
Hark to the song the night-winds make.
The bairns chaunt the fairy tune
A little one would love to croon.   5

'Yin that blew the thistle seed,
Yin that strung the rowans reid,
Yin that danced fu' daintily
Abune the green o' the blaeberries.'

Mirror, mirror, on the wall,   10
Shadows rise and shadows fall,
Who will answer when I call?

But the wind blows out the candles three
So that the better I may see
The little one look back at me.   15

ANNIE HONEY

When we gave him no 'Good-e'en'
At the cross or on the green,
Nor welcomed him with laughter for the love
Of the songs he once was making
At the brewing or the baking, 5
Songs we were a-wearied of,

It was Annie Honey who
Said he went at dawning thro'
The valley where the white mist chills.
Softly, so that none should waken, 10
He the secret road had taken,
For the country of the Kind Folk
That lies beyond the hills.

Annie Honey, heart of gold,
In the windy town acold, 15
Under drifting April moons,
Could not stay her eyes from weeping,
Sorrowed waking, sorrowed sleeping,
For his wild lamenting tunes.

Welladay and welladay! 20
Came October mournfully,
Brindled moths a-spinning
In a twilight green;
Every plane-tree mist-enfolden,
Black as velvet, amber-golden, 25
Was a leopard lithe and lean.

All a-tremble did she hear,
Now so far, now so near,
With a music rarer than the brown bird trills,
'Annie Honey, Annie Honey—Annie H-o-n-e-y.' 30
And she followed where it led her,
To the land beyond the hills.

PATRICK

Ye lads and ye lasses
That rins thro' the toon,
Hear ye aucht o' Auld Patrick
Wha mends the fouk's shoon?
Mendin' auld shoon,
Tinkerin' at shoon,
Grey o' the mornin'
Till evenin' reid;
An' the robin sings saft
In the green glen-heid.

Ye gentle an' simple
That walks in the wynd,
Wi' Patrick be hamely,
Wi' Patrick be kind.
Doon the lang wynd,
At the fit o' the wynd,
Grim wi' sorrow
And grey wi' greed . . .
An' there's gowd on the broom
In the green glen-heid.

I'll gang nivver mair
At morn, nicht or noon,
Lily-licht fitted
On dancin' shoon,
On elfin shoon,
On fairy shoon,
Whaur the rose burns bricht
An' the berry burns reid,
Tae the he'rt o' the warld
In the green glen-heid.

The lads and the lasses
That rins ower the toon
Cares nocht for Auld Patrick
Wha mends the fouk's shoon.
Puir auld shoon,   35
Weerin' dune!
Grim wi' sorrow
An grey wi' greed . . .
He was my ain luve
In the green glen-heid.   40

PENCHRISE

I shall be grave and old,
I shall be cold and wise,
When I forget the moorland
Lifting to Penchrise;
The lovely, ancient moorland
Beneath the dappled skies.

There every trembling willow
Can show a silver crest
To the bright crystal water
Streaming from the west.
And Joy, the Gypsy, found me there
And clasped me to her breast.

We tracked the green Catrail
Winding like a snake,
Where bluebells lisp and flutter
And solemn thistles quake,
For fear the buried hill-men
Should hear them and awake.

Wind kissed the heather,
Sun smote the pine,
They brewed the cup together,
Lusty, strong and fine;
And Joy, the mad Gypsy,
She's drunk the honey wine.

Sleek, silken creatures
Were peering thro' the leaves
(Oh, the darlings, the sly eyes,
Robbers, murderers, thieves!)
In and out the meshes
That Chance, their mother, weaves.

Deep was the thicket
Where the strange gods stirred
The flame of the world
To a magic chord,
In the pure high singing   35
Of the hidden bird.

I shall grow grave and old,
I may grow cold and wise,
Even now in distant dream
The moorland faints and dies;   40
The lovely, ancient moorland
Lifting to Penchrise,

Where cold crystal waters
Come streaming from the west,
And Joy, the wild Gypsy,   45
In tattered beauty dressed,
Has found some other lover
To gather to her breast.

AT CANDLEMAS

Lang syne at Candlemas
At first cam o' the mune,
I, a bit lassie,
Hame-gaun fae the toon,
Fell in wi' a stranger
Frail as ony reed,
Wi' a green mantle
Hapt aboot her heid.

Haste, I wad haste me,
The whinny road along,
Whinny, crookit road
Faur the grey ghaists gang.
Wi' her een fu' o' spells,
Her broo runkled sair,
She micht weel be the witch
O' the Braid Hill o' Fare.

Here cams Candlemas,
A wan deein' mune,
Eh! bit I'm weary.
Cauldrife wis the toon!

Yon's a blythe bairnie
Soople as a reed,
Rinnin' wi' a hankey
Tied aboot her heid,
Hastin', hastin',
Limber-licht fit,
Doon the crookit road
Faur the grey moths flit.

Quo' she, 'Ye'r sma'-bookit,
Yer broo's runkled sair,
Er' ye the auld witch
O' the Braid Hill o' Fare?'

MOST SAD IS SLEEP

In summer-time
Most sad is sleep,
When hawthorns still
Their blossoms keep;
So thin sleep's veil is,
Faint and rare,
Scarcely a dream
Can shelter there.

Only dim thoughts
Of sunny squares,
Marigold fields
And Country Fairs,
Of missing now
In every place,
The present comfort
Of your face.

In summer-time
Just at daybreak
How blessèd it
Would be to wake

In a fine world
Of towns and trees,
Marigold fields
And sunny seas,
Where flying rains
The blossoms kiss,
But yet a different
World from this!

Because beyond
The marigold,
Where little hills
Great woods enfold,
I run to push
The boughs apart
And fall a-weeping
On your heart.

THE FIDDLER

A fine player was he . . .
'Twas the heather at my knee,
The Lang Hill o' Fare
An' a reid rose-tree,
A bonnie dryin' green, 5
Wind fae aff the braes,
Liftin' and shiftin'
The clear-bleached claes.

Syne he played again . . .
'Twas dreep, dreep o' rain, 10
A bairn at the breist
An' a warm hearth-stane,
Fire o' the peat,
Scones o' barley meal
An' the whirr, whirr, whirr, 15
O' a spinnin'-wheel.

Bit aye, wae's me!
The hindmaist tune he made . . .
'Twas juist a dune wife
Greetin' in her plaid, 20
Winds o' a' the years,
Naked wa's atween,
And heather creep, creepin'
Ower the bonnie dryin' green.

THE LANE KIRKYAIRD

The lane kirkyaird
Kens naither buss nor tree,
Bit bonnie gowden whin
Glintin' til the sea,
An' grey heid-stanes 5
O' the auld kith an' kin,
Weet wi' the spindrift thin.

Ower the lane kirkyaird
Gin a flame licht hie
Wi' the hindmaist trumpet's blast 10
Soondin' fae the sea,
'Roose ye, roose ye,
Auld kith an' kin,
Sleepin' late amang the whin,'

Syne saft wad she maen, 15
Yon saut-mou'd sea,
'The auld kith an' kin
They hae lang won free—'
Oh, feat gangs the win'
An' the spindrift thin 20
An' the fine, cauld smell o' the whin!

ALAS! POOR QUEEN

She was skilled in music and the dance
And the old arts of love
At the court of the poisoned rose
And the perfumed glove,
And gave her beautiful hand 5
To the pale Dauphin
A triple crown to win—
And she loved little dogs
      And parrots
    And red-legged partridges 10
And the golden fishes of the Duc de Guise
And a pigeon with a blue ruff
She had from Monsieur d'Elbœuf.

Master John Knox was no friend to her;
She spoke him soft and kind, 15
Her honeyed words were Satan's lure
The unwary soul to bind.
'Good sir, doth a lissome shape
And a comely face
Offend your God His Grace 20
Whose Wisdom maketh these
Golden fishes of the Duc de Guise?'

She rode through Liddesdale with a song;
'Ye streams sae wondrous strang,
Oh, mak' me a wrack as I come back 25
But spare me as I gang.'
While a hill-bird cried and cried
Like a spirit lost
By the grey storm-wind tost.

Consider the way she had to go, 30
Think of the hungry snare,
The net she herself had woven,
Aware or unaware,
Of the dancing feet grown still,
The blinded eyes.— 35
Queens should be cold and wise,
And she loved little things,
    Parrots
   And red-legged partridges
And the golden fishes of the Duc de Guise 40
And the pigeon with the blue ruff
She had from Monsieur d'Elbœuf.

THINK LANG

Lassie, think lang, think lang,
Ere his step comes ower the hill.
Luve gi'es wi' a lauch an' a sang,
An' whiles for nocht bit ill.

Thir's weary time tae rue   5
In the lea-lang nicht yer lane
The ghaist o' a kiss on yer mou'
An' sough o' win' in the rain.

Lassie, think lang, think lang,
The trees is clappin' their han's,   10
The burnie clatterin' wi' sang
Rins ower the blossomy lan's.

Luve gi'es wi' a lauch an' a sang,
His fit fa's licht on the dew.
Oh, lass, are ye thinkin' lang,   15
Star een an' honey mou'?

THE GHOST

The wind that brings
The twilight in
Is musky-scented,
Faint and thin,
When light as dew
On tender herb
A footstep falls
Across the kerb.

Into the street
The children pack,
With, 'Here's the pedlar-
Man come back!
The pedlar with
The red balloons
And flutes that play
The dancing tunes.'

The wind that brings
The twilight home
Is frailer than
The drifted foam,
When light as vapour
On a glass
The footstep falls
Upon the grass.

'O Mary, loose
Your cloudy wrap!
The gate is shut,
No timorous tap
Comes on the empty
Window-pane,
To wake your life
To joy again.'

The old one broods
Beside the fire.
No grief has she,   35
And no desire.
With puckered lips
And crooked smile
She mutters to
Herself the while.   40

'A year, or two—
Or maybe three—
And I the pedlar-
Man shall be,
And I the baby   45
Soft and white
That Mary cries for
In the night,
And I the wind
So faint and thin,   50
The wind that blows
The twilight in.'

From *Sun and Candlelight (1927)*

COURTIN'

Luik ye, ma pretty, then luik ye,
   Ye s'all hae baith yaird an' bield,
Aipple an' curran' busses,
   Bees in the clover field.

   An' she sang till hersel',   5
   She sang till hersel',
      As she steppit ower the door:
   'There was a lad that in the green
      Spied a bonnie reid floo'er.'

But luik ye, ma pretty, luik ye,   10
   Gin ye're naither fond nor true,
Awa' through the warld an' tak yer chance
   O' a better man tae lo'e.

   An' she sang till hersel',
   She sang till hersel',   15
      As she keekit in the gless sae clear:
   'But whiles he thocht 'twas ower bonnie a rose
      For a lad like him to wear.'

But luik ye, ma pretty, luik ye,
   For a' sae sweet ye sing,   20
Cum nae tae me when yer bloom is ower,
   Cravin' for boord and ring.

   An' she sang till hersel',
   She sang till hersel',
      As she lay in the cruik o' his airm: 25
   'But the lad he s'all pu' his bonnie reid rose
      Gin he haud it safe frae hairm.'

THE WIFE

Ma son brings hame his bride
    At gloamin', saft wi' dew;
She boo's her comely heid,
    Wi' a kiss for ma mou'.

Lift, lift, ma hert,
    As bird upon the wing!
Ma son wi' his bride
    Is prooder nor a king.

She strauchtens up hersel',
    Tall as a lily floo'er—
Herk to the bairnie's han'
    Chap, chappin' at the door.

Lauch, lauch, ma hert!
    Afore the winter sna'
Ma son, sae prood o' ane,
    Wull syne be prood o' twa.

Noo sit ye by the fire,
    By the warm hearthstane;
Turn ye yer face tae mine,
    Dochter o' ma ane!

But it's no' the flickerin' flame
    That blin's me whaur I sit;
Cauld am I an' blin',
    Cauld frae heid tae fit.

Oh, better ye had deid,
    A happy lauchin' wean,
Ma son, your comely bride
    Hes the grey gled's e'en.

WAATER O' DYE

Waater o' Dye, whaur ye rin clear
I hear the cry—sae aft I hear—
O' ane wha lauched and lo'ed and sinned
And noo gangs sheda'less as wind.

Wi' her I traivel, straucht an' sure,
To the grey clachan yont the muir,
Hapt in the breckan and the whin,
Whaur dwalt the forbears o' my kin.

She gars me seek on Wirran's hill
The fern that sains the hert frae ill;
She p'ints whaur noddin' foxgloves stan'
Wi' heids a' turned tae elfinlan';
Syne queer auld-farrand tunes we'll sing
Amang the heather and the ling.

Waater o' Dye, whaur ye rin still
On me she warks her auncient will;
What I hae niver kent, I ken—
The feel o' babes, the luve o' men.

The sea-gaun bird forebodes me grief,
I moorn at sicht o' fa'in' leaf;
Intil the clood I luik, bricht-e'ed,
For wings o' Deith abune ma heid.

An' aye she hauds me for her ain,
Flesh o' her flesh, bane o' her bane—
Some lang-deid wumman o' my kin—
Waater o' Dye, hoo still ye rin.

SINGIN' WAATER

Singin' waater, rin oot o' the mist
   An' doon by the moorland bare;
The lass that lies in your siller kist
   S'all keep her body fair.
Ye rowed me ower and rowed me ower,   5
   Sweet o' the smellin' pine,
Till ma e'en was bricht as the marshy floo'er,
   Ma feet like the linen fine;
An' 'twas a' tae pleesure a licht luve,
     A licht luve o' mine.   10

Singin' waater, rin oot o' the sna',
   Syne doon by the breckan green;
Oh, wad ye bit tak ma grief awa'
   An' mak ma hert clean;
In yer glimmerin' fa' or yer dancin' lift   15
   Ma tanglet threids untwine,
An' smoor amang the windy drift
   The thochts I fain wad tyne;
It's a' for the sake o' a leal luve,
     A leal luve o' mine.   20

WORLD'S LOVE

'What gaed ye oot tae seek, my bonnie,
   By the wanin' mornin' moon?'
'I gaed to seek the fairy howe
   Whaur I danced in fairy shoon.'
'Ye cast your shoon fae ye, my bonnie,
   Ye waded ower the ford.'
'I heard my name cried on the hill
   An' kent my true luve's word.'

'What gae ye oot tae seek, my bonnie,
   This hoor sae cauld and mirk?'
'A green, green grave whaur thistles wave
   Near by Saint Mary's Kirk.'
'And is there nocht wull roose my bonnie
   Sleepin' sae deep an' soun'?'
'O gin my bairn greet in the nicht
   There's nane s'all haud me doon.'

THE SANG

The auld fouks praised his glancin' e'en,
Tae ilka bairn he was a frien',
A likelier lad ye wadna see,
Bit—he was nae the lad fur me.

He brocht me troots frae lochans clear,
A skep o' bees, a skin o' deer;
There's nane s'uld tak' wha canna gie,
An' he was nae the lad fur me.

He luiket aince, he luiket lang,
He pit his hert-brak in a sang;
He heard the soondin' o' the sea,
An' a' wis bye wi' him an' me.

The tune gaed soughin' thro' the air,
The shepherds sang't at Lammas fair,
It ran ower a' the braes o' Dee,
The bonnie sang he made fur me.

Sae lang 'twill last as mithers croon
And sweetherts seek the simmer's moon;
Oh, I hae gaen wha wadna gie,
For it s'all live when I maun dee.

THE PROOD LASS

The simmer's gaen,
Yon angry loorin' clood
Wull droon the warld in rain;
The sea-gaun birds are cryin' lang and lood.
     Gang ye yer lane 5
Up bye the green hill stair,
An' seek ma door nae mair—

Nor late, nor sune,
Wi' promise in yer e'en
Tae tak' frae me ma croon, 10
Croon o' a lass whae a' for luve has gi'en.
     Oor courtin's dune;
Gin winter wauk the tree,
Syne I'll keep tryst wi' ye.

Gang ony airt; 15
Ye're mine, ma lad, ye're mine,
Close faulded in ma hert.
Till a' the lan's lie naith the sauty brine,
     We s'all nae pairt.
But on yon green hill stair, 20
Wi' mortal fit—nae mair!

BARBARA

At mornin's furst cock-craw
   I hae won frae the land o' Dreid,
Sair fur the sicht o' ye, Barbara—
   The glint o' your gowden heid.

Yestreen wi' an elfin shaft,
   A wee sma arra' o' stane,
I hae stricken your breist sae white and saft
   And cleft your hert in twain.

Hae ye seen a wild rose fa'
   While yet its leaves was reid?
Sae hae I seen ye, Barbara,
   In the land o' dreams and Dreid.

Cum rinnin' the green hills doon,
   Linkin' your hand wi' mine,
And weer the bonnie braided goon
   And the beads o' coral fine!

As aince in the Spring o' the year,
   The sweet Spring, Barbara!—
Robin, singin' sae lood and clear
   Amang the blossoms' sna'—

Ere I socht an elfin dairt
   In the lands o' dream and Dreid
Or ye had won my ain luve's hert
   Wi' a lift o' your gowden heid.

WEE JOCK TODD

The King cam' drivin' through the toon,
Slae and stately through the toon;
He bo'ed tae left, he bo'ed tae richt,
An' we bo'ed back as weel we micht;
But wee Jock Todd he couldna bide,
He was daft tae be doon at the waterside;
Sae he up an' waved his fishin' rod—
    Och, wee Jock Todd!

But in the quaiet hoor o' dreams,
The lang street streekit wi' pale moonbeams,
Wee Jock Todd cam' ridin' doon,
Slae an' solemn through the toon.
He bo'ed tae left, he bo'ed tae richt
(It maun ha'e been a bonnie sicht)
An' the King cam' runnin'—he couldna bide—
He was mad tae be doon at the waterside;
Sae he up wi' his rod and gaed a nod
    Tae wee Jock Todd.

JEALOUSY

The new mune sma' an' slim,
  The win'-blawn leaf on the pane;
I micht hae gotten sleep
  But for they eerie twain.

For she wis like a leaf, 5
  Blawn oot o' the windy morn,
Wi' her wan new mune o' a face,
  Amang the stookit corn.

Wae's me! I turned ma heid
  Frae her tear-begrutten e'en; 10
Sae clear they were as the burn
  Whaur it rins ower mosses green.

She s'uld hae hed the plaid,
  Pit bye in the kist lang syne,
But for her yalla hair, 15
  Her fit ower slicht and fine.

The wee reid hungerry mou',
  It s'uld hae hed bite and sup,
But I hae seen the bee
  Ower aft at the rose's cup. 20

My skin is broun as a toad,
  E'en hae I shairp's a shrew,
Ma hert is bleck an' coorse,
  Coorse thro' an' thro'.

For better ye wad hae fared, 25
  Ma bonnie young barefit quean,
Hedna the lad I lo'e
  Cum whistlin' ower the green.

I lies awauk wi' the mune,
  Wi' the wind-blawn leaf on the pane; 30
I micht hae gotten sleep,
  But for yon eerie twain.

THE BLUE BOAT

A laddie his lane frae morn till nicht—
But I wad be hame by can'el-licht.
Siller eneuch hid I tae spare,
For a wee blue boat frae the Mairket Fair.

I bocht a brooch wi' a siller pin, 5
A kerchief for tyin' anaith ma chin;
A' the lave o' the money went
Tae the fortune wife in the gipsy tent.

The Corbie Burn's ayont the Dee—
Wi' cauld white lips it girned at me; 10
The witch frae oot o' the ha'thorn luikt,
Wi' a' her ten black fingers crookt.

The fouk that bides in the Deid Man's Cairn
They chittered, chittered amang the fern:
'Here cam's the maid that hadna' a groat 15
Tae buy a wee laddie a wee blue boat.'

Ma brooch lies deep in the Corbie Linn,
Ma kerchief I gi'ed tae the thornie whin.
O, Laddie alane frae morn till nicht,
I daurna' face the can'el-licht. 20

THE WILD LASS

Hameward ye're traivellin'
In the saft hill rain,
The day lang by
That ye wearied o' the glen;
Nae ring upon yer han', 5
Nae kiss upon yer mou'—
    Quaiet noo.

There's fiddlers an' dancin'
An' steps gaun by the doors,
Bit nane o' them s'all fret ye 10
In the lang nicht 'oors.
O, Peace cum on the wind,
Peace fa' wi' the dew,
    Quaiet noo.

Cauld was the lift abune ye, 15
The road baith rough and steep,
Nae farrer s'all ye wander
Nor greet yersel tae sleep,
Ma ain wild lass,
Ma bonnie hurtit do'o— 20
    Quaiet, quaiet noo.

'IN THE STREETS THEREOF'

Mirk at the oot ga'un;
   Fog and the frosty rime,
Can'el brunt tae a threid
   This lang, lang time.

Peace at the oot ga'un;
   A' things by wi' an' dune
Wark and steer; the clatter o' feet,
   Liltin' bairns' tune.

Lichtsome ga'un in,
   The bairns at their auld play
Linkit han's in the gowden street,
   Tae 'Gaitherin' Nuts in May'.

MEMORY

The howlet cries on Cloch-na-ben,
    The nicht fa's dark wi' rain;
I weary o' your becks an' boos,
    Grim Shedda' o' ma ain.

The mune wins clear o' driftin' clood,
    Clear licht frae hill tae sea;
I'm wanderin' by a singin' burn
    In bonnier company.

THE TREE

Happy walking it is when
Laughing girls go up the glen;
Grasses nodding, bluebells shy,
They were wishing they were I,
And one ancient thorny tree 5
It was watching, watching me.

Weary walking is it when
Sighing girls go down the glen;
Lonely cloud in evening sky
Was not lonelier than I, 10
Yet the strange and solemn tree
Still was watching, watching me.

Could I find some hidden bay
Many and many a mile away,
On the wet and salty strand 15
When the wind blows from the land
There would rise a hoary tree,
Always watching, watching me.

THE SILVER CITY

Yonder she sits beside the tranquil Dee,
Kindly yet cold, respectable and wise,
Sharp-tongued though civil, with wide-open eyes,
Dreaming of hills, yet urgent for the sea;
And still and on, she has her vanity,
Wears her grey mantle with a certain grace,
While sometimes there are roses on her face
To sweeten too austere simplicity.

She never taught her children fairy lore,
Yet they must go a-seeking crocks of gold
Afar throughout the earth;
And when their treasure in her lap they pour,
Her hands upon her knee do primly fold;
She smiles complacent that she gave them birth.

THE MOURNERS

They carried her to the little kirk
Through the autumn day—
The little kirk among the trees.
Sombre, sad and ill at ease
I heard the mourners say: 5
'She was once a fine lass;
All flesh is as grass.
We go down, every one,
In sorrow when our day is done.'

When they came to the little kirk 10
Very old and grey,
Fair shone the elder-trees,
Elm and oak and mulberries,
In beauty magical
Robed for the festival 15
Of this their dying day.
And still I heard them say:
'We go down, every one,
In sorrow when our day is done.'

WITHY WANDS

Up in the waste and eerie lands
Where I went, after withy wands,
Old Wind came through a bourtree hedge,
Crept down along the water's edge;
There lay so whist I fairly knew
How loud heart beat and grasses grew.

The world turned grey like smoky glass,
To let the queer wayfarers pass,
On tufty track, in murky air,
Not seen, nor heard, yet everywhere;
And feathers soft. Old Wind and I,
We held our breath till they were by.

At time for shining sun to rise,
Looking through windows in the skies,
I saw a house not built with hands,
Till birds awoke the eerie lands,
And down along the reedy sands
Old Wind went waving withy wands.

COWSLIPS SOON WILL DANCE

Cowslips soon will dance in rings
    Above the brimming dew;
Nesting birds will preen their wings
    And learn their tender notes anew.

Bees among the whin will flit
    Ere April's moon is old,
And all the dusty roads be lit
    With little lamps of starry gold.

The blade will quicken in the sod,
    The white moth in her cell,
For winds blow from the south, and God
    Is watching over Israel.

MARCH 21

THE CAPTIVE

If spirit is to body
   As music to the song,
Your soul should be a seraph,
   Bright-eyed and swift and strong.
But oh, it is a captive!
   A bird shut in a cage,
Beating with broken feathers
   In sorrow and in rage.

HERITAGE

When the rugged moor's my comrade
   And the barren hills my friends,
When I take delight in the winds of night
   And ghostly twilight ends,

The ancient folk are waking.
   They beat on my heart and brain;
From a handful of dust comes wanderers' lust
   For traffic with wind and rain.

Their eyes are watching when I watch
   The way that the wild deer went,
I hear their cry where the thin reeds sigh
   On wastes of the naked bent.

Lost and gone and forgotten,
   Old tracks by the bracken sown,
Mystical rites by the cold star lights
   On an altar shaped from a stone.

But the moor shall be my comrade
   And the hills my friends shall be,
Till life's last snow falls chill and slow
   On hill and moor and tree.

CHANGE

There came an unsought guest,
   And down the wind she blew
A joy, a hope, a jest—
   A song or two.

While mournful hearts had we,
   Lamenting overmuch
On many a face to see
   Her gentle touch.

For some there are obey
   Her will with great content,
Abide her yea and nay
   With sweet assent—

The stars, the hills, the seas
   And all the water springs,
Pale flowers of the may
   And fleeting, wingèd things.

WINTER

Down by the water-meadows
All on a winter's noon,
There was a naked thorn-bush
Sang a mournful rune;
She told the reeds a story   5
Of memories and sighs,
Of the robber bees' carousal
And the waft of butterflies.

All in a winter's gloaming
Down by the shingly shore,   10
There were two ancient sailormen
Outside a tavern door,
Complaining to each other
With lamentable lips
For the great dead captains,   15
And the old Sailing Ships.

TREES

Crooked grey village,
I loved every stone of you,
Friends of my youth, and the
Kin of my own in you;
Sorrowful-wise
The folk look in my eyes,
Their words are but wounds
Now, I'm stepping alone in you.

Glen up beyond there,
I know every fold of you,
Blossom of heather,
Broom of the gold in you;
The wild birds' long cry,
The hill waters' sigh
Are sadder than tears
For the fine days of old in you.

Wood of the birches,
The pretty shy trees in you,
Silver and grey, with the
Kind little breeze of you,
All the length of the day
There is nothing they say
But what I would hear
In the peace of you—peace of you.

COTTON GRASSES

Where seldom footstep passes
   By the lone lochan's edge,
   Foam-white above the sedge,
I hear the cotton grasses—

Whispering, whispering, whispering,
   Now summer days are long,
   The burden of a song
Too sorrowful for singing;

Of joyful tears unwept,
   Of tenderness unwist,
   Of lovers' lips unkissed
And promised trysts unkept.

Where seldom footstep passes,
   So bleak the heath and bare,
   In a cold scentless air
The whispering cotton grasses.

From *The Singin' Lass (1929)*

THE WEE SMA' GLEN

The water dreeped frae stane tae stane,
The wild rose bloomed and dee'd its lane,
But lip to praise it there was nane,
Till Mary cam' to the Wee Sma' Glen.

It wasna when she pu'ed the briar 5
Nor lauched to see the rowans' fire,
But when her e'en grew saft and weet
At sichts ower fair and soonds ower sweet,

The whisper gaed frae hill to hill,
The very herps o' Heaven grew still; 10
God minded on the Wee Sma' Glen,
And kenned it wasna wrocht in vain.

THE GHAIST

Tho' dear ye be an' kind
My hert ye ne'er sall bind,
Like drift o' rain on moorland stane or leaf upon the wind
Sae in yir ain my hand has lain—
Tho' dear ye be an' kind. 5

Tae me ye're but a ghaist.
Him that I lo'e the best
Can haunt at will the glen or hill or in his green grave rest.
For guid or ill, he hauds me still;
'Tis ye, that be the ghaist. 10

HEART-FREE

Sin' noo we twa maun twine
   Wi' nae mair troth tae keep
My hert wins oot o' the kist,
   Whaur ye lockit it doon sae deep.

My lauch to the laverock gangs,
   My grief's fur the hunted hare,
A licht fitstep to the dance,
   A kiss at ilka fair.

Here's shoon fur wanton Meg
   That ne'er hed hoose nor hame;
A gowden ring fur a nameless lass,
   To licht her o' her shame.

The lievin' sall hae my breid,
   The corp' my lily-floo'ers,
Some gangrel's bairn the sang o' my lips
   I suld hae gi'en to yours.

WINTER-TIME

Monday, at the gloamin',
    I saw a reid reid lowe,
Whaur tinker fouk wull ne'er set fit,
    Far ben in the ghaisty howe;
And yon that gaed ahint me
    Was nae sheda o' my ain.
It's eerie fa' the nichts
    Aifter Marti'mas is gane.

Twa e'en as bleck as howlets,
    A week past Marti'mas,
Glowered ower the new-lit can'els
    Frae oot the luikin'-glass;
And Three cam' creepin' doon the loan
    On Thursday in the mirk,
Whase shoon was wrocht in yon far toon
    That ne'er had Cross nor kirk.

I hard the elfin pipers
    Sae witchin', sweet an' sma'
On Sabbath wi' the warld asleep;
    They wiled my hert awa'.
They stilled the soughin' o' the burn—
    O, tae a lanesome lass
There's eerie freits on ilka road,
    When bye is Marti'mas.

HOGMANAY

Wha knocks at my door this Hogmanay?
A cannie young lassie, limber and gay.
Lips o' mine, e'en o' mine—
Come ben, come ben tho' ye're deid lang syne.

Whaur ha'e ye tint yir Sabbath shoon?
The fiddles is tuned and a' the toon
Is kissin' and courtin' and dancin'-fey
Tae the screich o' the reels on Hogmanay.

When the stars blaw oot an' the mune grauws wan,
It's ower the hills wi' a bonny young man
Whaur the floo'er o' love springs thorny an' sweet—
And tho' an auld wife maun awhilie greet
Ye'll aye gang limber an' licht an' free—
Canny bit lassie that aince wis me.

ANN GILCHRIST

As I gae by the Bleedie Burn
   Whaur's nayther leaf nor tree,
Lat me nae hear Ann Gilchrist's feet
   Nor sicht her evil e'e.

As I gaed by the Bleedie Burn
   Tae the witches' howff I cam'—
Ann Gilchrist's in among the whin
   Seekin' a wandert lamb.

She's ta'en it frae the thorny buss,
   Syne thro' the moss and fern
She's croonin' it and cuddlin' it
   As gin it were a bairn.

An' I wuss the whins wis nae sae shairp
   Nor the muckle moss sae weet,
For wha wull gie Ann Gilchrist fire
   Tae warm her clay-cauld feet?

WELCOME

Auld man frae the glens come ben,
    Lass wi' the raggit shoon—
I rowed a bairn in my airms yestreen
    Till the wanin' o' the moon.

In a dream o' the nicht it cam'
    Like a lamb to the howe o' the hill,
I crooned it ower wi' a cradlin' sang
    Till its weary cry was still.

My hert was a warm reid lowe
    For the wee cauld han's and feet:
Was ever a dream sae fair as yon,
    Gaed ever a nicht sae fleet?

Auld man frae the glens come ben,
    Ye're wae as a hameless wean;
Lass wi' the raggit shoon,
    Yir e'en's yon bairn's e'en.

THE EERIE HOOSE

Says she:—It is an eerie place
   This hoose I ca' ma hame
Wi' wa's baith stooter than the hills,
   An' frailer than the faem.

Says she:—It is an eerie hoose   5
   Wi' chaumers braid and blue,
Whaur I gang wi' a fearsome step,
   A han' afore ma mou'.

Sin' thir's ae word gain I suld speak—
   Hoo saft so e'er it fa'—   10
Wad gar its very stoops to rock,
   Syne melt like simmer snaw.

Says she:—It is an eerie hoose,
   Clear lichted wast an' east,
Whaur I gang wi' twa shakin' airms   15
   Close gruppit to ma breist.

Sin, thir's ae steekit door whase latch,
   Gin I tuk thocht to lift,
The corner-stanes wad slip awa'
   Like weeds in winter's drift.   20

Says she:—'Twad be a dowie hoose
   An' weary lang the day
Wis thir nae door I daurna try,
   Nae word I daurna say.

THE CAN'EL

She's ta'en her can'el frae the boord
   Wi' hands baith slim an' sma',
A gowden rose it bloomed and floo'red
   An' flamed atween us twa.

She's pluckt ma hert frae oot ma breist
   Wi' hands as white as faem,
She's pluckt ma hert oot o' ma breist
   An' warmed it at the flame.

Syne, when the can'el flickered laigh
   Wi' her twa hands she's ta'en
Ma hert, and at the dawnin' grey
   Gi'en it me back agen.

INVITATION

Lad, come kiss me
   Whaur the twa burns rin.
Am I no' sweet as honey,
   Wild as gouden whin,

Slim as the rowan,
   Lips like berries reid,
Fey as siller mune-floo'er
   That sprang frae fairy seed?

Luve, come clasp me
   Whaur the twa burns rin,—
A' but the white soul o' me
   That ye can never win.

THIS WOMAN

Gin I bring her beads o' amber
    For her neck sae fair,
Bricht as burnin' gowd
    Or the sunlicht in her hair,
She mocks me wi' a fancy
    For a siller willow wand,
Twisted like a croon
    In her slim broun hand.

On some droosy nicht in simmer
    Comes a tinker caird,
Creepin' like a thief
    Thro' the lang green yaird;
Syne its meal for him and can'els
    An' honey frae the bee,
Wi' the glimmer o' a tear
    In her young saft e'e.

Noo the bloom is on the hawthorn
    Whaur the clear burn rowes,
My ewes and lambs thegether
    Amang my ain knowes;
But no' at fa' o' gloamin'
    Will she tread the rashes weet,
The water rins ower cauld
    For her sma' white feet.

Hed I been fause and fickle,
    A' thing frae her ta'en,
Hed the lass been aye the loser
    An' mysel' the lad to gain,
Gin I cried on her she'd follow,
    Blew the wind frae winter's airt,
An' the water roarin' hie
    As her ain fond hert.

JEAN CAM'BELL

Blin' Jean Cam'bell
   To the kirk gaed
Lauchin' tae hersel'
   In her auld green plaid.

She hard the leaf reistlin'   5
   Cauld amang snaw,
Ae bird cheepin'
   'Tween a water an' a wa'.

She hard fouk rinnin',
   Soondless thir shoon,   10
Deid hands straikin',
   Puin' at her goon.

Wi' 'Haste Jeanie Cam'bell,
   The berry blooms sweet,
Young lads is singin'   15
   Castin' at the peat!

'Are ye for the gloamin'
   Munelicht an' dew,
Blythe Jeanie Cam'bell
   In yir plaid sae new?'   20

As blin' Jean Cam'bell
   To the kirk gaed
Lauchin' tae hersel'
   In her auld green plaid.

THE SINGIN' LASS

O lucky penny a mile ayont the mill
   I lifted frae the mosses o' the moor,
     Auld, an' bent and twisted, I tint ye in the hoor
That the stranger lass cam' singin' ower the hill.

My luve sits in her bien hoose sae modest as a floo'er,   5
   A lily floo'er that's growin' in the shade,
     The wind that blaws her can'el blaws through a ragged plaid;
The singin' lass gangs lauchin' by the door.

My luve she sleeps sae quait 'neath the munelicht's milky beams,
   White and sweet on linen sheets, till dawn comes to the east.   10
   O lucky penny that's swingin' on the breist
O' the singin' lass wha's liltin' thro' my dreams!

MOONLIGHT MEETING

The Hill by the Lochan
  A' gowd and green,
She's luiket at the Lochan
  An' gin she wis a queen.

'Lochan, Lochan, 5
  Tethered to yir bed,
Canna' rax yir cauld feet
  Ower ma green plaid.'

'Whist,' says the Lochan,
  'The moon's auld e'en 10
Sa' ye creepin' doon
  To ma airms yestreen.
Siller wis yir gowd then,
  Washen in dew;
Sleepit ye or waukit ye 15
  The hale nicht thro'?

'Tho' laigh,' says the Lochan,
  'An' lane is my bed,
An' I canna rax ma cauld feet
  Ower yir green plaid.' 20

WINDS OF THE WORLD

I heard my name at gloamin' late,
   I heard it cried sae clear and sma',
But ere my fit was at the yett
   The wind had blawn the soond awa'.

A rose o' love grew at my door,　　　　　　　　　　5
   I happit it frae frost and snaw;
A sough o' wind cam' ower the moor,
   The wind has blawn the rose awa'.

Nae cry to hear, nae floo'er to fa';
   Noo blaw the wind frae ony airt　　　　　　　　10
The thocht o' them it ne'er can blaw
   Frae the warm sheilin' o' my hairt.

A TRAVELLER

Gin ye're oot on unkent roads yir lane
    Wi' ne'er a freend ye can ca' yir ain
By field or dyke or naked quarry,
    Wearied feet on the shairp whin stane.

Gin ye greet at the mune's blin' face o' deith 5
    Glimmerin' ower the wan snaw-wreath,
An' curse the wind for an auld grey foumart
    Teerin' yir hairt wi' her hungry teeth,

May ye meet a lad by a thorny tree
    Wha'll cry yir name, as he cried on me 10
Ower the faded plaid aboot his shou'der,
    'God gang wi' ye, Mary McPhee!'

Syne ye maun bless the mune's frail horn,
    The unkent roads that yir feet hev torn,
The wind, an' a' puir traivellin' craturs, 15
    For the sake o' the lad by the wintry thorn.

HUNTLIE HILL

When I am deid an' gane
   An' ye suld crave me still
Gae seek me in a bonnie birk
   Grouin' on Huntlie Hill.

Clasp my sweet body slim
   Syne lie an' tak' your ease,
My droosy kisses on yir hair,
   Yir heid upon my knees.

Yon's but a pipin' bird
   Gangs moontin' ower the plain
Or but the liltin' hert o' me
   Ye never socht tae gain.

Farrer an' farrer yet,
   Aye soarin' as she sings,
Wi' glint o' rain upon her breist,
   Wi' sunlicht in her wings.

Sae turn ye tae yir sleep,
   Yir heid upon my knee,
Anaith the droosy kisses
   O' yir bonnie birkin tree.

ARRIVAL

Oh, three came to my darkened house
   By woodlands black and bare,
Who broke my bread and drank my wine,
   When leaves were green and fair.

And two came at the dusky hour,
   When winter twilight ends,
To knock with soft familiar touch
   Of long invited friends.

But never did my darkened house
   To light and glory spring,
Till One threw open wide the door,
   Unbidden like a King.

EVENING WALK

A mocking bird, the plover,
   To draw me to the bent,
And round, and round and over,
   Crying 'Content, Content';

With none there but the witches—
   Mad Heather, Whinney Thorn—
Striding both dykes and ditches
   To girn at yellow corn;

And running moonlight races,
   The Children of the Tide
From sunlit rosy places
   Come home unsatisfied.

AMONG THORNS

Starving field, so poor and thin
Barley would not grow therein;
Sower sowed the seed in vain,
Thorns sprang up and choked the grain.

Now the sun unsheathes his sword, 5
Poppies spring to meet their lord,
Proud, outrageous, and bold.
Marigold on marigold

Lights her clear courageous star
Till the thorns outnumbered are. 10
Come, ye thankful, come and bless
Miracle of barrenness.
Starving soil, so poor and thin
Barley would not grow therein.

CAMBUS WOODS

When nearer hills had shed their snow
And summer's flutes began to blow,
You gathered Orchis flowers that grow
    In Cambus Woods,

Where every footpath green and deep
Awaits a lover long asleep
Some unforgotten tryst to keep.

My dear acquaintance, tho' your eyes
Have learnt the paths of Paradise,
And how Elysium outvies
    Fair Cambus Woods,

Come when the hills to Beauty break
And tender flowers of Orchis wake,
Sudden, sweet, swift excursion make
    To Cambus Woods.

OF SORROWFUL THINGS

Swing of the wild blue-bell
   With her sweet beauty lost,
Brittle and grey as a shell,
   Sorrowful dancing ghost.

Empty nest of the wren
   Flung to the frosty briar;
Drip and spit of the rain
   On the ash of a tinker's fire.

Footsteps passing the gate,
   Passing into the wild—
Things that trouble me yet
   As they troubled me when a child.

DAWN AND TWILIGHT

She will not wear her silver gown for me
   Whose vagrant journey ends at candlelight,
So gracious is her secret courtesy
   Toward one who comes so late in sorry plight—

This was the constant thought I had of her,
   With darkness falling, mist upon the height,
A trifling wind, of leaves a distant stir—
   Oh such a night as any other night!

She would not put a single jewel on
   So sweet and cunning was her courtesy—
And she had risen up before the dawn
   And dressed herself in Immortality.

ANEMONES

Anemones, they say, are out
   By sheltered woodland streams,
With budding branches all about
   Where Spring-time sunshine gleams;

Such are the haunts they love, but I
   With swift remembrance see
Anemones beneath a sky
   Of cold austerity—

Pale flowers too faint for winds so chill
   And with too fair a name—
That day I lingered on a hill
   For one who never came.

From *The Turn of the Day (1931)*

SPRING

The green corn springs
In the warmth o' the rain.
The robin pipes
On a kirk yaird stane,
A ring o' gowd's   5
On the neck o' the doo,
The lammie suckles at the ewe,
An' ma he'rt's fu'
As I gang ma lane
Whaur robin sings   10
On a kirk yaird stane.

A BRETON WOMAN SINGS

On resurrection morning
When the Just are glorified,
We shall not dare to look at the saints
Walking side by side

Since in Our Lady's chapel 5
I bade my candles burn
For a kiss—a cry—a welcome,
A bonnie boat's return.

And prayed not for salvation
Nor for my spirit's food, 10
Only—'My man's a sinner,
Let Mary make him good.'

And that on Judgement morning
When the Just are glorified,
We two may creep to her white feet, 15
And kneel there side by side.

A SMALL THING

'A hurt so small,'
  Say you,
'A thread of grey
  On blue,
So slight a thing
Less than a wild rose sting
Nothing at all.'
  And yet,
When thrushes call,
  Or winds awake
And sigh—and sink—
  And fall—
Into the evening's grey
I think—
  And think
This small heartbreak
Will wear my life away.

THE BROKEN BRIG

Twa o' us met whaur the waters spring
This ae nicht o' a',
Ane to rage and ane to sing
At onding o' the snaw.

The twain o' us wi' never a moon
In the blin-drift and the sleet,
Ane wha gaed like thistle doon,
Ane wi' silly feet.

Me wi' a he'rt o' fear and dreid
Whaur the burns was rinnin' big,
Her to gang forrit wi' lifted heid
First ower the broken brig.

The twain o' us by the reid fire flame
Oot o' the mirk and snaw—
Oh wha' is this that lands me hame
This ae nicht o' a'?

A tinker wife wi' a dreepin' plaid
The candle stalks atween,
A whey-faced wife wi' a dreepin' plaid
And *twa sichtless e'en.*

THE LISSOME LEDDY

I h'ard a lissome leddy
Ower a blue hill heid
On a fine day, a fair day,
Spin a fairy threid.

Like saft water rinnin'
Naith faem white as meal
Was the sough o' the spinnin'
O' that fairy wheel.

Like a licht in a shady
Birk wood green,
Was the lissome leddy
Wi' her flick'rin' e'en.

A lad wadna wed her,
She likit him weel;
Noo she weaves oot her sorro'
On a fairy wheel.

In the wild wood shady
Ower a blue hill heid,
Hark tae the lissome leddy
Spinnin' at her threid.

THE DOORS OF SLEEP

Jenny come ower the hill,
Ye hae broke yer troth lang syne
An' ta'en yer hand frae mine,
But nichts are warm and still.

White as a flo'er in May 5
Gang glimmerin' by my bed—
White flo'er sae sune tae fade
At early dawnin' day.

Come by the doors o' sleep,
Whaur ne'er a word sall fa' 10
O' the ring ye gi'ed awa,
The tryst ye failed tae keep;
When nichts are clear and still,
Jenny—come ower the hill.

THE STRANGER

Oh, wha cam' doon the Dye Water
Yestreen, nae tryst to keep,
Wi' e'en maist like a bairnie's e'en
New waukened frae her sleep?

Thro' a cauld moss rins Dye Water, 5
Whaur the grey peewit cries,
Yestreen it ran a gowden burn,
Frae Hills o' Paradise.

A wild rose bloomed by Dye Water
Amang the thorny bent 10
To glimmer in her hands yestreen,
Like cup o' Sacrament.

She turned aboot Dye Water,
The road she cam' she gaed;
I h'ard the flittin' o' her feet, 15
The stirrin' o' her plaid.

JOAN THE MAID

Joan, Joan, the bonnie maid,
She rinses claes in the cauld mill-lade,
Strong i' the airm and straucht i' the thigh,
To kirn and weave and herd the kye,
By day on the croft by the waterside; 5
But, come the nicht and I hear her ride.

On a milk white horse in siller shoon,
She rides to Embro', Embro' toon
Amang the reid-coats ower the muir,
Wi' her gowden hair and her he'rt sae pure 10

Up to the yett o' the castle wa'
Whaur bolts and bars afore her fa',
Wi' step sae licht and cheek sae reid
Tae lay a croon on a prince's heid.

Oh gin they tak frae ye yer sword 15
And bind yer breist wi' a hempen cord,
Frae the fiery whin and the flamin' sark
Yer soul wull moont like a liltin' lark;
Joan, o' the croft by the waterside—
What ails me that I hear ye ride? 20

LOST THINGS

She borrowed roses' sweetness,
The birch and aspen tree
Lent her their grace, and little hills
Some magic glamourie.

But since that summer morning
On which I woke to weep,
The rose has claimed her loveliness,
The hills her beauty keep.

While high among the uplands
Or down the forest path
I long for her lost foolishness
Her quick impatient wrath.

CURIOS

Little old shops in Queer Street,
  Where nobody buys or sells—
Cupid might find his bow in one,
  Or Harlequin his bells.

Come Pan, and rummage for your pipes,
  Reddened and rimed with rust,
Sweet ladies all your fans and shoes
  Are tumbled into dust.

Here are keepsakes—beads as blue
  As sunny Southern Seas,
And silver keys to turn the locks
  On—Memories.

Little old shops in Queer Street,
  By some called Sorrow Lane,
Where all the leaves of Summers gone
  Whisper to the rain.

THE BLUE JACKET

When there comes a flower to the stingless nettle,
   To the hazel bushes, bees,
I think I can see my little sister
   Rocking herself by the hazel trees.

Rocking her arms for very pleasure
   That every leaf so sweet can smell,
And that she has on her the warm blue jacket
   Of mine, she liked so well.

Oh to win near you, little sister!
   To hear your soft lips say—
'I'll never tak' up wi' lads or lovers,
   But a baby I maun hae.

'A baby in a cradle rocking,
   Like a nut, in a hazel shell,
And a new blue jacket, like this o' Annie's,
   It sets me aye sae well.'

From *Lost Country* and *Other Verses (1937)*

LOST COUNTRY

Two mountain streams that swiftly pass
Thro' dark and hilly lands,
By secret names I named you, as
You slipped between my hands.

Footpath with the wondrous way									5
Of spreading sparse and sweet,
Even on a winter's day,
Wild thyme for my feet,

That climbed and climbed as if to find,
High on the moorland's lift,									10
One aged solitary tree
Swept by the stormy drift:

Cold moorland, vext by winds' alarms
Lost footpath, naked streams,
To you I'm stretching out my arms,									15
Country of my dreams.

CHANCE ACQUAINTANCE

'Wha'ever bides in this hoose,
Noo nicht is drawin' doon,
Rise up and tell a young man
The road to Forfar toon.'

She's ta'en a new candle 5
To licht him sweetly ben,
He thinks on stars at gloamin',
On summers in the glen.

The weary winds grow quaiet
To hear her bonnie words 10
That fill his he'rt wi' music
And the chaunt o' singin' birds,

And, oh, it is a sorrow
For a likely lad and wise,
To turn his face to Forfar, 15
His back on Paradise.

WHEN AT FAMILIAR DOORS

When at familiar doors
None answers to our call,
'Twere well to board the ship
That sails at evening-fall;

Chartless and rudderless, 5
To track the ocean broad,
Like them that dreaming go,
Borne by the winds of God;

To other country where,
By other journeys led, 10
Strangers shall light our evening fire,
Strange hands shall make our bed.

TWO IS COMPANY

We gaed and we gaed to the ha'thorn tree
That hings by the weepin' well,
Jean and Nelly o' Upper Stanehive
And the third ane was mysel'.

Quoth Jean, 'That silken goon o' mine   5
Had ye seen when it was new,
Ere the flitterin' moth won into the kist
And riddled it thro' and thro'!'

Says Nellie, 'My locks was like the corn
On the bonnie hairst fields o' hame;   10
The tides o' sorrow gaed ower my heid
And turned them white as faem.'

And never a sough, as we sat and sat
By the weary, weary well,
O' the braws I had lang syne, or hoo   15
I wasna' ill-faured mysel'.

CORRICHIE

By oor burnside a queen rade licht
Thro' moor and moss and saugh,
To see her gay lords win a fecht
In yon braid haugh.

The rowan tree its berry shed,
The leaft had tint its green,
When gallant wi' her lads lang syne
She rade, the bonnie queen.

The years gang roond; frae green to gowd
The moor and moss maun turn—
Oh, whaur dwalt I when she rade by
My ain Corrichie Burn?

NAOMI

All the city was moved about them, and they said, 'Is this Naomi?'—
   The Book of Ruth

Naomi, Naomi, what wait ye for?
The elders have steppit the causey ower,
Wi' a sigh and a froon and a mournfu' e'e,
Wailin', 'Naomi! It canna be!'

The wives have lookit ye up and doon,
Yer tremblin' mou' and yer faded goon,
Sorrowfu' steppin' the causey ower—
Naomi, Naomi, what wait ye for?

For some dear lass ye kent lang syne,
When days of youth were clear and fine,
To tak' yer hand in the twa o' her ain,
The tears upon her cheeks like rain,
Wi' a word o' comfort the he'rt to fill,
'It's yersel', Naomi, and bonnie still.'

THE BURDEN

'Set doon your pack,
Puir weary wife,'
Quoth I, 'and rest a wee.
Lang is the road,
Sair is the load,   5
And the wind
Sings in the tree.'

'A puir auld wife,
A weary wife,
And something frail and sma',   10
But I maun on
And tak' the hill
Wi' a fair
"Guid nicht to ye a'."

'The same as the wing   15
Is to the bird,
The sail to the ship
On the sea,
Sae is the burden
To the back,   20
Gin ye cairry it
Cannily,' quo' she,
'Gin ye cairry it cannily.'

THE WIDOW

John Andrew Davidson
Lies buried here,
Tenant in Easter Drum
For forty year.

The buss o' aipple-ringie 5
At your feet
Is growin' rare and sweet.
I'se hae anither at your heid the same.
I wad hae liked 'Respeckit' at your name,
'Respeckit Tenant'. 10

Man, your een o' grey
Glint into mine
Like rinnin' fire in strae!
Here in the kirkyaird lane;
'I daur ye put sic ony daftlike word 15
On Easter Drum's heidstane,'
I hear ye say.

DESIRES OF YOUTH

An auld wife cam' to oor door
The day and nicht atween,
She looked at me and looked awa'
Wi' her lang-sichted een.

Says she, 'I ken a young lass
Wha gangs her hamely ways,
Her thochts set on a fairer land
Ayont these hills and braes.

'Wha dances gay upon the green
And licht at countra fairs,
And hears abune the fiddler's tune
A bonnier lilt than theirs.

'And, wanderin' wi' her sweethe'rt
Doon by the rocky shore,
Thinks to hersel', "He's nae the luve
Sae long I've waited for."'

An auld wife cam' to oor hoose
When nicht was like to fa'.
I looked in her lang-sichted een
And syne I looked awa'.

GATHERING SHELLS

I aye likit my Grannie's sister,
Likit her rael weel,
Her, that cam' from a fisher toon
And carried the fisher creel.

Speer at her o' ships and sailors, 5
Storms on the sauty brine—
'It's far eneuch awa',' says she,
'And ower lang syne.'

Aince, when wind in the tree was soughin'
Like watters flowin' deep, 10
I h'ard her singin' to hersel',
Wauken or asleep.

'There's cowries and there's siller buckies,
Spinks and fairies' boats,
And a necklace for a leddy 15
O' the peerrie-weerie groats.'

She sang a wee thing rauch and timmer
Nor kent nae lilt nor reel.
She cam' from the cauld east countra,
I likit her rael weel. 20

THE PLAID

I had a plaid o' tartan
Frae ower the western sea,
As saft as silk, as warm as milk,
And happed me to the knee.

A ragged wife gaed by me   5
Ae cauld and wintry morn;
I gaithered in aboot my plaid
And passed her by wi' scorn.

Wae's me, she's cursed my plaidie!
For noo, come sun, come rain,   10
Mair rauch than sark o' tinker wife
It cuts me to the bane.

A WOMAN SINGS

My licht feet farin'
Ben the hoose and through,
Oh, will ye come at cock-craw,
Or wi' the fa' o' dew?

Will ye come a puir man,   5
A beggar, to my board,
Or wi' a lauch and wi' a toss
To tak' me like a lord?

There's a still day dawnin'
When I'll no' care   10
Gin ye come like lord or loon
Or gin ye come nae mair;

Wi' cauld hands weavin'
Oot the hoose and in
A bonnie white grave-goon   15
To fauld aneath my chin.

THE GREEN YAIRD

I had a green yaird
Wi' a sweet pink may,
Whaur a yella-breisted bird
Sang a' the simmer day.

And a wanderin' wind, 5
Saft as smirr o' rain,
In an' oot the may-tree
Gaed and cam' again.

Far hae I traivelled,
Mickle hae I seen, 10
Oh, it's 'Hame noo' seekin'
For my gairden green.

The bird's sang's ended,
The pink may's deid,
The wind blaws the soor leaf 15
O' the nettle weed.

Sae the laigh wind soughed,
Sae the licht wind stirred,
Ere a tree was shapit
Or a singin' bird 20
Or a he'rt to moorn
Ower a sma' green yaird.

THE MUSICIAN

The fiddler from Kilbirnie
He plays but ae tune,
Be it early, be it late,
Sunlicht or mune.

Nine bonnie bairnies
Were dancing in a ring,
He fiddled wi' the lilt
O' a laverock in the spring.

Twa wives sat weavin',
He garred them lauch and greet,
The birl o' a blythe reel
Stirrin' their auld feet.

Ower the dark muir, and
The deein' heather-bell,
Wi' a weary sough he
Fiddled to himsel'.

Lichtsome at mornin',
Dowie in the mirk,
He plays the tune o' Dauvid's Psalm,
Learned in Kilbirnie Kirk.

IN A LITTLE OLD TOWN

The haar creeps landward from the sea,
The laigh sun's settin' reid.
Wha's are the bairns that dance fu' late
On the auld shore-heid?

Wi' linkit hands and soople feet,　　　　　　　　　5
Slae turnin' in a ring,
Even on and even on
They sing and better sing.

'In gangs she' and 'Oot gangs she',
Their steps noo lood, noo saft,　　　　　　　　　10
Witless words to an eerie tune,
Sae solemn and sae daft.

And come they from the Windy Wynds
Or oot o' the years lang deid,
I harken wi' a stounin' he'rt　　　　　　　　　15
On the auld shore-heid.

NEWS

'Whaur hae ye been?
The nicht draws in.'
'At the back o' yon hill
Whaur twa burns rin.'
'What did ye hear, 5
What hae ye seen?'
'Lasses and lads
On the dancin'-green;
A woman singin'
Her bairn a sang; 10
The hush o' a hoose
Whaur mourners gang;
The piper that plays
To the naked air,
A bawdy tale, 15
And an auld wife's prayer.
The warld and a'
That's haud therein,
At the back o' yon hill
Whaur twa burns rin.' 20

NICHT O' NICHTS

Quiet by the fireside,
Warm the lowe o' peat,
Ne'er a cry upon the hill,
Rain nor snaw nor sleet.

Twa clear candles,   5
Bonnily they shine,
The loaf is o' the wheaten meal,
The cloth o' linen fine.

Strangers from the hill-roads,
Ye sall mak' the feast,   10
O puir man! O young lass
Wi' the baby at your breist!

Bless and break the white loaf
Atween the twa lichts;
Let me mysel' gang hungry,   15
This nicht o' a' the nichts.

THE SPAE-WIFE

The spae-wife cries at oor door
'Come, rise and let me ben;
I hev' the herb o' healin'
Will ease fouks o' their pain
And gar them thole nae langer
The hurt that they hev' ta'en.'

But whaur, O skilly spae-wife,
Whaur is growin' green
The sweet leaf o' healin'
Will soothe my sleepless een
And gar me greet nae langer
The hurt that I hev' gi'en?

NEW YEAR'S MORNING

The bells on new year's morning
Strike twelve and then are dumb;
Now lover turns to lover
With thoughts of days to come.

Now old folks sigh and wonder,
'Who sees the next year dawn?'
And wise folks say, 'There's comfort
Though half the best be gone.'

While one guest all unbidden
Keeps whispering in my ear,
'When little's left to hope for,
The less will be to fear.'

MARTHA'S HOUSE

And so at last I came to 'Martha's House'.
By the roadside it stands,
Where fields of corn creep to the mountain lands,
Silent and sweet and clean,
A table spread   5
With linen fair and fine,
Whereon was bread
And cups of country wine.

No sound, no stir save dove's soft whirr
Till, from a chamber high,   10
One clear quick cry
One name, one word,
'Mary'—yet nothing stirred,
Only small winds that blew,
Inward, the scent   15
Of mint and myrrh and rue.

'Twas 'Martha's House', folks said,
Yet why called so,
I never heard, nor read
Nor sought to know.   20

FOXGLOVES AND SNOW

Two things have set the world a-twist
And spoiled the music of the spheres;
One is a lovely secret missed,
And one a wrong beyond all tears.

Sweet secret—I shall never know,
Though seas run dry, and suns turn cold,
How many purple foxgloves grow
This summer by the ruined fold.

And—sorry wrong—though roses red
By western waters bloom and fall,
No more I watch the last snows fade
On a dark hill above Glen Doll.

MEMORY'S TRICK

Three of us on the hill-roads
From morn till evening's end,
You my kind acquaintance
And you my best friend.

Beyond the woods a stranger 5
Passed the time of day,
Lingered for a moment
And went upon his way.

Our voices woke the moorland,
The blue hills' lonely dream. 10
Now all the words are vanished
Like bubbles on the stream—

Your words, my dear acquaintance,
And yours, my friend the best—
All but the passing stranger, 15
His careless, heedless jest.

ONCE LONG AGO

Climbing on Cades-Muir
Before the town woke,
Seeking flinty arrows
Of the elfin folk,

You said that the curlew
Was a wicked bird
And when she whistles
Cries a bad word.

One or the other
Told how foxgloves stand
Pointing lost fairies
Home to fairy-land,

And of the junipers,
With sad twisted faces,
Wringing their lean hands
In wild haunted places.

But, oh! the sun darkened,
Birds hushed to hear
A soft drift, drifting,
Coming very near.

So last night I heard it,
Lisp, lisp of rain
And felt my small hand
In your hand again.

THE FAITHFUL HEART

There cam' a man from Brig o' Feugh,
Whaur I was wild and young;
I kent him by his heather step
And the turn upon his tongue.

He spak' o' crofters on the hill, 5
The shepherd from the fauld,
Simmers wi' the flourish sweet,
Winters dour and cauld;

O' this guid man and that guid wife,
Aince lads and lasses brave, 10
Hoo ane still whustles at the ploo'
And ane is in his grave;

O' them that's ower the faemy seas,
And them that bides at hame,
But I socht nae news o' my auld love 15
Nor named her bonnie name.

LINKS O' LUNAN

By the Links o' Lunan
On a clear simmer's eve
Young Annie Lizzie
Wad play at 'Mak Believe'.

Watch her on the white shore!   5
Licht, licht as faem,
She's the glimmer o' a wave,
The deep sea its hame.

Wi' lang saft fingers
Cunnin' noo it slinks,   10
Seekin' oot the wild rose
Blawin' in the links.

The sands o' Time rin doon—doon,
The years turn blin' and spare;
Annie Lizzie's gane and wi' her   15
A' that's young and fair.

But, gin ye gang by Lunan,
When the green tide flows,
And hear the whisper o' a wave
Tellin' to a rose,   20

Hereawa' or thereawa'
On midsimmer's eve,
Young Annie Lizzie's
At her game o' 'Mak' Believe'.

AT PARTING

Her body, lissom as a tree,
Its leaf wi' tempest tossed;
Her tearless een like water-springs
Smitten in winter's frost;

Her hand sae tender and sae young 5
As oot o' mine it slips;
I weel maun bear—but hoo to thole
The tremblin' o' her lips!

NOVEMBER IN EDINBURGH

A magic falls upon the town
On still November eves,
When down along the Water of Leith
Flutter the golden leaves.

There stands a little sombre house
With dusty ivy twined;
Last night Carlyle's grey shadow fell
Across the lamp-lit blind.

And whose the chaise, that down the Mound
This misty evening wends?
And whose the face that smiles from it
On all 'Rab's' faithful friends?

I walk beneath the Castle Rock
And in the 'Gardens'' glade
Linger to hear a halting step
And touch 'the Shirra's' plaid.

For there's a spell upon the town
On still November eves,
And one goes on expecting
Such sights and sounds as these.

ON A BIRTHDAY

Time, why are you going so fast?
I like not furious paces.
Milestones glimmer and then are past,
White, solemn faces.

I'm coming near to Forever and Ever,   5
With its flower and leaf unfalling,
Where you, poor Time, are an ancient measure,
Fit for a dream's recalling.

And fain am I to turn again,
Before this journey's ended,   10
For a long, long look at the road I came,
So rough and dark and—splendid!

Uncollected Poems

UNSEEN (c.1929)

Oft in the wild woods
Wi' primroses spread,
Licht hands abune me
Hae made me a bed—
Silken saft pillows,   5
Whaur dreamin' I've lain—
Like hands o' a mither,
Tho' mither I've nane.

When flooers o' the wild wood
Lie deid on the green,   10
Oh! licht hands abune me
Come steekin' ma e'en,
Frae the dreid o' the dark,
The waters that maen,
Like hands o' a lover,   15
Tho' lover I've nane.

WIZARDRY (c.1930)

The reaping after the sowing,
Moons that sail through the sky,
Morning, and cocks all crowing,
Nights with the owlet's cry,
Years with their wizardry
Parting you and me.

The years that will cover us over
In snows that come again,
The constant bloom of the clover,
The former and latter rain:
These with their wizardry
Hiding you from me.

Yesterday you were weeping,
To-day your tears are flown;
It is the Shadow creeping
Across the dial stone,
Turning tides of the sea
Estranging you and me.

THE KISS (c.1931)

Straying through the ragged bent
That lies at Journey's End,
Came one from dim and distant days,
Half enemy, half friend.

Straying through the ragged bent 5
Where Thorny Thistle is,
To start, and stare and touching lips
With hesitating kiss.

Frail kiss that came not to its birth
In love and constancy, 10
Yet blossomed sweet and passionless
Through Time's strange Alchemy.

Uncertain Provenance

THE DOVE (c.1922)

On a winter's nicht, on a winter's nicht,
When the candle flame burned lang and blue,
In the sough o' the wind, and the sigh o' the wind
There cam' to my pane a bonnie doo.

The saft wings beatin' ahint the glass 5
I thocht 'twas the buss' wi' the broken bough,
Through sough o' the wind an' sigh o' the wind,
I heard na' the plaint o' the bonnie doo.

I streiket her breest in the morning reid,
Her stane-cauld breest o' the bluebell's blue, 10
An' happit her roond in the mools o' the yaird,
Wi' 'Ye'll croon nae mair, ma bonnie doo.'

Noo simmer cloods creep ower the hills
And simmer lichtning glimmers through,
O'er glint o' muir an' gloom o' muir, 15
Gangs aye the croodlin' o' a doo.

Think ye, the silver lichtning's dart,
Wad strike my hert a sairer stoun.
O'er glint o' muir an' gloom o' muir
Ye croon—and—croon— 20
An' I streikit your breest o' the bluebell's blue—
Ma bonnie doo—ma bonnie doo!

AFTER THE STORM (c.1927)

The crashing breakers roar
And tumble on the sandy shore,
At the ocean's edge
Brown froth quivers and dances.
There was a storm last night. 5
See the long breakers running home!
See on the sand the lines of dull, brown foam!

Last night the wind blew strong,
Hurrying the heavy clouds along. 10
Over the pounding breakers
The spindthrift hung like a veil,
Glimmered with phosphorescent light
In the wild, moonless night
All the seagulls were asleep. 15
I could only hear the ceaseless roar
Of the breakers pounding on the shore!

THE POEMS OF VIOLET JACOB

Violet Jacob (*left*)
Violet Jacob in 1936, when she received an honorary degree from the University of Edinburgh

Reproduced by kind permission of the Angus Archives, Angus, Scotland

House of Dun (*below*)
The House of Dun, childhood home of Violet Jacob

Reproduced by kind permission of the National Trust for Scotland

From *Verses (1905)*

HALF-WAY

The world is not the dream of living gold
    We dreamed when we were young;
Then, all the glory that the west could hold
    Burned, fold on fold,
A molten veil across its portals flung
Behind whose shade the years lay sleeping still,
    Like tales untold;
But now, beyond the beeches bare and chill,
Beyond the woods set far upon the hill,
    The clouds are cold.

And life is not the journey that we planned
    As we set out with morn;
We said, 'We will rest here and view the land,
    Or take our stand
Upon these hills and see the ripening corn,
Or step aside along the mere to mark
    The wild-fowl band;'
But now, we know we must tread swift and stark,
If we would cross the desert ere the dark
    Creeps on the sand.

And death is not the dim and distant shade
    So far against the sky;
The half-seen trap for others waiting laid,
    While we, arrayed
In pride and plume of youth, go sweeping by.
We thought to meet him with a spirit braced
    By conquests made;
But now, we know, when half the road is traced,
Our hope is but to reach him undisgraced
    And unafraid.

THE SHADOW

What soul has swept your branches, cypress-tree,
   That you should point so high;
That you, whose root among the graves may be,
   Look ever to the sky?

Dark warden of the long-untended tomb
   Seen o'er some mouldering wall,
Or set where fountained gardens are abloom
   And roses blush and fall.

Scarcely the wind is voiceful as it sways
   Your column, dusk, austere;
Scarcely the evening breeze that round you plays
   Brings music to the ear.

Your earth-bound foot mortality retains
   Imprisoned in the sod,
Your earth-freed spirit to that ether strains
   Which is the breath of God.

The light o'er southern vineyards dying down
   Smiles on the landscape still,
And lays the lengthening shadow of your crown
   On many a Tuscan hill.

And, nearer home, where memory's deathless sun
   Enwraps some tear-sown mound,
Your shade, at day's decline, O silent one,
   Slants eastward on the ground.

By tomb or pleasance, convent-girdled height,
   In countries far or near,
You bear a message from eternal light
   To us whose souls are here.

O silent witness! dark where yonder sky
   In saffron splendour burns,
'Tis but the shadow that on earth must lie,
   The substance heavenward turns.

AN IMMORTELLE

There is a secret garden where I dwell
Hedged round about with thorn and Judas-tree,
   Barred in with iron like a prison cell
      And known to none but me.

Black rocks encircle it; the nightshade wreath
Twines in the bush its leaden-purple spray
   And the rank hellebore, with poisoned breath,
      Sighs on the air all day.

I loved it not, yet I was wont to go
To gaze my fill and all my plants compare,
   To taste the bitter herbs that thrive and grow,
      Spreading a carpet there.

        ❧ ❧ ❧

But now, 'tis years, since, in that sorry place,
I swung the wicket; for, all gloriously,
   A wingèd figure came with radiant face
      And bore away the key.

And still—I have a little poison-flower
I gathered there; and, though I would forget,
   I take it out in some friend-haunted hour
      To find it living yet.

BEYOND THE WALLS

The firelight plays since dusk began
    To gather in the room,
Beyond the pane the daylight's span
    Grows to the evening gloom;
But my heart is out with the gipsy man
    In his lair among the broom.

Beside the farm both barn and stack
    Dark in the steading rise,
Up in the loaning green, the track
    Along the firwood lies,
Where the gipsy sits with his brows of black,
    And the black light in his eyes.

He marks the swift owl skim the trees
    When twilight turns to grey,
He hears the whisper up the leas
    Before the coming day,
And the secret hours of the world he sees
    And the soul of night at play.

His ceiling is the drooping bough,
    The fir-trees' ragged limb,
When from the hills the western sough
    Sings o'er the lowlands dim;
And the polestar, hanging above the Plough,
    Is the lantern-flame for him.

O weary roof and crowding wall
    That bar the scented air!
O chain and key whose ceaseless thrall
    Lies on a world of care,
There are no bolts shot in the firwood tall
    But the joy of life is there!

O to be out when spring has drest
    The green moss for a bed,
To roam by plain and wooded crest
    Till the rose-hips turn to red;
And to lay me down for the last long rest,
    With the great sky overhead!

'COME ON, COME UP, YE ROVERS'

Come on, come up, ye rovers
    Whose ships at anchor ride,
The west wind stirs the clovers,
    And O! the world is wide:
So, up with your chains as the sun goes down 5
    And out upon the tide!

There drives on the Atlantic
    The torn scud of the rain,
And lines of foam leap frantic
    Against the coast of Spain, 10
Where the air is full of the souls of men
    Who sailed the Spanish Main.

Where Rocca's light is burning
    On plunging miles of sea,
Eastward and eastward turning, 15
    By Crete and Tripoli,
There is a spirit abroad in the wind
    That cries aloud to me.

The coast drops low behind you,
    The gull swoops round the spars; 20
Shall small men's limits bind you
    Whose milestones are the stars?
Whose signposts stand where Orion swings
    Above earth's locks and bars?

Come up, ye sons of morning, 25
    This world was built for you!
Far off, Heaven's light's adorning
    The lands where dreams come true;
And the Angel that sits at the Gates of the East
    Shall open and let you through. 30

AIRLIE KIRK

A little spot of tangled ground
Set in the folding hill,
From curlew-haunted braes the sound
Of flitting voices shrill;
The high October sky unrolled
Above the plough-land's crest,
Rank mallows by the hearthstone cold
With the field-mouse for guest;
Gudeman, it is long since the fire went out
And time that we went to rest.

The naked rafters overhead
Stand up like withered hands;
I mind me when the roof-tree spread
Where now the burdock stands.
The threshold's deep between the whin
And fast in briers twined;
Where little feet ran out and in
The track is hard to find;
Gudeman, it is long since we closed the door
And left what it held behind.

Down in the strath the kirk is set
Upon the running burn;
It's many roads we've trod, and yet
It's here we must return.
Old lights along the fields are laid,
Old shadows lie as deep,
But new eyes watch them as they fade
Among the grazing sheep,
And it's time we went down to Airlie kirk
And laid ourselves down to sleep.

IN LOWER EGYPT

Above the ancient waters of the Nile
The mists of earth and dusk of heaven meet,
Where, slow along the bank, the camel-file
Moves, like a passing dream, on velvet feet;
And, as the choral voices of a dream,   5
The night sounds play their chant upon the stream.

The crane stands silent; all the fields exhale
A band of fertile damp along the shore;
The same moon, red and low behind the veil,
That lit Old Egypt, lights for me once more   10
The mirage of a kingdom that has been,
And, through the mist, the shadow of a queen.

Rise up, O Royal Egypt, from the dusk
With all the weight of tresses on thine head
Heavy with golden nets and faint with musk,   15
Girt with the lotus from the river-bed,
And eyes that once, with their devouring fire,
Lit for men's hearts a sacrificial pyre.

O Serpent, by a serpent slain at last!
Come through the vaporous fields with garments trailed, 20
Embroidered with the lotus-leaf, made fast
With gems; with green and Tyrian purple veiled;
Turn but thy face, that I may see and know
The witchcraft throned in Egypt long ago.

There is a sound of flute and wavering reed,   25
The measured throb of falling oars that beat,
A tall prow swimming noiseless through the weed,
The shifting glimmer of a silken sheet;
And, from the dim luxuriance drawn nigh,
The feet of Royal Egypt passing by.   30

And now, her foot is set upon the barge,
The flutes play up, the fans ply to and fro,
The ripples, dying at the river-marge,
Curl, as the prow swings out upon the flow,
And its retreating music and its state   35
Leave, once again, the dusk inviolate:

Only, across the tillage lying low,
There comes the creak of well-wheels working late.

THE CALL

The stars above the apple boughs,
Like distant gazers, stand aloof,
Watching the white walls of the house,
Watching the room below the roof.

There is the night-hush over all 5
Beneath the crescent hanging low,
And, through the dark, there comes a call
From hidden lips whose voice I know.

And every root and stem and leaf,
Sends out its scented breath to me; 10
The fox is waiting like a thief,
The bird is watching from the tree.

And, in the room below the thatch,
While the white house in sleep is drowned,
Up to the open window-latch 15
There come strange whispers from the ground.

ॐ ॐ ॐ

   I will arise and steal upon the stair,
Where the tall clock counts up Time's gathered hoard
   Telling its numbers to the empty air,
   My naked feet upon the creaking board. 20
Out, out across the threshold I will go
   Into the night, the sighing, luring night,
   And all the eyes above, around, below,
Like lamps upon my path shall peer and glow
   Till thorn and thicket are alive with light. 25

   I will lie down upon my mother Earth,
Heart to her heart and soul upon her soul,
   Until the sounds that in the night have birth
   Above my head their harmonies unroll;
   And over me the little pattering feet 30
Shall come and go; and every bush and tree
Shall send from out its shades a cloudy fleet
Of flitting wings whose softly thronging beat
   Shall neither stay nor turn because of me.

THE VALLEY OF THE KINGS

Northward upon the stream our boat is creeping,
The sky above is pearl, the river pearl,
And soon will coming night her shades unfurl
Like some great bird on stealthy pinions sweeping,
As the effulgence chills 5
And young stars stand above the Theban hills
Within whose fastnesses the kings are sleeping.

To them the roll of time is but a dreaming,
To them the lotus, mouldered on their breasts,
Still dripping from the Nile, in beauty rests, 10
As when the mourners broke those blossoms streaming
And shook the silver shower,
The pallid glory of the royal flower
Fit guerdon for a royal spirit deeming.

To-night it seems that peak and rugged boulder 15
Stand o'er their soundless dwellings for a sign;
Surely some cipher of a hand divine
Is graven yonder on the mountain's shoulder,
Hidden in shadows vast
That melt to greyness as the boat slips past 20
With the slow current, and the sky grows colder.

Mayhap, the phantom of a past endeavour,
Born of that ancient striving to the light,
Has wrapt the secret sepulchres with might
And haunts the valley of the Nile for ever; 25
Breathing eternally
A note of immortality to be,
Resounding ceaselessly and dying never.

While, round the sleepers, sounds of feet have broken
The stillness that encompassed them so long, 30
And the loud voices of an idle throng
Within those halls of death have idly spoken;
While sacrilegious hands
Have loosed about them the funereal bands
To rob their bosoms of life's symbolled token, 35

From one unchanging hope can none divide them,
Although its outward emblem be despoiled;
Though silence and the peace for which they toiled
A world whose ways they knew not has denied them,
That hope its wings has spread 40
Within the rifled strongholds of the dead
As the wings shadowed on the wall beside them.

Changeless, unaltered still the soul's desire is,
Fixed as the hills whose heights we leave behind
To merge in fading colours undefined, 45
Purple and amethyst and rose and iris,
And, to the dripping oar,
The dusk is closing down along the shore,
The brooding dusk of Isis and Osiris.

THE LOWLAND PLOUGHMAN

The team is stabled up, my lass,
    The dew lies thick and grey;
Beyond the world, the long green light
    Clings to the edge of day.

By farm and fold the work is still,
    Their breath the beanflowers yield,
And, in the dusk, the gowans stand
    Like moons along the field.

A little ghost alone, my dear,
    The night moth flitters by;
Beside the hedge I'm lonely too,
    Although no ghost am I.

Leave the gudeman to mind the hearth,
    The wife to mend the fire,
Nor heed the lads whose voices come
    In mirth from yard and byre.

The evening star is up, my dear,
    And oh! the night is sweet,
Come through the heavy drops that bend
    The grasses at your feet.

For I am young and I am strong
    And well can work for two,
And 'tis a year, come Martinmas,
    I've loved no lass but you.

And, in a year, come Martinmas,
    Before the fields are sown,
I will not need to walk nor stray
    Between the lights alone.

For then the cot beyond the farm
    A happy man will hold,
A wife who wears a golden ring
    To match her hair of gold.

Selections from POEMS OF INDIA

II. NIGHT IN THE PLAINS

The plains lie in the furnace of the year
And sleep, repenting, hides from men his boon,
And flagging life strains fitfully to hear
The tardy footstep of the slow monsoon.
All day the stones, the dust upon the plain,
From never-changing skies the heat have drawn,
And darkness brings no solace in its train
—The breeze will rise an hour before the dawn.

There is no rest; from out the heavy skies
The burning planets hang; now near, now far,
Shrilly the women's voices fall and rise,
Crying to Kali in the hot bazaar.
There is no nightwatch but will end at last,
There is no vigil but will pass away,
The time wears on, the moon is setting fast
—The breeze will rise an hour before the day.

Life crouches low and fear is with the strong,
On every side the crawling time to mark,
There sound, like fevered pulses all night long,
The tom-toms, throbbing in the stifling dark;
A puff of odour from the jasmine-tree
Comes by the well across the parching lawn,
See where the hosts of heaven stand patiently,
—The breeze will rise an hour before the dawn.

The sick men toss, the breathless air is still;
Along the ward one slow, soft whisper falls,
Where Death's grim angel waits to have his will
Within the shadow of the whitewashed walls;
And women's steadfast eyes are fixed upon
The lurking shape whose hand they keep at bay,
Stand up, O souls of men, fight on, fight on!
—The breeze will rise an hour before the day.

Is that a shiver in the tamarind,
Or some awakening bird that stirs the leaves?
Turn, turn to sleep, there comes a breath of wind   35
And mainas talk by the verandah-eaves;
A little space to sleep and to forget
Before the tyrant sun begins his sway,
Ere in the heavens his brazen throne be set
—God give us strength to face the coming day.   40

III. THE RESTING-PLACE

Brother, beside the jungle track, thy stone
Half raised, a nameless, carven slab, I see,
Half hidden by the tangle, secretly;
Where roots join twisted hands above thy head,
Where scarce a footfall passes save my own,   5
   Nor white man's tread.

I have been wandering since noon was high,
And now, because the evening comes apace,
Thy tomb shall be my rest a little space;
From thy long-vanished hand this loan I take,   10
Across the years this hospitality
   That thou dost make.

The jungle has grown over thee, O friend,
For, scarce a furlong from thy buried dust,
Once stood a city where the great and just   15
Built high the parapet and mosque and dome,
Where now the creeper flings its tasselled end
   Around their home.

How many centuries have come and gone
Since first thou sawest, with awakened eyes,   20
The green-scarfed houris proffering Paradise;
Since thy young crescent moon, athwart this shade,
Son of the Prophet, has in silver shone
   Where thou art laid!

Mayhap, thy spirit loved what mine loves best; 25
The tread of horses and the pride of life,
The jungle's magic and the joy of strife,
The long nights spent beneath the spangled sky—
O dead Mahommedan! Thy passing guest
By these accepts from thee this meed of rest 30
  Salaam, O Bhai!

IV. EVENING IN THE OPIUM FIELDS

As pageants, marshalled by a masterhand,
So are the poppy-fields; in rose and red
And foam of white and livid purple spread,
Mile upon mile, they stretch on either hand;
Dark by the well the heavy mangoes stand, 5
Where labouring oxen pace with dusty tread
And dripping water-skins climb up to shed
Their gush upon the irrigated land.

So cool the labyrinthine channels run,
Flooding the grey stems with a maze of gold; 10
For, as he nears his end, the dying sun
Does all the plain within his arms enfold;
Beneath the mango-trees long shadows creep,
Like sleep's tread falling through the flowers of sleep.

V. 'GOD IS GREAT'

  'Allāh hu akhbar!
  Allāh hu akhbar!
  La ilahā illalāh!'
  Aslant upon the dusty way
The little mosque has thrown its shade, 5
A streak of blue at noontime laid,
  To lengthen tardily with day;
And now the hour has come to pray,
Soldier and prince and clod—
  'God is great, God is great, 10
  There is no god but God!'

He stands upon the outer wall,
His hands upraised, his sunken eyes
Look westward to where Mecca lies;
Ho! Islam's men, it is the call 15
To evening prayer; he cries to all,
Soldier and prince and clod—
  'God is great, God is great,
  There is no god but God!'

Close to the wall below his feet 20
A pomegranate, against the white,
Flaunts, green and scarlet, in the light,
Now glaring day has lost its heat;
Ho! Islam's men in field and street,
Soldier and prince and clod— 25
  'God is great, God is great,
  There is no god but God!'

Dark figure, seeing inwardly
Through evening mist and evening balms
To Mecca, white among the palms, 30
Across the rolling leagues of sea,
At thy long cry they bend the knee,
Soldier and prince and clod—
  'God is great, God is great,
  There is no god but God!' 35

Spread at thy feet, around, beneath,
The world wears on amid its tears,
And few and evil are their years
Fighting their way from birth to death,
Soldier and prince and clod— 40
What shining city canst thou see,
Far off, beyond the flood of fate,
Where none are poor or desolate
That thou dost cry eternally?

There comes no answer, early, late, 45
But 'God is great, God is great,
  There is no god but God!'
  'Allāh hu akhbar!
  Allāh hu akhbar!
  La ilahā illalāh!' 50

VII. CHERRY-BLOSSOM AT DAGSHAI

Far down below this range to-day
   A waft of morning pureness fills
The blue ravines that stretch away
   To lose themselves among the hills.

And, like a shrouded diadem,
   Beyond the peaks set row on row,
Looms northern India's mystic gem,
   The crown of Himalayan snow.

These lower heights which close us in
   A more ethereal jewel wear,
There seems, where sheer descents begin,
   A radiant mirage in the air,

For, with its veil of rose and foam
   A-quiver like transparent wings,
To the stern ramparts of its home
   The wild hill cherry-blossom clings.

Own sister to the clouds of dawn,
   Each magic tree o'erhangs the brink,
Its slender stems like lattice drawn,
   Dark, on a fairyland of pink.

Three days agone no sign was ours,
   No voice to cry the coming hope
That autumn's wave would break in flowers
   And roll in torrents down the slope;

But as, when darkness rends apart,
   A shaft of glory pierces through,
Joy's hand has pierced the mountain's heart
   And all the barren world is new.

IX. THE DISTANT TEMPLE

Branch of the henna-tree,
Blown in a temple garden far away
In that unfading East across the sea,
O for one waft of perfume from your spray
To cheer the heart in me! 5

Flower of the champa white,
Sown by the evening wind where dusky feet
Have worn the temple pavement with their beat,
I would lie down and give my soul to-night
Could I but breathe your sweet! 10

Note of the temple gong
At sunset clanging through the dusty gold,
Since last I heard your nightly music told
It seems as though the months were ages long
And joy itself grown old. 15

Heart of the East, my heart,
Laden with your remembrance, may not rest;
The very winds that blow from east to west
From out that far horizon-line, impart
Your whisper, trebly blest. 20

Sound of the temple drum,
Like distant beating of the march of fate,
Through the long years your voice is never dumb,
Calling, at sundown, from the temple gate
To me, who cannot come. 25

From *Songs of Angus (1915)*

TAM I' THE KIRK

O Jean, my Jean, when the bell ca's the congregation
Owre valley an' hill wi' the ding frae its iron mou',
When a'body's thochts is set on his ain salvation,
   Mine's set on you.

There's a reid rose lies on the Buik o' the Word 'afore ye   5
That was growin' braw on its bush at the keek o' day,
But the lad that pu'd yon flower i' the mornin's glory,
   He canna pray.

He canna pray; but there's nane i' the kirk will heed him
Whaur he sits sae still his lane at the side o' the wa',   10
For nane but the reid rose kens what my lassie gie'd him—
   It an' us twa!

He canna sing for the sang that his ain he'rt raises,
He canna see for the mist that's 'afore his een,
And a voice drouns the hale o' the psalms an' the
   paraphrases,   15
   Cryin' 'Jean, Jean, Jean!'

THE HOWE O' THE MEARNS

Laddie, my lad, when ye gang at the tail o' the plough
   An' the days draw in,
When the burnin' yellow's awa' that was aince a-lowe
   On the braes o' whin,
Do ye mind o' me that's deaved wi' the wearyfu' south   5
   An' its puir concairns
While the weepies fade on the knowes at the river's mouth
   In the Howe o' the Mearns?

There was nae twa lads frae the Grampians doon to the Tay
   That could best us twa;   10
At bothie or dance, or the field on a fitba' day,
   We could sort them a';
An' at courtin'-time when the stars keeked doon on the glen
   An' its theek o' fairns,
It was you an' me got the pick o' the basket then   15
   In the Howe o' the Mearns.

London is fine, an' for ilk o' the lasses at hame
   There'll be saxty here,
But the springtime comes an' the hairst—an it's aye the same
   Through the changefu' year.   20
O, a lad thinks lang o' hame ere he thinks his fill
   As his breid he airns—
An' they're thrashin' noo at the white fairm up on the hill
   In the Howe o' the Mearns.

Gin I mind mysel' an' toil for the lave o' my days   25
   While I've een to see,
When I'm auld an' done wi' the fash o' their English ways
   I'll come hame to dee;
For the lad dreams aye o' the prize that the man'll get,
   But he lives an' lairns,   30
An' it's far, far 'ayont him still—but it's farther yet
   To the Howe o' the Mearns.

Laddie, my lad, when the hair is white on yer pow
   An' the work's put past,
When yer hand's owre auld an' heavy to haud the plough 35
   I'll win hame at last,
And we'll bide our time on the knowes whaur the broom stands braw
   An' we played as bairns,
Till the last lang gloamin' shall creep on us baith an' fa'
   On the Howe o' the Mearns. 40

THE LANG ROAD

Below the braes o' heather, and far alang the glen,
The road rins southward, southward, that grips the souls
   o' men,
That draws their fitsteps aye awa' frae hearth and frae fauld,
That pairts ilk freen' frae ither, and the young frae the
   auld.
And whiles I stand at mornin' and whiles I stand at nicht, 5
To see it through the ghaisty gloom, gang slippin' oot o'
   sicht;
There's mony a lad will ne'er come back amang his ain to
   lie,
An' it's lang, lang waitin' till the time gangs by.

And far ayont the bit o' sky that lies abune the hills,
There is the black toon standin' mid the roarin' o' the
   mills.   10
Whaur the reek frae mony engines hangs 'atween it and
   the sun
And the lives are weary, weary, that are just begun.
Doon yon lang road that winds awa' my ain three sons
   they went,
They turned their faces southward frae the glens they aye
   had kent,
And twa will never see the hills wi' livin' een again,   15
An' it's lang, lang waitin' while I sit my lane.

For ane lies whaur the grass is high abune the gallant deid,
And ane whaur England's michty ships sail proud abune
   his heid,
They couldna' sleep mair saft at hame, the twa that sairved
   their king,
Were they laid aside their ain kirk yett, i' the flower o' the
   ling.   20
But whaur the road is twistin' through yon streets o' care
   an' sin,
My third braw son toils nicht and day for the gowd he
   fain would win,
Whaur ilka man grapes i' the dark to get his neebour's
   share,
An' it's lang, lang strivin' i' the mirk that's there.

The een o' love can pierce the mools that hide a sodger's
    grave, 25
An' love that doesna' heed the sod will neither hear the
    wave,
But it canna' see 'ayont the cloud that hauds my youngest
    doon
Wi' its mist o' greed an' sorrow i' the smokin' toon.

And whiles, when through the open door there fades the
    deein' licht,
I think I hear my ain twa men come up the road at nicht, 30
But him that bides the nearest seems the furthest aye frae
    me—
And it's lang, lang listenin' till I hear the three!

THE BEADLE O' DRUMLEE

Them that's as highly placed as me
(Wha am the beadle o' Drumlee)
Should na be prood, nor yet owre free.

Me an' the meenister, ye ken,
Are no' the same as a' thae men 5
We hae for neebours i' the glen.

The Lord gie'd him some lairnin' sma'
And me guid sense abune them a',
And them nae wuts to ken wha's wha.

Ye'd think, to hear the lees they tell, 10
The Sawbath day could mind itsel'
Withoot a hand to rug the bell,

Ye'd think the Reverend Paitrick Broun
Could ca' the Bible up an' doon
An' loup his lane in till his goon. 15

Whiles, gin he didna get frae me
The wiselike word I weel can gie,
Whaur wad the puir bit callant be?

The elders, Ross an' Weellum Aird,
An' fowk like Alexander Caird, 20
That thinks they're cocks o' ilka yaird,

Fegs aye! they'd na be sweir to rule
A lad sae newly frae the schule
Gin my auld bonnet crooned a fule!

But oh! Jehovah's unco' kind! 25
Whaur wad this doited pairish find
A man wi' sic a powerfu' mind?

Sae, let the pairish sleep at nicht
Blind wi' the elders' shinin' licht,
Nor ken wha's hand keeps a' things richt. 30

It's what they canna understan'
That brains hae ruled since time began,
An' that the beadle is the man!

THE WATER-HEN

As I gae'd doon by the twa mill dams i' the mornin'
The water-hen cam' oot like a passin' wraith
And her voice cam' through the reeds wi' a sound of
    warnin',
  'Faith—keep faith!'
'Aye, bird, tho' ye see but ane ye may cry on baith!'   5

As I gae'd doon the field when the dew was lyin',
My ain love stood whaur the road an' the mill-lade met,
And it seemed to me that the rowin' wheel was cryin',
  'Forgi'e—forget,
And turn, man, turn, for ye ken that ye lo'e her yet!'   10

As I gae'd doon the road 'twas a weary meetin',
For the ill words said yest're'en they were aye the same,
And my het he'rt drouned the wheel wi' its heavy beatin'.
  'Lass, think shame,
It's no for me to speak, for it's you to blame!'   15

As I gae'd doon by the toon when the day was springin'
The Baltic brigs lay thick by the soundin' quay
And the riggin' hummed wi' the sang that the wind was
    singin',
  'Free—gang free,
For there's mony a load on shore may be skailed at sea!'   20

        ಌ ಌ ಌ

When I cam' hame wi' the thrang o' the years 'ahint me
There was naucht to see for the weeds and the lade in
    spate,
But the water-hen by the dams she seemed aye to mind
    me,
  Cryin', 'Hope—wait!'
'Aye, bird, but my een grow dim, an' it's late—late!'   25

THE HEID HORSEMAN

O Alec, up at Soutar's fairm,
    You, that's sae licht o' he'rt,
I ken ye passin' by the tune
    Ye whustle i' the cairt;

I hear the rowin' o' the wheels,   5
    The clink o' haims an' chain,
And set abune yer stampin' team
    I see ye sit yer lane.

Ilk morn, agin' the kindlin' sky
    Yer liftit heid is black,   10
Ilk nicht I watch ye hameward ride
    Wi' the sunset at yer back.

For wark's yer meat and wark's yer play,
    Heid horseman tho' ye be,
Ye've ne'er a glance for wife nor maid,   15
    Ye tak nae tent o' me.

An' man, ye'll no suspec' the truth,
    Tho' weel I ken it's true,
There's mony ane that trails in silk
    Wha fain wad gang wi' you.   20

But I am just a serving lass,
    Wha toils to get her breid,
An' O! ye're sweir to see the gowd
    I braid about my heid.

My cheek is like the brier rose,   25
    That scents the simmer wind,
And fine I'd keep the wee bit hoose,
    'Gin I'd a man to mind!

It's sair to see, when ilka lad
    Is dreamin' o' his joe,   30
The bonnie mear that leads yer team
    Is a' ye're thinkin' o'.

Like fire upon her satin coat
   Ye gar the harness shine,
But, lad, there is a safter licht 35
   In thae twa een o' mine!

Aye—wark yer best—but youth is short,
   An' shorter ilka year—
There's ane wad gar ye sune forget
   Yon limmer o' a mear! 40

THE GEAN-TREES

I mind, when I dream at nicht,
Whaur the bonnie Sidlaws stand
Wi' their feet on the dark'nin' land
And their heids i' the licht;
And the thochts o' youth roll back
Like wreaths frae the hillside track
In the Vale of Strathmore;
And the autumn leaves are turnin'
And the flame o' the gean-trees burnin'
Roond the white hoose door.

Aye me, when spring cam' green
And May-month decked the shaws
There was scarce a blink o' the wa's
For the flower o' the gean;
But when the hills were blue
Ye could see them glintin' through
And the sun i' the lift;
And the flower o' the gean-trees fa'in'
Was like pairls frae the branches snawin'
In a lang white drift.

Thae trees are fair and gay
When May-month's in her prime,
But I'm thrawn wi' the blasts o' time
And my heid's white as they;
But an auld man aye thinks lang
O' the haughs he played amang
In his braw youth-tide;
And there's ane that aye keeps yearnin'
For a hoose whaur the leaves are turnin'
And the flame o' the gean-tree burnin'
By the Sidlaws' side.

THE TOD

There's a tod aye blinkin' when the nicht comes doon,
Blinkin' wi' his lang een an' keekin' roond an' roon',
Creepin' by the fairmyaird when gloamin' is to fa',
And syne there'll be a chicken or a deuk awa'—
Aye, when the guidwife rises, there's a deuk awa'!

There's a lass sits greetin' ben the hoose at hame,
For when the guidewife's cankered she gi'es her aye the
  blame,
An' sair the lassie's sabbin' an' fast the tears fa',
For the guidwife's tint her bonnie hen an' it's awa'—
Aye, she's no sae easy dealt wi' when her gear's awa'!

There's a lad aye roamin' when the day gets late,
A lang-leggit deevil wi' his hand upon the gate,
And aye the guidwife cries to him to gar the toddie fa',
For she canna thole to let her deuks an' hens awa'—
Aye, the muckle bubbly-jock himsel' is ca'd awa'!

The laddie saw the tod gang by an' killed him wi' a stane
And the bonnie lass that grat sae sair she sabs nae mair
  her lane,
But the guidwife's no contentit yet, her like ye never saw!
Cries she—'This time it is the lass, an' *she's* awa'!
Aye, yon laddie's waur nor ony tod, for Bell's awa'!'

THE BLIND SHEPHERD

The land is white, an' far awa'
    Abune ae bush an' tree
Nae fit is movin' i' the snaw
    On the hills I canna see;
For the sun may shine an' the darkness fa',   5
    But aye it's nicht to me.

I hear the whaup on windy days
    Cry up amang the peat
Whaur, on the road that speels the braes,
    I've heard my ain sheep's feet,   10
An' the bonnie lambs wi' their canny ways
    An' the silly yowes that bleat.

But noo wi' them I mauna' be,
    An' by the fire I bide,
To sit and listen patiently   15
    For a fit on the great hillside,
A fit that'll come to the door for me
    Doon through the pasture wide.

Maybe I'll hear the baa'in' flocks
    Ae nicht when time seems lang,   20
An' ken there's a step on the scattered rocks
    The fleggit sheep amang,
An' a voice that cries an' a hand that knocks
    To bid me rise an' gang.

Then to the hills I'll lift my een   25
    Nae matter tho' they're blind,
For Ane will treid the stanes between
    And I will walk behind,
Till up, far up i' the midnicht keen
    The licht o' Heaven I'll find.   30

An' maybe, when I'm up the hill
    An' stand abune the steep,
I'll turn aince mair to look my fill
    On my ain auld flock o' sheep,
An' I'll leave them lyin' sae white an' still   35
    On the quiet braes asleep.

THE DOO'COT UP THE BRAES

Beside the doo'cot up the braes
    The fields slope doon frae me,
And fine's the glint on blawin' days
    O' the bonnie plains o' sea.

Below's my mither's hoosie sma', 5
    The smiddy by the byre
Whaur aye my feyther dings awa'
    And my brither blaws the fire.

For Lachlan lo'es the smiddy's reek,
    An' Geordie's but a fule 10
Wha' drives the plough his breid to seek,
    And Rob's to teach the schule;

He'll haver roond the schulehoose wa's,
    And ring the schulehoose bell,
He'll skelp the scholars wi' the tawse 15
    (I'd like that fine mysel'!)

They're easy pleased, my brithers three—
    I hate the smiddy's lowe,
A weary dominie I'd be,
    An' I canna thole the plough. 20

But by the doo'cot up the braes
    There's nane frae me can steal
The blue sea an' the ocean haze
    An' the ships I like sae weel.

The brigs ride out past Ferryden 25
    Ahint the girnin' tugs,
And the lasses wave to the Baltic men
    Wi' the gowd rings i' their lugs.

My mither's sweir to let me gang.
    My feyther gi'es me blame, 30
But youth is sair and life is lang
    When yer he'rt's sae far frae hame.

But i' the doo'cot up the braes,
    When a'tumn nichts are mirk,
I've hid my pennies an' my claes   35
    An' the Buik I read at kirk,

An' come ae nicht when a' fowks sleep,
    I'll lift them whaur they lie,
An' to the harbour-side I'll creep
    I' the dim licht o' the sky;   40

An' when the eastern blink grows wide,
    An' dark still smoors the west,
A Baltic brig will tak' the tide
    Wi' a lad that canna rest!

LOGIE KIRK

O Logie Kirk amang the braes,
   I'm thinkin' o' the merry days
Afore I trod thae weary ways
   That led me far frae Logie!

Fine do I mind when I was young
   Abune thy graves the mavis sung
An' ilka birdie had a tongue
   To ca' me back to Logie.

O Logie Kirk, tho' aye the same
   The burn sings ae remembered name,
There's ne'er a voice to cry 'Come hame
   To bonnie Bess at Logie!'

Far, far awa' the years decline
   That took the lassie wha was mine
An' laid her sleepin' lang, lang syne
   Amang the braes at Logie.

THE PHILOSOPHY OF THE DITCH

Aweel, I'm couped. But wha' could tell
    The road wad rin sae sair?
I couldna gang yon pace mysel',
    An' I winna try nae mair!

There's them wad coonsel me to stan',   5
    But this is what I say:
When Nature's forces fecht wi' man,
    Dod, he maun just give way!

If man's nae framed to lift his fit
    Agin' a nat'ral law,   10
I winna' lift my heid, for it
    Wad dae nae guid ava'.

Puir worms are we; the poo'pit rings
    Ilk Sawbath wi' the same,
Gin airth's the place for sic-like things,   15
    I'm no sae far frae hame!

Yon's guid plain reas'nin'; an' forbye,
    This pairish has nae sense,
There's mony traiv'lin wad deny
    Nature and Providence;   20

For loud an' bauld the leears wage
    On men like me their war,
Elected saints to thole their rage
    Is what they're seekin' for.

But tho' a man wha's drink's his tea   25
    Their malice maun despise,
It's no for naething, div ye see,
    That I'm sae sweir to rise!

THE LOST LICHT
(A PERTHSHIRE LEGEND)

The weary, weary days gang by,
    The weary nichts they fa',
I mauna rest, I canna lie
    Since my ain bairn's awa'.

The soughing o' the springtide breeze   5
    Abune her heid blaws sweet,
There's nests amang the kirkyaird trees
    And gowans at her feet.

She gae'd awa' when winds were hie,
    When the deein' year was cauld,   10
And noo the young year seems to me
    A waur ane nor the auld.

And, bedded, 'twixt the nicht an' day,
    Yest're'en, I couldna bide
For thinkin', thinkin' as I lay   15
    O' the wean that lies outside.

O, mickle licht to me was gi'en
    To reach my bairn's abode,
But heaven micht blast a mither's een
    And her feet wad find the road.   20

The kirkyaird loan alang the brae
    Was choked wi' brier and whin,
A' i' the dark the stanes were grey
    As wraiths when I gae'd in.

The wind cried frae the western airt   25
    Like warlock tongues at strife,
But the hand o' fear hauds aff the he'rt
    That's lost its care for life.

I sat me lang upon the green,
    A stanethraw frae the kirk,   30
And syne a licht shone dim between
    The shaws o' yew and birk.

'Twas na the wildfire's flame that played
    Alang the kirkyaird land,
It was a band o' bairns that gae'd
    Wi' lichts in till their hand.

O white they cam', yon babie thrang,
    A' silent o'er the sod;
Ye couldna hear their feet amang
    The graves, sae saft they trod.

And aye the can'les flickered pale
    Below the darkened sky,
But the licht was like a broken trail
    When the third wee bairn gae'd by.

For whaur the can'le-flame should be
    Was neither blink nor shine—
The bairnie turned its face to me
    An' I kent that it was mine.

An' O! my broken he'rt was sair,
    I cried, 'My ain! my doo'!
For a' thae weans the licht burns fair,
    But it winna' burn for you!'

She smiled to me, my little Jean,
    Said she, 'The dule and pain,
O mither! frae your waefu' een
    They strike on me again:

'For ither babes the flame leaps bricht
    And fair and braw appears,
But I canna keep my bonnie licht,
    For it's droukit wi' your tears!'

There blew across my outstreeked hand
    The white mist o' her sark,
But I couldna reach yon babie band
    For it faded i' the dark.

My ain, my dear, your licht shall burn 65
    Although my een grow blind,
Although they twa to saut should turn
    Wi' the tears that lie behind.

O Jeanie, on my bended knee
    I'll pray I may forget, 70
My grief is a' that's left to me,
    But there's something dearer yet!

THE LAD I' THE MUNE

I.
O gin I lived i' the gowden mune
   Like the mannie that smiles at me,
I'd sit a' nicht in my hoose abune
And the wee-bit stars they wad ken me sune,
For I'd sup my brose wi' a gowden spune
   And they wad come out to see!

II.
For weel I ken that the mune's his ain
   And he is the maister there;
A' nicht he's lauchin', for, fegs, there's nane
To draw the blind on his windy-pane
And tak' an' bed him, to lie his lane
   And pleasure himsel' nae mair.

III.
Says I to Grannie, 'Keek up the glen
   Abune by the rodden tree,
There's a braw lad 'yont i' the mune, ye ken.'
Says she, 'Awa' wi' ye, bairn, gang ben,
For noo it's little I fash wi' men
   An' it's less that they fash wi' me!'

IV.
When I'm as big as the tinkler-man
   That sings i' the loan a' day,
I'll bide wi' him i' the tinkler-van
Wi' a wee-bit pot an' a wee-bit pan;
But I'll no tell Grannie my bonnie plan,
   For I dinna ken what she'll say.

V.
And, nicht by nicht, we will a' convene
   And we'll be a cantie three;
We'll lauch an' crack i' the loanin' green,
The kindest billies that ever was seen,
The tinkler-man wi' his twinklin' een
   And the lad i' the mune an' me!

THE GOWK

*I see the Gowk an' the Gowk sees me
Beside a berry-bush by the aipple-tree.*
—Old Scots Rhyme

Tib, my auntie's a deil to wark,
   Has me risin' 'afore the sun;
Aince her heid is abune her sark
   Then the clash o' her tongue's begun!
Warslin', steerin' wi' hens an' swine,   5
Naucht kens she o' a freend o' mine—
But the Gowk that bides i' the woods o' Dun
   He kens him fine!

Past the yaird an' ahint the stye,
   O the aipples grow bonnilie!   10
Tib, my auntie, she canna' spy
   Wha comes creepin' to kep wi' me.
Aye! she'd sort him, for, dod, she's fell!
Whisht now, Jimmie, an' hide yersel'
An' the wise-like bird i' the aipple-tree   15
   He winna' tell!

Aprile-month, or the aipples flower,
   Tib, my auntie, will rage an' ca';
Jimmie lad, she may rin an' glower—
   What care I? We'll be far awa!   20
Let her seek me the leelang day,
Wha's to tell her the road we'll gae?
For the cannie Gowk, tho' he kens it a',
   He winna' say!

THE JACOBITE LASS

My love stood at the loanin' side
   An' held me by the hand,
The bonniest lad that e'er did bide
   In a' this waefu' land—
There's but ae bonnier to be seen
   Frae Pentland to the sea,
And for his sake but yestere'en
   I sent my love frae me.

I gi'ed my love the white white rose
   That's at my feyther's wa',
It is the bonniest flower that grows
   Whaur ilka flower is braw;
There's but ae bonnier that I ken
   Frae Perth unto the main,
An' that's the flower o' Scotland's men
   That's fechtin' for his ain.

Gin I had kept whate'er was mine
   As I hae gi'ed my best,
My he'rt were licht by day, and syne
   The nicht wad bring me rest;
There is nae heavier he'rt to find
   Frae Forfar toon to Ayr,
As aye I sit me doon to mind
   On him I see nae mair.

Lad, gin ye fa' by Chairlie's side
   To rid this land o' shame,
There winna be a prooder bride
   Than her ye left at hame,
But I will seek ye whaur ye sleep
   Frae lawlands to the peat,
An' ilka nicht at mirk I'll creep
   To lay me at yer feet.

MAGGIE

Maggie, I ken that ye are happ'd in glory
    And nane can gar ye greet;
The joys o' Heaven are evermair afore ye,
    It's licht about yer feet.

I ken nae waefu' thochts can e'er be near ye
    Nor sorrow fash yer mind,
In yon braw place they winna let ye weary
    For him ye left behind.

Thae nichts an' days when dule seems mair nor double
    I'll need to dae my best,
For aye ye took the half o' ilka trouble,
    And noo I'd hae ye rest.

Yer he'rt'll be the same he'rt since yer flittin',
    Gin auld love doesna tire,
Sae dinna look an' see yer lad that's sittin'
    His lane aside the fire.

The sky is keen wi' dancin' stars in plenty,
    The New Year frost is strang;
But, O my lass! because the Auld Year kent ye
    I'm sweir to let it gang!

But time drives forrit; and on ilk December
    There waits a New Year yet,
And naething bides but what our he'rts remember—
    Maggie, ye'll na forget?

THE WHUSTLIN' LAD

There's a wind comes doon frae the braes when the licht is
    spreadin'
  Chilly an' grey,
An' the auld cock craws at the yett o' the muirland
    steadin'
  Cryin' on day;
The hoose lies sound an' the sma' mune's deein' an' weary   5
  Watchin' her lane,
The shadows creep by the dyke an' the time seems eerie,
But the lad i' the fields he is whustlin' cheery, cheery,
  'Yont i' the rain.

My mither stirs as she wauks wi' her twa een blinkin',   10
  Bedded she'll bide,
For foo can an auld wife ken what a lassie's thinkin'
  Close at her side?
Mither, lie still, for ye're needin' a rest fu' sairly,
  Weary an' worn,   15
Mither, I'll rise, an' ye ken I'll be warkin' fairly—
An' I dinna ken *wha* can be whustlin', whustlin', airly
  Lang or it's morn!

Gin ye hear a sound like the sneck o' the back-door turnin',
  Fash na for it;   20
It's just the crack i' the lum o' the green wood burnin',
  Ill to be lit;
Gin ye hear a step, it's the auld mear loose i' the stable
  Stampin' the strae,
Or mysel' that's settin' the parritch-spunes on the table,   25
Sae turn ye aboot an' sleep, mither, sleep while ye're able,
  Rest while ye may.

Up at the steadin' the trail of the mist has liftit
  Clear frae the ground,
Mither breathes saft an' her face to the wa' she's shiftit—   30
  Aye, but she's sound!
Lad, ye may come, for there's nane but mysel' will hear ye
  Oot by the stair,
But whustle you on an' I winna hae need to fear ye,
For, laddie, the lips that keep whustlin', whustlin' cheery   35
  Canna dae mair!

CRAIGO WOODS

Craigo Woods, wi' the splash o' the cauld rain beatin'
   I' the back end o' the year,
When the clouds hang laigh wi' the weicht o' their load o' greetin'
   And the autumn wind's asteer;
Ye may stand like ghaists, ye may fa' i' the blast that's cleft ye   5
   To rot i' the chilly dew,
But when will I mind on aucht since the day I left ye
   Like I mind on you—on you?

Craigo Woods, i' the licht o' September sleepin'
   And the saft mist o' the morn,   10
When the hairst climbs to yer feet, an' the sound o' reapin'
   Comes up frae the stookit corn,
And the braw reid puddock-stules are like jewels blinkin'
   And the bramble happs ye baith,
O what do I see, i' the lang nicht, lyin' an' thinkin'   15
   As I see yer wraith—yer wraith?

There's a road to a far-aff land, an' the land is yonder
   Whaur a' men's hopes are set;
We dinna ken foo lang we maun hae to wander,
   But we'll a' win to it yet;   20
An' gin there's woods o' fir an' the licht atween them,
   I winna speir its name,
But I'll lay me doon by the puddock-stules when I've seen them,
   An' I'll cry 'I'm hame—I'm hame!'

THE WILD GEESE

'O tell me what was on yer road, ye roarin' norlan' Wind,
As ye cam' blawin' frae the land that's niver frae my mind?
My feet they traivel England, but I'm deein' for the north.'
'My man, I heard the siller tides rin up the Firth o' Forth.'

'Aye, Wind, I ken them weel eneuch, and fine they fa' an'
    rise, 5
And fain I'd feel the creepin' mist on yonder shore that
    lies,
But tell me, ere ye passed them by, what saw ye on the
    way?'
'My man, I rocked the rovin' gulls that sail abune the
    Tay.'

'But saw ye naething, leein' Wind, afore ye cam' to Fife?
There's muckle lyin' 'yont the Tay that's mair to me nor
    life.' 10
'My man, I swept the Angus braes ye ha'ena trod for
    years.'
'O Wind, forgi'e a hameless loon that canna see for tears!'

'And far abune the Angus straths I saw the wild geese flee,
A lang, lang skein o' beatin' wings, wi' their heids towards
    the sea,
And aye their cryin' voices trailed ahint them on the air—' 15
'O Wind, hae maircy, haud yer whisht, for I daurna listen
    mair!'

From *More Songs of Angus and Others (1918)*

TO A. H. J.

Past life, past tears, far past the grave,
   The tryst is set for me,
Since, for our all, your all you gave
   On the slopes of Picardy.

On Angus, in the autumn nights,   5
   The ice-green light shall lie,
Beyond the trees the Northern Lights
   Slant on the belts of sky.

But miles on miles from Scottish soil
   You sleep, past war and scaith,   10
Your country's freedman, loosed from toil,
   In honour and in faith.

For Angus held you in her spell,
   Her Grampians, faint and blue,
Her ways, the speech you knew so well,   15
   Were half the world to you.

Yet rest, my son; our souls are those
   Nor time nor death can part,
And lie you proudly, folded close
   To France's deathless heart.   20

JOCK, TO THE FIRST ARMY

O Rab an' Dave an' rantin' Jim,
    The geans were turnin' reid
When Scotland saw yer line grow dim,
    Wi' the pipers at its heid;
Noo, i' yon warld we dinna ken,
    Like strangers ye maun gang—
'We've sic a wale o' Angus men
    That we canna weary lang.'

An' little Wat—my brither Wat—
    Man, are ye aye the same?
Or is yon sma' white hoose forgot
    Doon by the strath at hame?
An' div' ye mind foo aft we trod
    The Isla's banks before?—
—'My place is wi' the Hosts o' God,
    But I mind me o' Strathmore.'

It's deith comes skirling through the sky,
    Below there's naucht but pain,
We canna see whaur deid men lie
    For the drivin' o' the rain;
Ye a' hae passed frae fear an' doot,
    Ye're far frae airthly ill—
—'We're near, we're here, my wee recruit,
    An' we fecht for Scotland still.'

THE FIELD BY THE LIRK O' THE HILL

    Daytime an' nicht,
        Sun, wind an' rain;
    The lang, cauld licht
        O' the spring months again.
    The yaird's a' weed,
        An' the fairm's a' still—
    Wha'll sow the seed
I' the field by the lirk o' the hill?

    Prood maun ye lie,
        Prood did ye gang;
    Auld, auld am I,
        But O! life's lang!
    Ghaists i' the air,
        Whaups cryin' shrill,
    An' you nae mair
I' the field by the lirk o' the hill—
    Aye, bairn, nae mair, nae mair,
I' the field by the lirk o' the hill!

MONTROSE

    Gin I should fa',
    Lord, by ony chance,
And they howms o' France
Haud me for guid an' a';
    And gin I gang to Thee,
    Lord, dinna blame,
But oh! tak' tent, tak' tent o' an Angus lad like me
    An' let me hame!

    I winna seek to bide
    Awa owre lang,
Gin but Ye'll let me gang
Back to yon rowin' tide
    Whaur aye Montrose—my ain—
    Sits like a queen,
The Esk ae side, ae side the sea whaur she's set her lane
    On the bents between.

    I'll hear the bar
    Loupin' in its place
An' see the steeple's face
Dim i' the creepin' haar;
    And the toon-clock's sang
    Will cry through the weit,
And the coal-bells ring, aye ring, on the cairts as they gang
    I' the drookit street.

    Heaven's hosts are glad,
    Heaven's hames are bricht,
And in yon streets o' licht
Walks mony an Angus lad;
    But my he'rt's aye back
    Whaur my ain toon stands,
And the steeple's shade is laid when the tide's at the slack
    On the lang sands.

THE ROAD TO MARYKIRK

To Marykirk ye'll set ye forth,
An' whustle as ye step alang,
An' aye the Grampians i' the North
Are glow'rin' on ye as ye gang.
By Martin's Den, through beech an' birk,   5
A breith comes soughin', sweet an' strang,
   Alang the road to Marykirk.

Frae mony a field ye'll hear the cry
O' teuchits, skirlin' on the wing,
Noo East, noo West, amang the kye,   10
And smell o' whins the wind'll bring;
Aye, lad, it blaws a thocht to mock
The licht o' day on ilka thing—
For you, that went yon road last spring,
   Are lying deid in Flanders, Jock.   15

THE BRIG

I whiles gang to the brig-side
    That's past the briar tree,
Alang the road when the licht is wide
    Owre Angus an' the sea.

In by the dyke yon briar grows
    Wi' leaf an' thorn, it's lane
Whaur the spunk o' flame o' the briar rose
    Burns saft agin the stane.

An' whiles a step treids on by me,
    I mauna hear its fa';
And atween the brig an' the briar tree
    Ther gangs na' ane, but twa.

Oot owre yon sea, through dule an' strife,
    Ye tak' yer road nae mair,
For ye've crossed the brig to the fields o' life,
    An' ye walk for iver there.

I traivel on to the brig-side,
    Whaur ilka road maun cease,
My weary war may be lang to bide,
    An' you hae won to peace.

There's ne'er a nicht but turns to day,
    Nor a load that's niver cast;
An' there's nae wind cries on the winter brae,
    But it spends itsel' at last.

O You that niver failed me yet,
    Gin aince my step ye hear,
Come to yon brig atween us set,
    An' bide till I win near!

O weel, aye, weel, ye'll ken my treid,
    Ye'll seek nae word nor sign,
An' I'll no can fail at the Brig o' Dreid,
    For yer hand will be in mine.

THE KIRK BESIDE THE SANDS

It was faur-ye-weel, my dear, that the gulls were cryin'
    At the kirk beside the sands,
Whaur the saumon-nets lay oot on the bents for dryin',
    Wi' the tar upon their strands;

A roofless kirk i' the bield o' the cliff-fit bidin',   5
    And the deid laid near the wa';
A wheen auld coupit stanes i' the sea-grass hidin',
    Wi' the sea-sound ower them a'.

But it's mair nor deith that's here on the haughs o' Flanders,
    And the deid lie closer in;   10
It's no' the gull, but the hoodit craw that wanders
    When the lang, lang nichts begin.

It's ill to dee, but there's waur things yet nor deein';
    And the warst o' a's disgrace;
For there's nae grave deep eneuch 'mang the graves in bein' 15
    To cover a coward's face.

Syne, a' is weel, though my banes lie here for iver,
    An' hame is no' for me,
Till the reid tide brak's like the spate in a roarin' river
    O'er the micht o' Gairmanie.   20

Sae gang you back, my dear, whaur the gulls are cryin',
    Gie thanks by kirk an' grave,
That yer man keeps faith wi' the land whaur his he'rt is lyin',
    An' the Lord will keep the lave.

GLORY

I canna' see ye, lad, I canna' see ye,
   For a' yon glory that's aboot yer heid,
Yon licht that haps ye, an' the hosts that's wi' ye,
   Aye, but ye live, an' it's mysel' that's deid!

They gae'd frae mill and mart; frae wind-blawn places,   5
   And grey toon-closes; i' the empty street
Nae mair the bairns ken their steps, their faces,
   Nor stand to listen to the trampin' feet.

Beside the brae, and soughin' through the rashes,
   Yer voice comes back to me at ilka turn,   10
Amang the whins, an' whaur the water washes
   The arn-tree wi' its feet amangst the burn.

Whiles ye come back to me when day is fleein',
   And a' the road oot-by is dim wi' nicht,
But weary een like mine is no for seein',   15
   An', gin they saw, they wad be blind wi' licht.

Deith canna' kill. The mools o' France lie o'er ye,
   An' yet ye live, O sodger o' the Lord!
For Him that focht wi' deith an' dule afore ye,
   He gie'd the life—'twas Him that gie'd the sword.   20

But gin ye see my face or gin ye hear me,
   I daurna' ask, I maunna' seek to ken,
Though I should dee, wi' sic a glory near me,
   By nicht or day, come ben, my bairn, come ben!

THE SHEPHERD TO HIS LOVE

Abune the hill ae muckle star is burnin',
  Sae saft an' still, my dear, sae far awa,
There's ne'er a wind, noo day to nicht is turnin',
  To lift the branches of the whisperin' shaw;
    Aye, Jess, there's nane to see,
    There's just the sheep an' me,
And ane's fair wastit when there micht be twa!

Alang the knowes there's no a beast that's movin',
  They sheep o' mine lie sleepin' i' the dew;
There's jist ae thing that's wearyin' an' rovin',
  An' that's mysel', that wearies, wantin' you.
    What ails ye, that ye bide
    In-by—an' me ootside
To curse an' daunder a' the gloamin' through?

To haud my tongue an' aye hae patience wi' ye
  Is waur nor what a lass like you can guess;
For a' yer pranks I canna but forgi'e ye,
  I fegs! there's naucht can gar me lo'e ye less;
    Heaven's i' yer een, an' whiles
    There's heaven i' yer smiles,
But oh! ye tak' a deal o' courtin', Jess!

A CHANGE O' DEILS

'A change o' deils is lichtsome'—Scots Proverb

My Grannie spent a merry youth,
   She niver wantit for a joe,
And gin she tell't me aye the truth,
   Richt little was't she kent na o'.

An' whiles afore she gae'd awa'   5
   To bed her doon below the grass,
Says she, 'Guidmen I've kistit twa,
   But a change o' deils is lichtsome, lass!'

Sae dinna think to maister me,
   For Scotland's fu' o' brawlike chiels,   10
And aiblins ither folk ye'll see
   Are fine an' pleased to change their deils.

Aye, set yer bonnet on yer heid,
   An' cock it up upon yer bree,
O' a' yer tricks ye'll hae some need   15
   Afore ye get the best o' me!

Sma' wark to fill yer place I'd hae,
   I'll seek a sweethe'rt i' the toon,
Or cast my he'rt across the Spey
   An' tak' some pridefu' Hieland loon.   20

I ken a man has hoose an' land,
   His airm is stoot, his een are blue,
A ring o' gowd is on his hand,
   An' he's a bonnier man nor you!

But hoose an' gear an' land an' mair,   25
   He'd gie them a' to get the preen
That preened the flowers in till my hair
   Beside the may-bush yestere'en.

Jist tak' you tent, an' mind forbye,
   The braw guid sense my Grannie had,   30
My Grannie's dochter's bairn am I,
   And a change o' deils is lichtsome, lad!

THE LAST O' THE TINKLER

Lay me in yon place, lad,
   The gloamin's thick wi' nicht;
I canna' see yer face, lad,
   For my een's no richt,
But it's ower late for leein',
An' I ken fine I'm deein',
Like an auld craw fleein'
   To the last o' the licht.

The kye gang to the byre, lad,
   An' the sheep to the fauld,
Ye'll mak' a spunk o' fire, lad,
   For my he'rt's turned cauld;
An' whaur the trees are meetin',
There's a sound like waters beatin',
An' the bird seems near to greetin',
   That was aye singin' bauld.

There's jist the tent to leave, lad,
   I've gaithered little gear,
There's jist yersel' to grieve, lad,
   An' the auld dog here;
An' when the morn comes creepin',
An' the wauk'nin' birds are cheipin',
It'll find me lyin' sleepin'
   As I've slept saxty year.

Ye'll rise to meet the sun, lad,
   An' baith be traiv'lin' west,
But me that's auld an' done, lad,
   I'll bide an' tak' my rest;
For the grey heid is bendin',
An' the auld shune's needin' mendin',
But the traiv'lin's near its endin',
   And the end's aye the best.

FRINGFORD BROOK

The willows stand by Fringford brook,
   From Fringford up to Hethe,
Sun on their cloudy silver heads,
   And shadow underneath.

They ripple to the silent airs
   That stir the lazy day,
Now whitened by their passing hands,
   Now turned again to grey.

The slim marsh-thistle's purple plume
   Droops tasselled on the stem,
The golden hawkweeds pierce like flame
   The grass that harbours them;

Long drowning tresses of the weeds
   Trail where the stream is slow,
The vapoured mauves of water-mint
   Melt in the pools below;

Serenely soft September sheds
   On earth her slumberous look,
The heartbreak of an anguished world
   Throbs not by Fringford brook.

All peace is here. Beyond our range,
   Yet 'neath the selfsame sky,
The boys that knew these fields of home
   By Flemish willows lie.

They waded in the sun-shot flow,
   They loitered in the shade,
Who trod the heavy road of death,
   Jesting and unafraid.

Peace! What of peace? This glimpse of peace
   Lies at the heart of pain,
For respite, ere the spirit's load
   We stoop to lift again.

O load of grief, of faith, of wrath,
   Of patient, quenchless will,
Till God shall ease us of your weight   35
   We'll bear you higher still!

O ghosts that walk by Fringford brook,
   'Tis more than peace you give,
For you, who knew so well to die,
   Shall teach us how to live.   40

PRISON

In the prison-house of the dark
    I lay with open eyes,
And pale beyond the pale windows
    I saw the dawn rise.
From past the bounds of space
    Where earthly vapours climb,
There stirred the voice I shall not hear
    On this side Time.
There is one death for the body,
    And one death for the heart,
And one prayer for the hope of the end,
    When some links part.
Christ, from uncounted leagues,
Beyond the sun and moon,
Strike with the sword of Thine own pity—
    Bring the dawn soon.

PRESAGE

The year declines, and yet there is
   A clearness, as of hinted spring;
And chilly, like a virgin's kiss,
   The cold light touches everything.

The world seems dazed with purity,
   There hangs, this spell-bound afternoon,
Beyond the naked cherry tree
   The new-wrought sickle of the moon.

What is this thraldom, pale and still,
   That holds so passionless a sway?
Lies death in this ethereal chill,
   New life, or prelude of decay?

In the frail rapture of the sky
   There bodes, transfigured, far aloof,
The veil that hides eternity,
   With life for warp and death for woof.

We see the presage—not with eyes,
   But dimly, with the shrinking soul—
Scarce guessing, in this fateful guise,
   The glory that enwraps the whole,

The light no flesh may apprehend,
   Lent but to spirit-eyes, to give
Sign of that splendour of the end
   That none may look upon and live.

THE BIRD IN THE VALLEY

Above the darkened house the night is spread,
    The hidden valley holds
  Vapour and dew and silence in its folds,
And waters sighing on the river-bed.
    No wandering wind there is
  To swing the star-wreaths of the clematis
    Against the stone;
Out of the hanging woods, above the shores,
One liquid voice of throbbing crystal pours,
    Singing alone.

A stream of magic through the heart of night
    Its unseen passage cleaves;
  Into the darkened room below the eaves
It falls from out the woods upon the height,
    A strain of ecstasy
  Wrought on the confines of eternity,
    Glamour and pain,
And echoes gathered from a world of years,
Old phantoms, dim like mirage seen through tears,
    But young again.

'Peace, peace,' the bird sings on amid the woods,
  'Peace, from the land that is the spirit's goal,—
  The land that none may see but with his soul,—
Peace on the darkened house above the floods.'
Pale constellations of the clematis,
    Hark to that voice of his
      That will not cease,
  Swing low, droop low your spray,
Light with your white stars all the shadowed way
    To peace, peace!

BACK TO THE LAND

Out in the upland places,
 I see both dale and down,
And the ploughed earth with open scores
 Turning the green to brown.

The bare bones of the country 5
 Lie gaunt in winter days,
Grim fastnesses of rock and scaur,
 Sure, while the year decays.

And, as the autumn withers,
 And the winds strip the tree, 10
The companies of buried folk
 Rise up and speak with me;—

From homesteads long forgotten,
 From graves by church and yew,
They come to walk with noiseless tread 15
 Upon the land they knew;—

Men who have tilled the pasture
 The writhen thorn beside,
Women within grey vanished walls
 Who bore and loved and died. 20

And when the great town closes
 Upon me like a sea,
Daylong, above its weary din,
 I hear them call to me.

Dead folk, the roofs are round me, 25
 To bar out field and hill,
And yet I hear you on the wind
 Calling and calling still;

And while, by street and pavement,
 The day runs slowly through, 30
My soul, across these haunted downs,
 Goes forth and walks with you.

THE SCARLET LILIES

I see her as though she were standing yet
    In her tower at the end of the town,
When the hot sun mounts and when dusk comes down,
    With her two hands laid on the parapet;
The curve of her throat as she turns this way,
    The bend of her body—I see it all;
And the watching eyes that look day by day
    O'er the flood that runs by the city wall.

The winds by the river would come and go
    On the flame-red gown she was wont to wear,
And the scarlet lilies that crowned her hair,
    And the scarlet lilies that grew below.
I used to lie like a wolf in his lair,
    With a burning heart and a soul in thrall,
Gazing across in a fume of despair
    O'er the flood that runs by the river wall.

I saw when he came with his tiger's eyes,
    That held you still in the grip of their glance,
And the cat-smooth air he had learned in France,
    The light on his sword from the evening skies;
When the heron stood at the water's edge,
    And the sun went down in a crimson ball,
I crouched in a thicket of rush and sedge
    By the flood that runs by the river wall.

He knew where the stone lay loose in its place,
    And a foot might hold in the chink between,
The carven niche where the arms had been,
    And the iron rings in the tower's face;
For the scarlet lilies lay broken round,
    Snapped through at the place where his tread would fall,
As he slipped at dawn to the yielding ground,
    Near the flood that runs by the river wall.

I gave the warning—I ambushed the band
    In an alder-clump—he was one to ten—
Shall I fight for my soul as he fought then,
    Lord God, in the grasp of the devil's hand?
As the cock crew up in the morning chill,
    And the city waked to the watchman's call,
There were four left lying to sleep their fill
    At the flood that runs by the city wall.

Had I owned this world to its farthest part,
    I had bartered all to have had his share;
Yet he died that night in the city square,
    With a scarlet lily above his heart.
And she? Where the torrent goes by the slope,
    There rose in the river a stifled call,
And two white hands strove with a knotted rope
    In the flood that runs by the river wall.

Christ! I had thought I should die like a man,
    And that death, grim death, might himself be sweet,
When the red sod rocked to the horses' feet,
    And the knights went down as they led the van;—
But the end that waits like a trap for me,
    Will come when I fight for my latest breath,
With a white face drowned between God and me
    In the flood that runs by the banks of death.

FROSTBOUND

When winter's pulse seems dead beneath the snow,
    And has no throb to give,
Warm your cold heart at mine, beloved, and so
    Shall your heart live.

For mine is fire—a furnace strong and red;   5
    Look up into my eyes,
There shall you see a flame to make the dead
    Take life and rise.

My eyes are brown, and yours are still and grey,
    Still as the frostbound lake   10
Whose depths are sleeping in the icy sway,
    And will not wake.

Soundless they are below the leaden sky,
    Bound with that silent chain;
Yet chains may fall, and those that fettered lie   15
    May live again.

Yes, turn away, grey eyes, you dare not face
    In mine the flame of life;
When frost meets fire, 'tis but a little space
    That ends the strife.   20

Then comes the hour, when, breaking from their bands,
    The swirling floods run free,
And you, beloved, shall stretch your drowning hands,
    And cling to me.

'THE HAPPY WARRIOR'

I have brought no store from the field now the day is ended,
    The harvest moon is up and I bear no sheaves;
When the toilers carry the fruits hanging gold and splendid,
    I have but leaves.

When the saints pass by in the pride of their stainless
    raiment, 5
    Their brave hearts high with the joy of the gifts they bring,
I have saved no whit from the sum of my daily payment
    For offering.

Not there is my place where the workman his toil delivers,
    I scarce can see the ground where the hero stands, 10
I must wait as the one poor fool in that host of givers,
    With empty hands.

There was no time lent to me that my skill might fashion
    Some work of praise, some glory, some thing of light,
For the swarms of hell came on in their power and passion, 15
    I could but fight.

I am maimed and spent, I am broken and trodden under,
    With wheel and horseman the battle has swept me o'er,
And the long, vain warfare has riven my heart asunder,
    I can no more. 20

But my soul is still; though the sundering door has hidden
    The mirth and glitter, the sound of the lighted feast,
Though the guests go in and I stand in the night, unbidden,
    The worst, the least.

My soul is still. I have gotten nor fame nor treasure, 25
    Let all men spurn me, let devils and angels frown,
But the scars I bear are a guerdon of royal measure,
    My stars—my crown.

From *Bonnie Joann and Other Poems (1921)*

BONNIE JOANN

We've stookit the hairst an' we're needin'
    To gaither it in,
Syne, gin the morn's dry, we'll be leadin'
    An' wark'll begin;
But noo I'll awa doon the braeside
    My lane, while I can—
Wha kens wha he'll meet by the wayside,
    My bonnie Joann?

East yonder, the hairst-fields are hidin'
    The sea frae my een,
Gin ye keek whaur the stooks are dividin'
    Ye'll see it atween.
Sae douce an' sae still it has sleepit
    Since hairst-time began
Like my he'rt—gin ye'd tak' it an' keep it
    My bonnie Joann.

Owre a'thing the shadows gang trailin',
    Owre stubble an' strae;
Frae the hedge to the fit o' the pailin'
    They rax owre the way;
But the sun may gang through wi' his beamin'
    An' traivel his span,
For aye, by the licht o' my dreamin',
    I see ye, Joann.

Awa frae ye, naebody's braver,
    Mair wise-like an' bauld,
Aside ye, I hech an' I haver,
    I'm het an' I'm cauld;
But oh! could I tell wi'out speakin'
    The he'rt o' a man,
Ye micht find I'm the lad that ye're seekin',
    My bonnie Joann!

THE WIND FRAE THE BALTIC

Below the wa's, oot-by Montrose,
    The tides ca' up an' doon
And mony's the gallant mairchantman
    Lies in aside the toon;
Oh, it's fine alang the tideway
    The loupin' waters rin
When the wind is frae the Baltic wi' the brigs comin' in.

I'd gie the ring upon my hand
    To hide me frae the sea
That manes by nicht an' cries by day
    The dule that's come to me,
For I'll hear nae mair the fit-fa'
    When hame the brigs may win
O' a man that sailed the Baltic, nor his step comin' in.

And noo the toon is fair asteer,
    The weans rin doon the street,
And I may turn my face aboot
    An' get me hame to greet,
There's sic a joy wi' a' fowk
    My tears wad be a sin,
For the wind is frae the Baltic—an' the brigs comin' in.

THE TRAMP TO THE TATTIE-DULIE

Thrawn-leggit carle wi' airms on hie
And jist a hole for ilka ee,
Ye needna lift yer hand to me
   As though ye'd strike me;
Ye're threits abune an' strae below,   5
But what-like use is sic a show?
Ye maun respec' me, bogle, tho'
   Ye mauna like me!

To gutsy doo or thievin' craw
Ye mebbe represent the law   10
When the come fleein' owre the wa'
   To tak' an airin',
Dod, I'll no say they arena richt
When sic a fell, unchancy sicht
Gars them think twice afore they licht—   15
   But *I'm* no carin'!

Yer heid's a neep, yer wame's a sack,
Yer ill-faured face gars bairnies shak',
But yet the likes o' you can mak'
   A livin' frae it;   20
Sma' use to me! It isna fair
For though there's mony wad declare
That I'm no far ahint ye there,
   I canna dae it!

Life's a disgust wi' a' its ways,   25
For free o' chairge ye get yer claes,
Nae luck hae I on washin'-days—
   There's plenty dryin',
But gin I see a usefu' sark
An' bide or gloamin' help my wark,   30
The guidwife's oot afore it's dark—
   And leaves nane lyin'.

Weel, weel, I'm aff. It's little pleasure
To see ye standin' at yer leisure
When I've sae mony miles to measure 35
   To get a meal!
Ye idle dog! My bonnet's through,
An' yours is no exac'ly new,
But a' the same I'll hae't frae you,
   And faur-ye-weel! 40

HALLOWE'EN

The tattie-liftin's nearly through,
They're ploughin' whaur the barley grew,
   And aifter dark, roond ilka stack,
   Ye'll see the horsemen stand an' crack
O Lachlan, but I mind o' you!   5

I mind foo often we hae seen
Ten thoosand stars keek doon atween
   The nakit branches, an' below
   Baith fairm an' bothie hae their show,
Alowe wi' lichts o' Hallowe'en.   10

There's bairns wi' guizards at their tail
Clourin' the doors wi' runts o' kail,
   And fine ye'll hear the skreichs an' skirls
   O' lassies wi' their droukit curls
Bobbin' for aipples i' the pail.   15

The bothie fire is loupin' het,
A new heid horseman's kist is set
   Richts o' the lum; whaur by the blaze
   The auld ane stude that kept yer claes—
I canna thole to see it yet!   20

But gin the auld fowks' tales are richt
An' ghaists come hame on Hallow nicht,
   O freend o' freends! what wad I gie
   To feel ye rax yer hand to me
Atween the dark an' caun'le licht?   25

Awa in France, across the wave,
The wee lichts burn on ilka grave,
   An' you an' me their lowe hae seen—
   Ye'll mebbe hae yer Hallowe'en
Yont, whaur ye're lyin' wi' the lave.   30

There's drink an' daffin', sang an' dance
And ploys and kisses get their chance,
   But Lachlan, man, the place I see
   Is whaur the auld kist used to be
And the lichts o' Hallowe'en in France!   35

THE DAFT BIRD

When day is past an' peace comes doon wi' gloamin'
    An' twa by twa the young fowk pass the yett,
Auld stocks like me maun let their thochts content them,
    Mindin' o' coortin's that they'll no forget.
Ye're no sae far awa the nicht, my Marget,
    Tho' on the brae-heid, past the dyke ye lie,
Whaur ae daft bird is singin' i' the kirkyaird
    And ae star watches i' the evenin' sky.

Late bird, daft bird, the likes o' you are bedded,
    The daylicht's deid, it's hame that ye should be,
Yer voice is naucht to them that canna hear ye;
    But sing you on, it isna naucht to me.
Dod, like yersel', it's time that I was sleepin',
    Sae lang it is since Marget laid her doon,
And ilka year treids up ahint anither
    Like evenin's ghaist ahint the aifternoon.

For rest comes slaw to you an' me, I'm thinkin',
    Oor day's wark's surely lang o' wearin' through,
The gloamin's had been wearier an' langer,
    Thae nichts o' June, late warker, wantin' you.
I maun hae patience yet, I'll no be grievin',
    There's them that disna fail tho' day be spent,
An' yon daft bird's aye singing i' the kirkyaird—
    Lord, I will bide my time, an' bide content.

'KIRRIE'

Comin' oot frae Kirrie, when the autumn gowd an' siller
   At the hindmaist o' September month has grips o' tree an' shaw,
The mune hung, deaved wi' sunset, no a spunk o' pride in till her,
   Nae better nor a bogle, till the licht was awa;
An' the haughs below the Grampians, i' the evenin' they were lyin'   5
   Like a lang-socht Land o' Promise that the cauld mist couldna smoor;
An' tho' ye didna see it, ye could hear the river cryin'
   If ye stood a while to listen on the road to Kirriemuir.

There's an auld wife bides in Kirrie—set her up! a pridefu' crater—
   And she's crackin' aye o' London an' the grand fowk ye may see;   10
O' the King, an' syne his palace, till I'm sure I'm like to hate her,
   For the mairket-day in Kirrie is the sicht for me.
But ye ken I'm sweir to fash her, an' it's best to be agreein',
   For gin ye dinna heed her, then she's cankered-like an' soor,
Dod, she tells o' muckle lairnin'—but I doot the bizzar's leein',   15
   For it's fules wad bide in London when they kent o' Kirriemuir.

O, the braw, braw toon o' Kirrie! What a years that I hae lo'ed it!
   And I winna seek to leave it tho' I'm spared anither score;
I'd be greetin' like a laddie for the auld reid hooses croodit
   Lookin' down upon the steadin's and the fields o' Strathmore.   20
Ye may speak o' heavenly mansions, ye may say it wadna grieve ye
   When ye quit a world sae bonnie—but I canna jist be sure,
For I'll hae to wait, I'm thinkin', or I see if I believe ye,
   For my first braid blink o' Heaven, an' my last o' Kirriemuir!

THE END O'T

There's a fine braw thistle that lifts its croon
   By the river-bank whaur the ashes stand,
An' the swirl o' water comes whisp'rin' doon
   Past birk an' bramble an' grazin' land.
But simmer's flittit an' time's no heedin'
   A feckless lass nor a pridefu' flow'r;
The dark to hide me's the grace I'm needin',
     An' the thistle's seedin'
        An' my day's owre.

I redd the hoose an' I meat the hens
   (Oh, it's ill to wark when ye daurna tire!)
An' what'll I get when my mither kens
   It's niver a maiden that biggs her fire?
I mind my pray'rs, but I'm feared to say them,
   I hide my een, for they're greetin' fast,
What though I blind them—for wha wad hae them?
     The licht's ga'en frae them
        An' my day's past.

Oh, wha tak's tent for a fadin' cheek?
   No him, I'se warrant, that gar'd it fade!
There's little love for a lass to seek
   When the coortin's through an' the price is paid.
Oh, aince forgotten's forgotten fairly,
   An' heavy endit what's licht begun,
But God forgie ye an' keep ye, Chairlie,
     For the nicht's fa'en airly
        An' my day's done!

THE KELPIE

I'm feared o' the road ayont the glen,
   I'm sweir to pass the place
Whaur the water's rinnin', for a' fowk ken
There's a kelpie sits at the fit o' the den,
   And there's them that's seen his face.

But whiles he watches an' whiles he hides
   And whiles, gin na wind manes,
Ye can hear him roarin' frae whaur he bides
An' the soond o' him splashin' agin the sides
   O' the rocks an' the muckle stanes.

When the mune gaes doon at the arn-tree's back
   In a wee, wee weary licht,
My bed-claes up to my lugs I tak',
For I mind the swirl o' the water black
   An' the cry i' the fearsome nicht.

And lang an' fell is yon road to me
   As I come frae the schule;
I daurna think what I'm like to see
When dark fa's airly on buss an' tree
   At Martinmas and Yule.

Aside the crusie my mither reads,
   'My bairn,' says she, 'ye've heard
The Lord is mindfu' o' a' oor needs
An' His shield an' buckler's abune the heids
   O' them that keeps His word.'

But I'm a laddie that's no that douce,
   An' fechtin's a bonnie game;
The dominie's pawmies are little use,
An' mony's the Sawbath I'm rinnin' loose
   When a'body thinks I'm hame!

Dod, noo we're nearin' the shorter days,
   It's cannie I'll hae to gang,
An' keep frae fechtin' an' sic-like ways,
And no be tearin' my Sawbath claes
   Afore that the nichts grow lang.   35

Richt guid an' couthie I'll need to be,
   (But it's leein' to say I'm glad),
I kent there's troubles that fowk maun dree,
An' the kelpie's no like to shift for me,
Sae, gine thae warlocks are fear'd o' Thee,   40
   Lord, mak' me a better lad!

BALTIC STREET

My dainty lass, lay you the blame
    Upon the richtfu' heid;
'Twas daft ill-luck that bigg'd yer hame
    The wrang side o' the Tweed.
Ye hae yer tocher a' complete,
    Ye're bonnie as the rose,
But I was born in Baltic Street,
    In Baltic Street, Montrose!

Lang syne on mony a waefu' nicht,
    Hie owre the sea's distress,
I've seen the great airms o' the licht
    Swing oot frae Scurdyness;
An' prood, in sunny simmer blinks,
    When land-winds rase an' fell,
I'd flee my draigon on the links
    Wi' callants like mysel'.

Oh, Baltic Street is cauld an' bare
    An' mebbe nae sae grand,
But ye'll feel the smell i' the caller air
    O' kippers on the land.
'Twixt kirk an' street the deid fowk bide
    Their feet towards the sea,
Ill nee'bours for a new-made bride,
    Gin ye come hame wi' me.

The steeple shades the kirkyaird grass,
    The seamen's hidden banes,
A dour-like kirk to an English lass
    Wha kens but English lanes;
And when the haar, the winter through,
    Creeps blind on close and wa'
My hame micht get a curse frae you,
    Mysel' get, mebbe, twa.

I'll up an' aff the morn's morn
   To seek some reid-haired queyn,
Bauld-he'rted, strang-nieved, bred an' born   35
   In this auld toon o' mine.
And oh! for mair I winna greet,
   Gin we hae meal an' brose
And a but an' ben in Baltic Street,
   In Baltic Street, Montrose!   40

BAILIE BRUCE

Ye'd winder, when creation's plan
Seems sae acceptable to man,
And the Creator, in His power,
Made brute an' bird, an' fruit an' flower;
When e'en the wasps that bigg their bike   5
An' clocks an' golachs, an' the like
O' a' yon vairmin has their use,
What gar'd Him fashion Bailie Bruce?

He couldna thole to see a wean
Wheepin' his pearie on the green,   10
Nae sweethe'rts coorted but he saw
Auld Hornie's tail ahint the twa.
In godly wrath he aye wad show
His hate o' sinfu' men; but tho'
The wicked fled afore his face   15
The guid aye passed them i' the race.

Oot frae the foremaist seat at kirk
He roared the psalms like ony stirk,
For gripp'd was he by sic a zeal
As nane but the elect micht feel;   20
An' when the kirk-door plate was set,
Wi' looks o' pride ye'd ne'er forget,
When puir fowk laid their pennies doon
He'd gi'e his Maker half a croon.

Weel, whiles oor ancient customs change   25
An' fowk accep' what's new an' strange;
Oor decent plate awa was laid
For bonny baggies—English made.
Sawbath cam' roond; the kirk was in;
The Bailie sat an' glow'red on sin;   30
The Elder brocht wi' reverent feet
His baggie to the foremaist seat.

In drapp'd the money; Bailie Bruce
Wi' open hand an' purse-strings loose
And e'en upliftit, kept his place;   35
The bag passed on its road o' grace.
Weel was't he couldna see the smile
That a' yon kirk-fu' had the while
Nor yet the Elder's twisted mou'
That wrocht him a' the journey through!   40

For oh! ahint the Bailie's back
Was done a deed o' shame to mak'
His righteous he'rt wi' anger swell
Nane gie'd a bodle but himsel'!
An' at the coontin', plain to see,   45
The baggie held but ae bawbee!

        ઇ ઇ ઇ

His health noo gars him keep the hoose;
Losh-aye! what ails him, Bailie Bruce?

CHARLEWAYN

Yestere'en was Hallowe'en,
  To-day is Hallow-day,
It's nine free nichts to Martinmas,
  And then we'll get away.
—Old song among Angus farm servants

Frae Hallowe'en to Martinmas
  There's little time to fill,
And yet there's mony a warkin' lass
  Thinks a' the days stand still.

Oh, cauld the mornin' creeps on nicht
  Alang the eerie skies,
An' cauld the blink o' caun'le-licht
  That lets me see to rise.

For late an' airly at the fairm
  The wark seems niver past,
But a week, come Monday, brings the tairm
  When I may flit at last.

My mither hauds her dochters ticht,
  My mither's hoose is sma',
An' I niver lo'ed my mither richt
  Until I gaed awa.

But yestere'en was Hallowe'en
  When a' may dance an' sing;
The auld guidwife shut doon her e'en,
  The young anes got their fling;

Set up, the fiddler wrocht. Below,
  The reel swang ilka ane,
But my feet danced oot to meet my joe
  By the licht o' Charlewayn.

My mither's hame's a happy hame
  Whaur easy I may lie,
And o' mysel' I'm thinkin' shame,
  Sic a feckless queyn am I.

For, by the licht o' Charlewayn,
  It's Rab that gar'd me lairn 30
To see a lover's lass mair plain
  E'en than a mither's bairn.

Aye, yestere'en was Hallowe'en,
  An' Martinmas is near;
It's wae for Martinmas I've been 35
  But it's like to find me here!

THE GANGEREL

It's ye maun whustle for a breeze
    Until the sails be fu';
They bigg yon ships that ride the seas
    To pleasure fowk like you.

For ye hae siller i' yer hand
    And a' that gowd can buy,
But weary, in a weary land,
    A gangerel-loon am I.

Ye'll feel the strang tides lift an' toss
    The scud o' nor'land faem,
And when ye drap the Southern Cross
    It's a' roads lead ye hame.

And ye shall see the shaws o' broom
    Wave on the windy hill,
Alang the strath the hairst-fields toom
    And syne the stackyairds fill.

Ye'll hear fu' mony a raittlin' cairt
    On Forfar's causey-croon,
Wi' young stirks loupin' to the Mairt
    That roars in Forfar toon.

O' nichts, ayont yer snibbet door,
    Ye'll see in changeless band,
Abune Craig Oule, to keep Strathmore,
    The stars of Scotland stand.

But tho' ye think ye sicht them fine
    Gang ben an' tak' yer rest,
Frae lands that niver kent their shine
    It's me that sees them best!

For they shall brak' their ancient trust,
    Shall rise nae mair nor set,
The Sidlaw hills be laid in dust
    Afore that I forget.

Lowse ye the windy-sneck a wheen,
   An' glowre frae ilka airt
Fegs! Ye may see them wi' yer een—   35
   I see them wi' my he'rt!

THE TINKLER'S BALOO

Haud yer whisht, my mannie,
   Hide yer heid the noo,
There's a jimp young mune i' the branches abune
   An' she's keekin' at me an' you.
Near she is to settin', 5
   Waukin' she shouldna be,
An' mebbe she sees i' the loan by the trees
   Owre muckle for you an' me.

Dinna cry on Daddie,
   Daddie's by the fairm, 10
There's a specklie hen that strays i' the den
   An' he's fear'd she may come to hairm.
Thieves is bauld an' mony,
   That's what guid fowk say,
An' they'd a' complain gin the limmer was ta'en 15
   An' cheughit afore it's day.

Sleep, an' then, come Sawbath,
   A feather o' grey ye'll get
Wi' specklies on it to set i' yer bonnet
   An' gar ye look brawer yet. 20
Sae hide yer heid, my mannie,
   Haud yer whisht, my doo,
For we'll hae to shift or the sun's i' the lift
   An' I'm singin' baloo, baloo!

THE BANKS O' THE ESK

Gin I were whaur the rowans hang
   Their berried heids aside the river,
I'd hear the water slip alang,
   The rowan-leaves abune me shiver;
And winds frae Angus braes wad sail
To blaw me dreams owre peat an' gale.

An' blawn frae youth, thae dreams o' mine
   Wad find me, tho' the rowans hide me,
Like hoolets grey they'd flit, an' syne
   They'd fauld their wings an' licht aside me;
And aye the mair content I'd be
The closer that they cam' to me.

Aside the Esk I'd lay me doon,
   Atween the rowans and its windin',
An' tho' the waters rase to droon
   A weary carle, I'd no be mindin';
For I wad sleep, my rovin' past,
Upon thae banks o' dreams at last.

INVERQUHARITY

Aside the Quharity burn
   I ken na what I'm seein'
   Wi' the licht near deein'
An' the lang year at the turn;
   But the dog that gangs wi' me
   Creeps whingein' at my knee,
And we baith haud thegither
Like a lad an' his brither
   At the water o' Quharity.

Alang the Quharity glen
   I mind on warlock's faces,
   I' the still, dark places
Whaur the trees hae airms like men;
   And I ken the beast can see
   Yon een that's watchin' me,
Whaur the arn-boughs darken
An' I'm owre fear'd to harken
   I' the glen o' Quharity.

By Quharity Castle wa's
   The toor is like a prison,
   Or a deid man risen
Amang the birken shaws;
And the sweit upon my bree
Is drappin' cauld frae me
   Till the ill spell's broken
   By the Haly Word spoken
At the wa's o' Quharity.

Alang the Valley o' Deith
   There'll be mony a warlock wait'n
   Wi' the thrangin' hosts o' Sat'n
Till I tak' my hin'maist breith;
   An' I'm fear'd there winna be
   The dog to gang wi' me
An' I doot the way is wearier
An' the movin' shadows eerier
   Than the jaws o' Quharity.

But I'll whisper the Haly Name
   For thae list'nin' lugs to hear me,
   An' the herds o' Hell'll fear me
An' tak' the road they came;   40
   For the wild dark wings'll flee
   Frae their bield in branch an' tree—
Nae mair the black airms thrawin'!
Nae mair the ill sough blawin'!
For my day o' days is dawin'   45
   Owre the Castle o' Quharity!

FAUR-YE-WEEL

As ye come through the Sea-Gate ye'll find a hoose we ken
Whaur, when a man is drouthy, his drouth an' he gang ben,
And whiles o' nichts there's dancin' and aye there's drink
    by day
And a fiddler-carle sits yonder an' gars his fiddle play:
    'Oh come, ye ancient mariners,
      Nae maitter soond or lame,
    For tho' ye gae on hirplin' tae
      Ye'll syne gang dancin' hame;
    The years are slippin' past ye
      Like water past the bows,
*Roond half the warld ye've toss'd yer dram but sune ye'll hae to
    lowse.'*

The toon is like a picture, the sea is bonnie blue,
The fiddle's cryin' aff the shore to captain, mate, an' crew,
An' them that's had for music the swirl o' gannets' wings,
The winds that drive frae Denmark, they dootna what it
    sings:
    'Oh come, ye dandy Baltic lads
      That sail to Elsinore,
    Ye're newly in, ye'll surely win
      To hae a spree ashore;
    Lairn frae the sea, yer maister,
      When fortune's i' yer debt,
The cauld waves washin' past the bar tak' a' that they can get!'

And when the quays are lichtit an' dark the ocean lies,
The daft mune, like a feckless fule, keeks doon to mock
    the wise;
Awa' in quiet closes the fiddle's voice is heard
Whaur some that should be sleepin' are listenin' for its
    word:
    'Sae haste ye noo, ye rovin' queyns,
      An' gie yer dads the slip,
    Tho' dour auld men sit girnin' ben
      There's young anes aff the ship,
    Come, tak' yer fill o' dancin',
      Yer he'rts at hame maun bide,
For the lad that tak's a he'rt to sea will drap it owre the side!'

And aye the fiddle's playin', the auld bow wauks the string,
The auld carle, stampin' wi' his fit, gies aye the tune a
    swing; 35
Gang East, gang West, ye'll hear it, it lifts ye like a reel:
It's niver dumb, an' the tune sings 'Come,' but its name is
    Faur-ye-weel!

THE SHADOWS

Boughs of the pine and stars between,
   In woods where shadows fill the air,
Oh, who may rest that once has been
     A shadow there?

Sounds of the night and tears between,
   The grey owl hooting, dimly heard;
Can footsteps reach those lands unseen,
     Or wings of bird?

Days of the year and worlds between,
   Still through the boughs the stars may burn,
The heart may break for lands unseen,
   For woods wherein its life has been,
     But not return.

A WINTER PHANTASY

The day was all delight,
   Chorus and golden tune;
Rides the steep night
   The white ship of the moon.

Now that the night is come
   And silence wakes to power,
All that was dumb
   Has its triumphal hour.

My soul, behold a sail
   The seas of Heaven upon,
Rise up and hail
   That roving galleon.

High above winter frost
   Speed on uncharted ways,
Enraptured, lost,
   Past thrall of nights and days.

Burnt fervent-white with rime,
   The blurred earth hangs beneath,
Frost-light sublime,
   Frost-tapers lit for death.

Look down the mists and see
   The orchards mazed with snow;
Grey, tangled tree,
   Lichen and mistletoe.

But, ere the dim world falls
   Engulfed, upon your track,
Even at Heaven's walls,
   Turn back, turn back!

And as the miles decrease,
   But all that foils regret,
By all that is your peace,
   My soul, forget.

From *Two New Poems (1924)*

ROHALLION

Ma buits are at rest on the midden,
    I haena a plack,
Ma breeks are no dandy anes, forrit,
    And waur at the back;
On the road that comes oot o' the hielands
    I see as I trayvel the airth,
Frae the braes at the back o' Rohallion,
    The reek abune Pairth.

There's a canny wee hoose wi' a gairden
    In a neuk o' Strathtay;
Ma mither is bakin' the bannocks,
    The weans are at play;
And at gloamin', ma feyther, the shepherd,
    Looks doon for a blink o' the licht
When he gethers the yowes by the shielin'
    Tae fauld them at nicht.

There's niver a hoose that wad haud me
    Frae this tae the sea
When a wind frae the knowes by Rohallion
    Comes creepin' tae me,
And niver a lowe frae the ingle
    Can draw like the trail an' the shine
O' the stars i' the loch o' Rohallion
    A fitstep o' mine.

There's snaw i' the wind an' the weepies
    Hang deid on the shaw,
And pale the leaves left on the rowan,
    I'm soothward awa;
But a voice like a wraith blaws ahint me
    And sings as I'm liftin' my pack
'I am waitin'—Rohallion, Rohallion—
    My lad, ye'll be back!'

From *The Northern Lights and Other Poems (1927)*

THE NORTHERN LICHTS

'Ma daddy turns him tae the sky
   And cries on me tae see
They shiftin' beams that dance oot-by
   And fleg the he'rt o' me.'
'Laddie, the North is a' a-lowe
   Wi' fires o' siller green,
The stars are dairk owre Windyknowe
   That were sae bricht the streen,

'The lift is fu' o' wings o' licht
   Risin' an' deein' doon—'
'Rax ye yer airm and haud it ticht
   Aboot yer little loon,
For oh! the North's an eerie land
   And eerie voices blaw
Frae whaur the ghaists o' deid men stand
   Wi' their feet amangst the snaw;

And owre their heids the midnicht sun
   Hangs like a croon o' flame,
It's i' the North yon licht's begun
   An' I'm fear'd that it's the same!
Haud ye me ticht! Oh, div ye ken
   Gin sic-like things can be
That's past the sicht o' muckle men
   And nane but bairns can see?'

THE NEEP-FIELDS BY THE SEA

Ye'd wonder foo the seasons rin
   This side o' Tweed an' Tyne;
The hairst's awa; October month
   Cam' in a whilie syne,
But the stooks are oot in Scotland yet,   5
   There's green upon the tree,
An' oh! what grand's the smell ye'll get
   Frae the neep-fields by the sea!

The lang lift lies abune the warld,
   On ilka windless day   10
The ships creep doon the ocean line,
   Sma' on the band o' grey;
And the lang sigh heaved upon the sand
   Comes pechin' up tae me,
And speils the cliffs tae whaur ye stand   15
   I' the neep-fields by the sea.

Oh, time's aye slow, tho' time gangs fast
   When siller's a' tae mak',
An' deith, afore ma poke is fu',
   May grip me i' the back;   20
But ye'll tak' ma banes an' ma Sawbith braws,
   Gin deith's owre smairt for me,
And set them up amang the shaws
   I' the lang rows plantit atween the wa's,
A tattie-dulie for fleggin' craws,   25
   I' the neep-fields by the sea.

THE ROWAN

When the days were still as deith
   And ye couldna see the kye
Though ye'd maybe hear their breith
   I' the mist oot-by;
When I'd mind the lang grey een
   O' the warlock by the hill
And sit fleggit like a wean
   Gin a whaup cried shrill;
Tho' the he'rt wad dee in me
   At a fitstep on the floor,
There was aye the rowan tree
   Wi' its airm across the door.

But that is far, far past
   And a'thing's just the same,
There's whisper up the blast
   O' a dreid I daurna name;
And the shilpit sun is thin,
   Like auld man deein' slow
And a shade comes creepin' in
   When the fire is fa'in' low;
Then I feel thae lang een set
   Like a doom upon ma heid,
For the warlock's livin' yet—
   But the rowan's deid!

THE LICHT NICHTS

Ye've left the sun an' the can'lelicht an' the starlicht,
    The wuds baith green an' sere,
And yet I hear ye singin' doon the braes
    I' the licht nichts o' the year.

Ye were sae glad; ye were aye sae like the laverock   5
    Wha's he'rt is i' the lift;
Nae mair for you the young green leaves will dance
    Nor yet the auld anes drift.

What thocht had you o' the ill-faur'd dairk o' winter
    But the ingle-neuks o' hame?   10
Love lit yer way an' played aboot yer feet,
    Year in, year oot, the same.

And noo, ma best, ma bonniest and ma dearest,
    I'll lay ma he'rt tae sleep
An' let the warld, that has nae soond for me,   15
    Its watch o' silence keep.

But whiles—and whiles—i' the can'lelicht an' the starlicht,
    I'll wauken it tae hear
The liltin' voice that's singin' doon the braes
    I' the licht nichts o' the year.   20

THE JAUD

'O what are ye seein', ye auld wife,
  I' the bield o' the kirkyaird wa'?'
'I see a place whaur the grass is lang
  Wi' the great black nettles grawn fierce an' strang
    And a stane that is clour'd in twa.'   5

'What way div ye glower, ye auld wife,
  Sae lang on the whumml'd stane?
Ye hae nae kin that are sleepin' there,
  Yer three braw dochters are swak an' fair
    And ilk wi' a man o' her ain!   10

There's dule an' tears i' yer auld een
  Tho' little eneuch ye lack;
Yer man is kindly, as weel ye ken,
  Yer fower bauld laddies are thrivin' men
    And ilk wi' a fairm at his back.   15

Turn, turn yer face frae yon cauld lair
  And back tae yer plenish'd hame;
It's a jaud lies yont i' the nettle shaws
  Whaur niver a blink o' the sunlicht fa's
    On the mools that hae smoor'd her name.'   20

'Her hair was gowd like the gowd broom,
  Her een like the stars abune,
Sae prood an' lichtsome an' fine was she
  Wi' her breist like the flowers o' the white rose tree
    When they're lyin' below the mune.'   25

'Haud you yer havers, ye auld wife,
  Think shame o' the words ye speak,
Tho' men lay fast in her beauty's grip
  She brocht the fleer tae the wumman's lip
    An' the reid tae the lassie's cheek.   30

Ye've lived in honour, ye auld wife,
  But happit in shame she lies,
And them that kent her will turn awa
  When the Last Day brak's tae the trumpet's ca'
    And the sauls o' the righteous rise.' 35

'Maybe. But lave me tae bide my lane
  At the fit o' the freendless queyn;
For oh! wi' envy I'm like tae dee
  O' the warld she had that was no for me
    And the kingdom that ne'er was mine!' 40

THE DEIL

Beside the birks I met the Deil,
  A wheen o' words I niffered wi' him
And, clear and lang, the wuds amang
  The merle sang whaur ye couldna see him;
The pale spring licht was late when he
  Was whustling tae the Deil and me.

I didna think it was himsel',
  I thocht he had been auld an' crookit,
Sae thrawn an' grim in ilka limb
  Ye'd ken him by the way he lookit;
Wha'd think the Deil wad linger on
  Tae listen till a bird like yon?

They tell't me that the Deil was black
  And blacker nor the corbie's feather,
But, loopin' doon, a-lowe wi' noon,
  Nae burn broun frae the peat an' heather,
Had e'er the shine ye wad hae seen
  Laid sleepin' i' the Deevil's een.

'The polestar kens ma bed,' says he,
  'I hae the rovin' gled for brither,
The hill crest is ma hoose o' rest,
  An' it's far west that I'd seek anither;
Alang the edge o' simmer nicht
  The wildfire is ma ingle-licht.'

The wuds were still, the merle was hame,
  The mist abune the strath was hangin',
Yet I could see him smile tae me
  When syne he turned him tae be gangin',
And ne'er a faur-ye-weel he spak'
  As he gaed frae me, lookin' back.

Ma feyther's hoose is puir an' cauld,
   The winter winds blaw lang and sairly,
The muircocks ca' and hoodie craw,
   It's nichtfa' sune, we're workin' airly;
Oot i' the wuds, the lee lang year   35
   Nae treid amang the birks ye'll hear.

Fu' mony a man has speir'd at me
   And thocht a wife he micht be findin',
But na—there's nane I could hae ta'en
   But just ane that I'll aye be mindin';   40
Him that ma mither kens richt weel
   Had been nae ither nor the Deil!

GEORDIE'S LAMENT

Oh, I was fou at Martinmas
    And fou at Halloween
And fouer yet at Hogmanay
    Than iver I hae been;

For Hogmanay's a time o' dule
    Altho' yer he'rt be licht,
And whiles ye canna mind at morn
    O' what ye did at nicht.

My feyther's wud, ma mither's daft;
    It's no for that I care,
But the bonnie lass I've lo'ed sae long
    Will tryst wi' me nae mair!

Oft hae we seen the Hunter's mune
    Rise reid ahint the stacks,
An' the nakkit tree-taps sweep the sky
    Wi' the cauld stars at their backs;

And whiles, frae oot the sleepin' hoose
    She's stown when nane could see
Tae daunder doon the misty fields
    I' the simmer nichts wi' me.

Oh Bell—ma ain, ma denty Bell,
    Ye winna turn yer heid,
And sic a clour ye've gi'en ma he'rt
    That I can feel it bleed!

What'll I dae when spring is back
    Wi' voice o' birds again,
And ilka craw has got his jo
    But me that's wantin' ane?

Oh Bell! had I, come Hogmanay,
    A bonnie wife at hame,
I'd no be sweir tae steik ma door
    When aince the evenin' came.

For a' the warld micht drink its best
   Tae gar the Auld Year flit,
And Hogmanay micht wauk the deid   35
   An' I wadna stir for it!

THE HELPMATE

I hae nae gear, nae pot nor pan,
   Nae lauchin' lips hae I;
Forbye yersel', there's ne'er a man
   Looks roond as I gang by.

An' a' folk kens nae time I've gie'd
   Tae daft strathspey an' reel,
Nor idle sang nor ploy, for dreid
   O' pleasurin' the deil.

Wi' muckle care ma mither bred
   Her bairn in wisdom's way;
On Tyesday first, when we are wed,
   A wiselike wife ye'll hae.

The best ye'll get baith but an' ben,
   Sae mild an' douce I'll be;
Yer hame'll be yer haven when
   Ye're married upon me.

Ye'll find the kettle on the fire,
   The hoose pit a' tae richts,
An' yer heid i' the troch at the back o' the byre
   When ye come back fou o' nichts.

STEENHIVE

Steenhive's an awfae place
   Wi' the sea at its chin
And the cauld faem on its blind bree
   When the gales blaw in.

Steenhive is stane deif
   Wi' the waves an' the years;
Een weit wi' scuds o' rain
   But owre haird for tears.

An' Steenhive's waur nor that,
   God gar it droon!
For its curst wa's stand yet
   Tho' ma ship's gane doon.

THE GUIDWIFE SPEAKS

Gudeman, ye sit aside the lum
   Sookin' yer pipe, yer doag at heel,
And gin the Lord should strike ye dumb
   Wha'd be the waur, ye soor auld deil?
And wha wad ken the dandy lad
   That, a' the preachin', socht ma ee,
When twa poond ten was a' we had
   And ye was cried in kirk wi' me?

Sae soople an' sae licht o' fit,
   The smairtest carles their pranks micht try
They got nae profit oot o' it—
   Nane thocht o' them gin ye was by!
They'd step, o' Sawbiths, tae the bell,
   Their gravats braw wi' spots an' stripes,
But there was nane forbye yersel'
   Could dance curcuddoch tae the pipes.

I'm risin' airly, workin' late;
   The best o' bannocks tae yer tea
Gang doon yer craig like leaves in spate
   And ne'er a word o' thanks tae me!
And here, oot-by, the teuchats greet,
   Dumb is the hoose through a' the day,
Ye'll maybe speak tae curse yer meat
   Or dunt yer pipe agin' yer tae.

An' yet, an' yet—I dreid tae see
   The ingle standin' toom. Oh, then
Youth's last left licht wad gang wi' ye...
   What wad I dae? I dinna ken.

THE LAST ANE

I gaed me doon the heid o' the wynd,
    Oot-by, below the stair,
But there was nane o' the fowk I'd kent
    Tae crack wi', there.

I set my face tae the bield o' the dock
    Whaur the brigs wad wait the tide;
There was niver a man that had sailed wi' me
    At the waterside.

I took the road to the toon-hoose wa'
    An' the seat whaur the auld men sit;
The broun leaves skailed frae the kirkyaird trees
    Across ma fit.

I turned me doon the path by the kirk
    Wi' the stanes set close at hand,
Whaur the freends that liena their fill at sea
    Are laid on land.

The yett was wide but the kirkyaird bars
    Had gotten their toonsfowk fast,
And the auld stanes there for the man tae see
    That's left the last.

              ಊ ಊ ಊ

There was Ane in yonder. Oh, straicht an' fine
    He stude by the cowpit thrang,
And my sair he'rt loup'd as He looked on me,
    For I'd kent him lang!

DONALD MACLANE

The ling for bed and the loan for bield
   And the maist o' the winter through
The wild wind sabbin' owre muir an' field,
There's lang lang drifts on the braes I've speil'd,
   O Donald Maclane, wi' you!   5

Fu' mony trayvels in sun and rain
   Wi' a sang for the gait they treid;
But the blythest gangers step aye their lane,
No twa thegither but ane by ane,
   When gangin's their daily breid.   10

A dancin' ee and a daffin' tongue,
   A voice i' the loanin' green,
Aye, fules think lichtly when fules are young
Tae pu' the nettle and no be stung,
   An' it's nocht but a fule I've been.   15

A crust for meat an' a curse for cheer,
   The weicht o' a heavy hand;
A skirl o' pipes i' the mornin' clear,
The rose-hip reid wi' the fadin' year
   And the breith o' the frozen land.   20

There was nane tae see when I set ma face
   Till a road that has ne'er an end,
There's a door that's steekit and toom's the place
That minds ma ain o' a black disgrace
   And an ill that they canna mend.   25

Ma feyther's bent wi' his broken pride
   And the shame that he'll no forgie,
But the love o' mithers is deep an' wide
And there's maybe room for a thocht tae hide
   An' a prayer for the likes o' me.   30

Play up, play up noo, Donald Maclane,
   And awa till oor rovin' trade;
For the wild pipes gie me a he'rt again
In a breist sae weary that whiles there's nane,
The wailin' pipes and the bairnies twain   35
   That are happit intill ma plaid.

THE CROSS-ROADS

'Wha bides in yon hoose we hae tae pass
    Yont—div ye see it?'
'There's nae hoose there. It's a theek o' grass
    And auld stanes wi' it.'
'But O! yon thing by the wa' that lurks!
    Is it soond or sicht?'
'It's just the breith o' the grazin' stirks
    Or the white haar crawlin' amang the birks
        Wi' the fa' o' nicht.'

'There's a windy keekin' amang the thorn
    And the branches thrawin—
' 'Twill be tae seek when the morn's morn
    Comes tae the dawin'!'
'But man, foo that? For it's there the noo
    And I see it plain—'
'Gin ye be sober, I doot I'm fou,
    For I see nane.'

'There's an auld wife's lee that I fain wad loss,
    Sae sair I fear it,
O' an ill man's hoose whaur the twa roads cross
    And his lair that's near it;
Yet gin ye'll meet him by birk or broom
    Ye canna tell—'
'It's nocht but havers. The road is toom
    And there's nane ye'll meet sic a nicht o' gloom
        But just mysel'.'

'But bide a wee till we kneel and pray,
    For I'd fain be prayin'.'
'Stand up, stand up—for I daurna say
    The words ye're sayin'!
But rise and gang tae the kirkyaird heid
    And plead yer best
Whaur they wadna bury the ootcast deid
    For a sad saul spent wi' the weird it's dree'd,
        And I'll maybe rest!'

From *The Scottish Poems of Violet Jacob (1944)*

THE WARLD

The warld's aboot the queerest place—
   Ye couldna just say foo tae tak it—
And queer the fowk o' human race
    Mak it.

Ye'll hae a plack for them that beg,   5
   Ye'll lift a lame dog owre the stiles,
He'll roond an' hae ye by the leg
    Whiles.

Ye'll dae yer best—ye can nae mair—
   Ill-gittit fowk will hae ye huntit   10
And niver lowse until ye're fair
    Affrontit.

And whiles I've thocht 'I winna wait
   Tae gie them back as guid's they gie,'
But a' the same I didna dae't—   15
    No me!

The women's tongues, baith loud an' saft,
   Bring oot the thrawness o' their naturs,
But fine I see they're nocht but daft,
    Puir craturs.   20

Lord! I hae wished Eliza dumb,
   Her ragin' was that strang and stoot;
Yet, at her kistin', I was some
    Pit oot.

The mair ye gie the less ye'll get,   25
   The road's aye reuch, whaure'er ye strike it,
The warld's a heap o' durt—an' yet
    Ye like it.

THE POOR SUITOR

When spring comes loupin' doon the braes
    And nakit trees are gettin' claes,
The sun—ill-gettit deevil—seeks
    Tae shame the patches in my breeks.

The birds gang courtin', brawly drest
    By natur in their verra best,
But my auld coat can no be seen
    Affrontin' Isabella's een.

And when the Sawbath day is near
    Tae tak her oot I daurna speir,
Lest soor auld wives should say she had
    A tattie-dulie for a lad!

My mither tells me no tae fash,
    That worth is a', appearance trash;
Weel, worth may mak a decent fella—
    It winna gie me Isabella!

Oh, for a dandy suit o' blue
    And buits that let nae water through!
Oh, that frae ony airt micht fa'
    A wheen bawbees tae mak me braw!

As round the year the seasons creep
    I mind the swine, I drive the sheep;
E'en tho' my luck a turn micht tak,
    'Twad come owre late tae pay me back.

'Twad find the same auld sheep an' swine,
    And Isabella wed lang syne,
And me like Daddy Black that begs,
    Thrawn i' the he'rt and i' the legs!

THE NEEBOUR

Auld Kate's awa'. November-month
   They laid her oot an' got her kistit
And had her pitten east the kirk
   (There wasna ane that wad hae miss'd it!)
Her door is lockit, cauld's the lum,
There's nane tae gang and nane tae come.

Her yett hangs rattlin' i' the wind,
   The tattie-shaws are black and rotten,
For wha's tae lift them? 'Let them bide,'
   The neebours say, 'she's best forgotten.'
They'll tell ye that her hoose is toom,
Forbye the rats in ilka room.

'Twixt her and me was just the wa',
   A wheen o' bricks oor hames dividit,
This lanesome loanin' held us baith,
   My but-an'-ben wi' hers aside it;
But ne'er a wean cam' nigh the place
For dreid he'd see her evil face.

The verra doags gaed fleein' by,
   And, gin that Kate was oot an' tryin'
Tae cast a bodle till a tink,
   He wadna touch't—he'd leave it lyin'!
Mysel', I let sic havers be.
I didna care a curse—no me.

          ಞ ಞ ಞ

But noo—but noo—I wauk o' nichts
   And smoor my heid; I daurna lift it
Lest yont the wa' there comes a soond
   O' ane that's deid but hasna shiftit
And aye seeks hameward through the mirk—
She'll no lie easy by the kirk!

And when my workin' day is by
   I seek my door as daylicht's deein',
It's sweir I am tae lift my een,
   I'm like the bairns—I'm no for seein'!
Lord mind o' me—I ken there's ane
At the dairk side o' the windy-pane!

THE POACHER TO ORION

November-month is wearin' by,
   The leaves is nearly doon;
I watch ye stride alang the sky
   O' nichts, my beltit loon.

The treetaps wi' their fingers bare
   Spread between me and you,
But weel in yonder frosty air
   Ye see me keekin' through.

At schule I lairnd richt wearilie,
   The Hunter was yer name;
Sma' pleasure were ye then tae me,
   But noo oor trade's the same.

But ye've a brawer job nor mine
   And better luck nor me,
For them that sees ye likes ye fine
   And the pollis lets ye be;

We're baith astir when men's asleep;
   A hunter aye pursued,
I hae by dyke an' ditch tae creep,
   But ye gang safe an' prood.

What maitter that? I'll no complain,
   For when we twa are met
We hae the nicht-watch for oor ain
   Till the stars are like tae set.

Gang on, my lad. The warlds owreheid
   Wheel on their nichtly beat,
And ye'll mind ye as the skies ye treid
   O' the brither at yer feet.

THE BALTIC

'Whaur are ye gaen sae fast, my bairn,
    It's no tae the schule ye'll win?'
'Doon tae the shore at the fit o' the toon
    Tae bide till the brigs come in.'

'Awa' noo wi' ye and turn ye hame,
    Ye'll no hae the time tae bide;
It's twa lang months or the brigs come back
    On the lift o' a risin' tide.'

'I'll sit me doon at the water's mou'
    Till there's niver a blink o' licht,
For my feyther bad' me tae tryst wi' him
    In the dairkness o' yesternicht.

' "Rise ye an' rin tae the shore," says he,
    "At the cheep o' the waukin' bird,
And I'll bring ye a tale o' a foreign land
    The like that ye niver heard." '

'Oh, haud yer havers, ye feckless wean,
    It was but a dream ye saw,
For he's far, far north wi' the Baltic men
    I' the hurl o' the Baltic snaw;

And what did he ca' yon foreign land?'
    'He tell'tna its name tae me,
But I doot it's no by the Baltic shore,
    For he said there was nae mair sea.'

CAIRNEYSIDE

I turned my een tae the lift
When nicht was on the glen
As I steppit oot frae my feyther's door
Tae tryst wi' Chairlie's men;
I thocht the stars like a gallant line   5
That fechts for a country's pride,
And they shone mair clear nor the lichts o' hame
In the water o' Cairneyside.

There was never a star tae see
When the heather happ'd my heid   10
And the wild wind grat owre Culloden muir
For the deein' and the deid;
My mou' was dry wi' the drouth o' hell
And I grippit the moss and cried
For the cauld, sweet taste on my burnin' lips   15
O' the water o' Cairneyside.

I turned my fitsteps hame
When the huntit were at rest
And the shots rang oot owre the land nae mair
On the hillsides o' the west;   20
And I socht the place at my mither's hairth
Whaur a broken lad micht hide—
There was naucht left standin' but nakit wa's
By the water o' Cairneyside.

Uncollected Poems

THE BARLEY (c.1906)

The grain stands bonny where the cliffs are sheer
And the blue North Sea is sleeping;
The stooks are yellow in a golden ear
With their shadows inward creeping.
The tide lies silent on the sands below
And the autumn mists hang early
To fade in heaven o'er the distant row
Of the low red roofs beyond the barley.

O late last harvest-time, when days were long,
Worked men and maids by the steading;
And gulls sailed landward in a screaming throng,
To the river pastures heading.
Soft was the footstep that beside me trod
In the dew of morning early,
For Love walked there beneath the smile of God
And the high blue sky above the barley.

The stalks fall mellow to the sweeping blade
With their weeds laid shorn beside them,
And eyes meet stealthily as lad and maid
Glance over where the stooks divide them;
But mine turn ever while I work alone
Through the long day, late and early,
To a low mound lying by a standing stone
Where the wall shuts out the barley
Where the Nether Kirk is grey, Janet,
By the long blue sea beyond the barley.

BINDWEED (c.1919)

Thou art not come from heaven, but fairyland,
   Creature of pearl and snow and magic dew,
Thou full-blown trumpet of some elfin crew
     Flung by the passing band
In petulant idleness when noonday sleep 5
     Broods on the woodlands deep,
To swing, unheeded, all the long day through.

Dreams—dreams—the day-dreams and the dreams of night
   Are spun, enwoven in thy frail festoon
And from the heart of thy translucent white 10
     Spirits come out to parley with the moon,
        Enchantment, fantasy,
The things that are not and will never be!

Where is the soul of fairyland confined?
   In what fell stronghold are its accents lost? 15
They vanished in the child-world left behind
     With but an echo tost
   Upon the tumult of a later day
To float awhile, and floating, die away.

But when the wandering of some idle hour 20
   Reveal thy fragile trail across the bough,
To long-forgotten paths, familiar now,
   Thy presence lures us, long-remembered flower,
And, with our feet beside these thresholds set,
   We pause one flying moment, children yet. 25

Notes for Individual Poems

The notes offer information intended to shed light upon the content, structure and origin of the poetry in the volume. Where possible, details of a poem's original periodical publication appear. Although this volume is not designed to be a variorum, alternate versions of selected poems are given to illuminate the different revision practices of Marion Angus and Violet Jacob. Angus revised her poetry more publicly than Jacob did, sometimes publishing several different versions of the same poem. As a result, alternate versions of poems appear in the notes for Angus's work more frequently than in the notes for Jacob's poems. In Angus's case, records relating to the production of two of her volumes of poetry have been preserved in the National Library of Scotland and the notes make reference to these invaluable documents.

Neither Angus nor Jacob produced manifestos on writing; to give readers a better sense of a poem's connection to the individual writer's body of work, the notes feature excerpts from their personal writings, including letters, journal entries and essays. The comments of contemporaneous and recent critics are included to draw attention to repeated themes or motifs in the poems and to give readers a sense of the evolution of each poet's writing style.

For considerations of space, the sources of quotations and paraphrases are provided in an abbreviated form within the notes. A complete list of sources cited in the notes and in the introduction itself is available at the end of the book. Line numbers for references to specific poems are provided. All biblical citations refer to the King James Bible.

List of abbreviations

OED – *Oxford English Dictionary*
NLS – National Library of Scotland
AUSC – Aberdeen University Special Collections
TLS – *Times Literary Supplement*

Marion Angus volumes

CD – *Christabel's Diary*
LC – *Lost Country and Other Verses*
SC – *Sun and Candlelight*
RG – *Round About Geneva*
SL – *The Singin' Lass*
SPMA – *Selected Poems of Marion Angus*
TD – *The Turn of the Day*
TL – *The Lilt and Other Verses*
TR – *The Tinker's Road and Other Verses*

Violet Jacob volumes

BM – *The Bailie MacPhee*
BJ – *Bonnie Joann and Other Poems*
DLI – *Diaries and Letters from India, 1895–1900*
MSA – *More Songs of Angus and Others*
NL – *The Northern Lights and Other Poems*
SA – *Songs of Angus*
SPVJ – *The Scottish Poems of Violet Jacob*
TNP – *Two New Poems*
V – *Verses*

The Poems of Marion Angus

THE LILT AND OTHER VERSES (1922)

The smallest of Angus's poetry volumes, *TL* draws together poems she had published previously in *Scots Pictorial* and *Scottish Chapbook*; it gives a sense of her revision process as she altered many of the poems between initial publication in periodicals and republication in the book.

BY CANDLE LIGHT

'The Mother', *Scots Pictorial*, 15 October 1921, p. 342. By changing the title to 'By Candle Light', Angus shifts attention away from the mother to the 'witchin', watchin' Flame' (line 31).

Janet Caird suggests that Angus in 'By Candle Light' 'blends witchcraft, a mother's sinister dominance of her son, and sadness of the young man parted from his love. Dread and evil are suggested by references to the "wrinkled leaves of the rowan-bush"'. She notes that the poem recalls the ballad 'Lord Randal'; the 'sleety rain' and 'candle-light' also reference similar elements in 'The Lyke-Wake Dirge', a 'favourite' of Angus's ('The Poetry of Marion Angus', p. 46).

Candles recur in Angus's poetry. Janet Caird surmises that they were 'commonplace' in Angus's youth and notes how even for modern readers candles have 'overtones of tranquillity and happiness, of mystery and the unseen' ('The Poetry of Marion Angus', p. 46). Helen Cruickshank associates candles with Angus herself; in *Octobiography*, she describes a meeting between her mother, who had senile dementia, and Angus. After Angus left, Cruickshank's mother reportedly commented: 'I'm glad that auld body's awa'. There was a man wi' a tray o' lichtit candles standin' ahint her a' the time, and I was feart he'd set her on fire' (p. 135).

THE DROVE ROAD

'On the Sheep Track', *Scots Pictorial*, 16 July 1921, p. 30.

Drove roads are used by herders to move their animals from one location to another. Culblean, located in Aberdeenshire, is the site of a famous fourteenth-century battle in the wars for Scottish independence. 'The Drove Road' is one of many poems in which Angus describes a palpable historical presence in the landscape (cf. 'The Fox's Skin', 'Joan the Maid' and 'Corrichie').

REMEMBRANCE DAY
'Remembrance Day', Scots Pictorial, 12 November 1921, p. 438.

Janet Caird, in 'The Poetry of Marion Angus', identifies 'Remembrance Day' as the one poem in Angus's body of work that is tied to a specific historical event (p. 47). Remembrance Day, observed on the second Sunday in November, commemorates the lives of soldiers lost in battle. The first year it was celebrated was 1921.

THE FOX'S SKIN
'The Same', Scots Pictorial, 28 January 1922, p. 78. The Scots Pictorial version refers to the 'Howe' rather than the 'Hame' of 'the Pictish Men' (line 4).

In 'The Fox's Skin', Angus compares the speaker's lifespan with that of the landscape, suggesting, as she does in other poems in TL, that the presence of the past is palpable for those sensitive enough to observe it.

TREASURE TROVE
'Treasure Trove', Scots Pictorial, 11 March 1922, p. 226.

Janet Caird suggests that 'Treasure Trove' represents the 'fairly disastrous results' of Angus's depiction of 'wee folk and fairies' ('The Poetry of Marion Angus', p. 47). While 'Treasure Trove' certainly is not one of Angus's more successful poems, it is not without merit. One reviewer argues that 'Treasure Trove' exhibits Angus's 'gift of blending the real and unreal' (S., p. 10). 'Treasure Trove' recalls a story she wrote years before; in 1906, *Pearson's Magazine* featured her 'Green Beads: The Story of a Lost Love' which describes a strand of beads divided as a 'love bond' between two people who later separate (p. 561). The daughter of one, left with half the necklace, accidentally meets the other lover; he slips her the beads he has saved for thirty years. The setting and the beads in 'Treasure Trove' closely echo this earlier story, suggesting that green beads were a personal symbol for Angus.

THE TURN OF THE DAY
'The Turn of the Day' became the title poem for her 1931 volume. In 'An Appreciation', J. B. Salmond suggests that there is 'one strange wistful thread running through' Angus's work – 'a kind of suggestion of frustration – something lost, something missed, something betrayed' (p. 6). His comments are helpful when reading 'The Turn of the Day', which addresses the loss of a lover without specifying the cause for separation. For the speaker, the frozen winter seems rich with nuptial symbolism; spring, the usual season of fertility and love, now brings only reminders of the speaker's loneliness.

MOONLIGHT
Wild thyme recurs in Angus's poetry (cf. 'Loneliness' and 'Lost Country'). She could be playing on the sound of thyme/time or it could be a personal symbol. In traditional folk symbolism, thyme represents 'spontaneous emotion' (Lehner and Lehner, p. 126). As does 'Among Thorns', 'Moonlight' celebrates the ability to find 'Paradise' in unpromising circumstances (line 31).

THE LILT
'The Lilt', *Scottish Chapbook*, 1 (1922), 37, and *Scots Pictorial*, 12 August 1922, p. 102. Angus's name is not given in the *Scots Pictorial* version.

'The Lilt', like many of her poems, compares the speaker's memories of a youthful romance to her present situation. Janet Caird notes that 'one of the recurring images' in Angus's poetry is 'that of a secret place in the hills where lovers meet' ('The Poetry of Marion Angus', p. 45). Weaving also figures frequently in Angus's poetry and often is associated with singing (cf. 'By Candle Light', 'The Lissome Leddy', 'A Woman Sings').

ALL SOULS' EVE
All Souls' Eve is celebrated on 1 November when prayers are offered for the dead. In Scottish folk tradition, Hallowe'en (31 October) is the time when the dead are thought to return to visit the living. For comparison, see Jacob's poem 'Hallowe'en'. The eerie appearance of the 'chalice of delight' (line 11) and the speaker's decision to 'drink

content' (line 16) suggest that the speaker interacts with the 'guests who wait / and pass, on All Souls' Eve' (lines 19–20).

THE TINKER'S ROAD AND OTHER VERSES (1924)

TR builds upon the work Angus began in TL and includes one of her most famous poems, 'Alas! Poor Queen'. The volume also reproduces nine of the poems from TL: 'By Candle Light', 'The Drove Road', 'Remembrance Day', 'The Fox's Skin', 'Treasure Trove', 'The Turn of the Day', 'The Lilt', 'Loneliness' and 'The Graceless Loon'. The poems in TR are in both English and Scots, as in all of Angus's books; in later publications, however, titles in Scots are more common than in her earliest volumes.

Writing to Charles Graves, her editor at Porpoise Press, Angus tells him that 'several' of the 'English papers spoke favourably of the book and the *Scotsman* pronounced it "a most appealing book".' She also admits:

> I am sorry not to have kept the Scots newspapers review of *The Tinker's Road*. They were very kind except perhaps our *Aberdeen Press and Journal* which will give no quarter to anyone whom Mr. C. M. Grieve has been good enough to say a word for. (Perhaps I should not have mentioned this). (NLS, MS 27476, folios 28–30, c. 20 June, no year)

The *Scotsman* review of TR observes that 'some of the vernacular verses in particular are striking in their emotional reality and imaginative intensity', calling them 'convincing proof, if such be needed, that the vernacular as a poetic medium is of high value'. The *TLS* review of TR argues her English poems are marked with a 'delicate, often ghostly, suggestiveness' (p. 123).

THE TINKER'S ROAD

Charles Graves, in 'The Poetry of Marion Angus', claims that the 'landscape behind [Angus's] poetry' is 'essentially Scottish. The moon and the drifting clouds, the wind and "the saft hill rain" are never far away, and there are places lonely in their eeriness like the Tinker's Road' (p. 107).

THE SEAWARD TOON

When Angus republished 'The Seaward Toon' in *TD*, she omitted stanza seven, the stanza that makes more explicit references to biblical figures and also establishes a more specifically female-centric focus. The poem appears here as it appeared in *TR* because this extra stanza gives greater insight into the poem's elusive subtext.

In 'The Seaward Toon', Angus dramatises two distinct outlooks – the speaker's and the unidentified 'ye'. The poem turns on the double meaning of 'seaward toon': geographically, the town resembles Angus's Arbroath; its twin, located 'ayont the blawing sand' (line 18), exists within the mind. The latter is a numinous other world that is suffused, like many ballads, with images from both the New Testament and pre-Christian legend. It is not clear whether the 'ye' is singular or plural; Colin Milton, in 'Modern Poetry in Scots Before MacDiarmid', considers 'ye' to mean 'most people', arguing for a wider reading of the poem's significance (p. 34). The references to specifically female activities or items – spinning and a 'breist-knot' (line 15) – suggest that the intended subject is a woman or several women.

My article 'Women "Wha' Lauched and Lo'ed and Sinned": Women's Voices in the Work of Violet Jacob and Marion Angus' discusses 'The Seaward Toon' in greater depth.

MARY'S SONG

'So Soft She Sings', *Scottish Chapbook*, 2 (1923), p. 16. In the *Scottish Chapbook* version, four lines gloss the poem: 'Mary sings by her candle's light / in the quiet night – the quiet night – ' prefaces the poem while the final two lines read, 'So soft she sings by her candle light / in the quiet night – the quiet night' (p. 16). Using English glosses and an English title is curious given the *Scottish Chapbook*'s Scottish nationalist stance. J. Derrick McClure suggests 'something must have been intended by the language change', proposing that the original version features an English speaker who transmits Mary's 'song'. He suggests that 'Scots itself, conceivably, has a deeper emotional resonance for a poem of unrequited love than English' (*Language, Poetry, and Nationhood*, p. 72). Whatever her reasons, her decision to omit these lines in *TR* suggests she did not think they were necessary for the poem's meaning.

Charles Graves, in 'The Poetry of Marion Angus', praises the 'delicacy' of 'Mary's Song' that 'had been lacking in the spirit and the technique of Scots verse for many years' (p. 97). The *Scotsman* review of *TR* contends that 'Mary's Song' has a 'physical reality' to it; it 'has blood coursing through its veins'. Hugh MacDiarmid draws attention to the 'pure and poignant [...] note' of the poem ('The New Movement', p. 62). Angus here references both the ballads and the Christian celebration of the Eucharist with her evocation of 'barley breid and elder wine' (line 3).

In 'Mary's Song', Angus gives one of her earliest examples of the mysterious love lyrics that continue to provoke debate among her readers. J. Derrick McClure speculates that the poem's speaker is 'Mary of Bethany', the sister of Martha described in the New Testament; this possibility, McClure argues, opens 'a whole field of potent implications' (*Language, Poetry, and Nationhood*, p. 69). One also can read the poem as a meditation upon desire written in response to the relationship between lovers depicted in the Song of Solomon. Many of Angus's lines echo passages from the Song of Solomon; for example, what the bird in 'Mary's Song' 'cries at evenin's fa" (line 7) is a near direct quotation of what Solomon calls to his beloved, the Shulamite (2:13).

The introduction discusses Angus's love poetry in more depth.

IN ARDELOT
Hardelot is located in northern France and was a popular destination for British tourists at the start of the twentieth century. Angus makes reference in *CD*, among other texts, to areas of France suggesting she had travelled there although she does not mention Hardelot specifically.

GEORGE GORDON, LORD BYRON
The year 1924 was the centenary of Byron's death. Angus's 'George Gordon, Lord Byron' refers to Byron's childhood in Aberdeen. He grew up in Scotland but moved to England when he was a child (McConnell, p. 479). Perhaps Angus recognised a similarity between his childhood move and hers from one country to another. Angus was well aware of Byron's work; she gave a BBC radio talk on Byron's connec-

tion to Aberdeen and in *RG* she describes visiting the Castle of Chillon:

> His wild heart must have been akin to the mountains, for we remember another home of his – a farm-house far away in Deeside, from where, in younger and perhaps happier days, 'He climbed the wild summits of dark Lochnagar'. (n/p)

In Byron's 'Lochnagar' the speaker describes his longing for Scotland. In *TR*, Angus included a footnote explaining that Byron knew the rhyme quoted at the end of 'George Gordon, Lord Byron' 'as a child'. Byron references this rhyme in the tenth canto of his *Don Juan*.

Angus begins 'George Gordon, Lord Byron' with a phrase from the ballad 'The Lyke-Wake Dirge', 'this ae nicht'. Helen Cruickshank in 'A Personal Note' recalls hearing Angus perform 'The Lyke-Wake Dirge' with 'terrifying urgency' at a gathering. She notes that 'this particular ballad seemed to haunt her, and "this ae nicht" creeps into several of her poems' (p. xix).

IN A MIRROR
'The Little One', *Scottish Chapbook*, 1 (1923), p. 257. The version in the present volume differs significantly from the *Scottish Chapbook* version; the earlier draft is reproduced below:

> The flame of my candle sways and shakes;
> A whistling song the night wind makes,
> I whistle it back to the night again,
> Peering out through my window pane;
> A bairn's chaunt—a fairy tune
> That a little one would softly croon—
>
> 'There was yin that blew the thistle seed,
> And yin strung rowans on a threid,
> And yin that danced sae daintily
> Amang the green o' the blae-berry'.
>
> Then turn, turn the candle white
> Till it shines into the mirror bright,
> And peering in the glass I see
> The Little One smile back at me.

In this earlier version, the capitalisation of 'Little One' suggests that the apparition is a unique, even holy, figure. Could it be the child Christ? or a fairy? It is not clear. In the *TR* version, the wind blows out the candles so the only illumination is provided by the spectral figure. It is not clear in the *TR* version if the 'little one' is merely a younger version of the speaker or a longed-for child. It also may be an otherworldly visitor. The third stanza suggests that this is a divination rite and the numinous visitor is not entirely discernible; the speaker asks: 'who will answer when I call?' (line 12). F. Marian McNeill's four-volume *The Silver Bough: A Study of the National and Local Festivals of Scotland* and J. M. McPherson's *Primitive Beliefs in the North-East of Scotland* discuss divination rituals in greater depth.

ANNIE HONEY
One of Angus's sisters was named Annie and while her name appears in 'Annie Honey' and other poems including 'The Blue Jacket' and 'Links o' Lunan', there is little information about the whereabouts of Angus's own sister after 1902. 'Annie Honey' perhaps falls into the category Maurice Lindsay refused to include in *SPMA* because of its interest in 'trafficking with elves and their kind' ('Introduction', p. xii). Despite the poem's comparative lightness, it is worth reading for its evocation of a child's perspective.

PATRICK
In 'Patrick', the speaker begs the residents of the town to treat the shoemaker well; it is not until the final stanza one discovers they were once lovers. Nan Shepherd in 'Marion Angus' suggests that Angus sees people 'with tenderness, as in the auld wife asking the bairns for news of the old cobbler, whom nobody likes' (p. 41). In this poem and others, shoes have symbolic significance. Here the speaker conflates youthful romance with walking 'on dancin' shoon' (line 24). In 'Heart-Free', where the absence of shoes connotes poverty and social rejection, the speaker gives her shoes to 'wanton Meg / that ne'er hed hoose nor hame' (lines 9–10). In 'Ann Gilchrist' the 'clay-cauld feet' of the suspected witch signify not only poverty but also the absence of love (line 16). Finally, in 'Winter-Time', shoes suggest the

conjunction of fairy presences and erotic possibility: the speaker sees alluring creatures wearing 'shoon' that were 'wrocht in yon far toon / that ne'er had Cross nor kirk' (lines 15–16).

PENCHRISE
Penchrise is located in the Borders near Hawick, where Angus volunteered during World War One. The Catrail is an ancient earthwork in the Borders.

AT CANDLEMAS
Candlemas is celebrated on 2 February; a quarter day in the Scottish folk calendar, it has roots in pre-Christian festivals (McNeill, *The Silver Bough*, II, p. 29). The weather during Candlemas day offers a premonition of the weather to come: 'gin Candlemas be fair and clear, / there'll be twa winters in the year' (McNeill, *The Silver Bough*, II, p. 77).

'At Candlemas' is one of Angus's most powerful examples of a dual time narrative. Charles Graves praised it for its 'peculiar lilt' ('Scottish Poets of To-Day: The New Makars', p. 219). In 'At Candlemas', the day serves as a threshold space between one end of the speaker's life (spring and youth) and the other (winter and old age). The parallels between the 'bit lassie' (line 3) the speaker recalls herself once being, and the 'blythe bairnie' (line 21) she observes, demonstrate the cyclical nature of time in Angus's poetry. The 'Braid Hill o' Fare' is a hill near Banchory in Aberdeenshire.

THE FIDDLER
In 'The Fiddler', Angus explores how a musician's tunes transport the speaker to three episodes in her past. Christopher Whyte wonders why the speaker is a 'witness rather than a protagonist', believing she is 'entirely passive' throughout the poem (p. 377). One can see, however, that the fiddler's songs elicit a visceral response in the speaker; she relives, rather than merely recalls, her past selves. The ellipses in each stanza serve as a typographical representation of the speaker's thoughts moving backwards into memory. In the first stanza, the imagery is almost entirely visual, reflecting a child's immediate perceptions: the speaker describes the heather with reference to her height and sees

in the landscape a connection between natural elements and emblems of domestic security (clothes drying on the line). In the second stanza, the imagery is primarily aural and tactile, exhibiting in its concision the oppressive closeness of a domestic interior. Angus evokes here a mother's listening ear; the rain, the spinning wheel, and the warmth of 'bairn' (line 11) and 'hearth-stane' (line 12) are the speaker's primary sensations. In the final stanza, the speaker distances herself from physical sensation. In contrast to the child's universe in stanza one, here the observer is old and 'dune' (line 19). Angus draws attention to how little there is left for this woman to sense: only 'wind' (line 21) and 'naked wa's' (line 22). She implies that the old woman lacks the sharpened senses of her younger selves perhaps because of age and infirmity, but more likely because of her deprivation.

THE LANE KIRKYAIRD
Comparing 'The Lane Kirkyaird' (1924) to Hugh MacDiarmid's poem 'Crowdieknowe' from *Sangschaw* (1925) reveals two different representations of the same scene: Last Judgement in a country cemetery. MacDiarmid's poem presents the dead dismissing with some annoyance 'God an' a' his gang' (line 9); Angus's, by contrast, offers a quiet celebration of place and the 'auld kith an' kin' who live there (line 13). MacDiarmid certainly was aware of Angus's work; this is not his only poem that suggests his indebtedness to Angus, Jacob and other poets writing in Scots. (See also the notes for Jacob's 'The Last Ane' and 'A Winter Phantasy'.)

ALAS! POOR QUEEN
'Alas! Poor Queen' is one of Angus's most anthologised poems. Marion Lochhead in 'Feminine Quartet' praises it as one of her 'unforgettable portraits in verse', 'the greatest' in Angus's collection (p. 26); she argues that 'there has rarely been a better apologia for Mary Stuart' (p. 25). A *Scotsman* article claims that the 'simply worded but touching tribute' suggests 'the theme of Mary Stuart is one which haunted' Angus ('A Scotsman's Log', p. 4). Charles Graves reminds her readers that the poem's title comes from a John Keats poem ('The Poetry of Marion Angus', p. 97); Keats's

poem 'Faery Song' ('Ah, Woe is Me! Poor Silver-Wing') includes the lines 'Alas! Poor Queen'.

Angus highlights several facets of Mary Stuart's life: her childhood in France, her relationship with her relatives (including her uncles the Duc de Guise and Monsieur d'Elboeuf), her interactions with John Knox and her complex romantic life. The reference to the 'triple crown to win' (line 7) refers to Mary's connection to the Scottish, English and French thrones (the latter through her marriage to the French Dauphin). In the third stanza, Angus refers to the journey Mary made to see James Hepburn, the Earl of Bothwell (who later became her third husband) as he recuperated at Hermitage Castle from an injury. The trip both made Mary ill and scandalised her subjects who believed the visit – made while the queen was still married to her second husband – was inappropriate. In the poem Angus has Mary sing an excerpt from the ballad 'The Drowned Lovers' in which two lovers, separated by the cruelty of their mothers, seek each other out and then perish in the 'deepest pot in Clyde's water' (Lyle, p. 210). Ultimately, Angus draws attention to the queen's difficulty of trying to balance the conflicting needs of both a political and a human, *female* body.

Angus's poem has been interpreted in choral form in Ian Venable's 1994 composition 'At the Court of the Poisoned Rose'.

THINK LANG
Janet Caird remarks that in 'Think Lang', as in many of Angus's love poems, 'the delight of love is followed by sadness and loss'; she writes, 'the girl is warned of the sadness to come [...] and at the same time the joy of love is expressed in the imagery of the trees clapping their hands' (p. 45).

THE GHOST
'The Ghost', *Glasgow Herald*, 5 November 1924, p. 8.

SUN AND CANDLELIGHT (1927)

SC showcases the continued evolution of Angus's style; her interest in experiences of desire and time remains but is deepened by stark images of speakers *in extremis*. Many poems feature interactions with enigmatic, often supernatural figures. Contemporaneous reviewers expressed interest in Angus's treatment of the supernatural; the *Scotsman* review notes the 'elfin light' of the poems, and argues that the volume 'augurs well for the future of Scottish poetry' ('Three Scottish Poets', p. 2). Charles Graves, in 'The Poetry of Marion Angus', indicates that the 'vivid green-papered boards' and 'crimson spine and endpapers' of SC were picked intentionally 'to typify the faery quality of the verse the book contained' (p. 97).

The review of SC in the *TLS* refers to her work's 'sincerity of feeling', calling attention to her 'kinship with the old ballad makers' and her poetry's evocation of the 'starkly primitive, eerie, or desolate' (p. 795). The *Scots Observer* notes that Angus's poems feature 'three things in them: beauty, a thrill of the heart, and the kind of symbolism that Blake meant when he sang of seeing a world in a grain of sand, and heaven in a wild flower' ('Porpoise Press Poets', p. 15).

Charles Graves's papers in the NLS, including typescripts of SC, shed light onto the book's production. In one letter Angus tells Graves that as she is 'always doubtful of the reliability' of her 'elusive imagination', she cannot guarantee him additional poems for the proposed volume but she hopes for 'a little collection out by the end of November in time for the Xmas sale'; she adds: 'please understand that I feel the end of November, or the beginning of December a good time for such small craft as mine' to be 'setting sail' (MS 27476, folios 21–24, c. 1 June 1927). A fortnight later, she tells him that 'Candlelight' in the title is 'better sounding than Can'el licht' (NLS, MS 27376, folios 25–27, c. 16 June 1927). The title emphasises Angus's interest in the balance of joy and sorrow, light and dark that 'Sun and Candlelight' connotes. The title also may refer to Elizabeth Barrett Browning's Sonnet 43 from *Sonnets from the Portuguese*: 'I love thee to the level of everyday's / most quiet need, by sun and candle-light' (lines 5–6).

C. M. Grieve makes direct reference to SC in a 1930 letter to Charles Graves. On Vox letterhead, he writes: 'Would you care to consider for early publication a volume of poems by me entitled *Fier Comme Un Ecossais* and equal

in voice to Marion Angus'[s] *Sun and Candlelight?*'; he tells
Graves: 'I should like them produced if possible in very
similar format to Miss Angus's volume in question' (NLS,
MS 27476, folio 87, no date [c. February 1930]). Porpoise
Press had published *Lucky Bag* (1927) by Hugh MacDiarmid
but a change in the press's leadership meant that MacDiarmid's project was not realised as proposed.

COURTIN'
In an earlier draft, 'Courtin'' was titled 'Courtship' (NLS,
MS 27479, folio 4). (See the note for 'Tam i' the Kirk'
regarding rose symbolism.)

THE WIFE
A *Scots Observer* article claims that 'a whole tragic romance
is summed up in the seven short stanzas of "The Wife"'
('Porpoise Press Poets', p. 15). Janet Caird considers 'The
Wife' to be Angus's 'most successful ballad'. She writes:
'the speaker is an ordinary woman, welcoming the [bride]
of her much-loved son. The first five stanzas express the
mother's eagerness to show her happiness for her self and
her son and her joy in receiving the girl'. Caird observes
that the speaker in 'The Wife' 'sees the girl's face in the
fire-light' and senses that her power over the son is ominous
and possibly supernatural in origin ('The Poetry of Marion
Angus', p. 46).

WAATER O' DYE
'Waater o' Dye' explores the speaker's relationship with a
'lang-deid wumman' (line 25) who brings to the speaker
what Nan Shepherd calls an 'imaginative apprehension':
supernatural knowledge and an awareness of her own mortality ('Marion Angus', p. 39). Angus emphasises the disruptive nature of the rituals the speaker learns by including an
extra couplet in stanza three, highlighting the 'queer auld-farrand tunes' she learns (line 13).
  The speaker experiences 'the feel o' babes' and the 'luve
o' men' (line 18) not through interaction with a man, but
rather through the kinswoman's 'auncient will' (line 16).
The woman's control over the speaker becomes more
problematic when one considers the Scottish children's
rhyme it recalls:

> Tweed said to Till,
> 'What gars ye rin sae still?'
> Till said to Tweed,
> 'Though ye rin wi' speed,
> And I rin slaw,
> Yet whaur ye droon ae man,
> I droon twa!' (McPherson, p. 64)

Read in light of this rhyme, the 'still' (line 15) river no longer seems idyllic. This rhyme implies 'still' waters are dangerous; the connection Angus makes between the spirit woman and the water seems more ominous – the woman's 'still' presence 'droon[s]' the speaker. The images of drowning and possession in 'Waater o' Dye' highlight how destructive this desire is; the speaker learns to see the presence of 'wings o' Deith' (line 22) around her. The poem's final stanza, with its reference to Genesis, chapter 2, suggests the boundaries between the two women are erased; the speaker is lost in the presence of the 'lang-deid wumman'.

SINGIN' WAATER

'Singin' Waater' offers another depiction of desire that parallels 'Waater o' Dye.' Here the lover is absent but the speaker is similarly overwhelmed by both her 'leal luve' (line 20) and the water representing it. Nan Shepherd in 'Marion Angus' explains that 'Singin' Waater' highlights the 'despairing self-disgust of a smirched woman to whom a second chance has come' (p. 39). The poem makes reference to the ballad 'Sir Patrick Spens' in which the grieving women left behind 'tore their hair, / a' for the sake of their true loves' (Lyle, p. 53). It also may refer to 'Edom of Gordon' in which Edom of Gordon, after he kills a woman, 'turned hir owr and owr again / O gin hir face was wan!' (Lyle, p. 58). See my 'Women "Wha' Lauched and Lo'ed and Sinned": Women's Voices in the Work of Violet Jacob and Marion Angus' for more extensive commentary on 'Singin' Waater'.

WORLD'S LOVE

See the notes for 'Patrick' regarding the significance of shoes in Angus's work. 'World's Love' perhaps references the ballad 'The Douglas Tragedy' in which the hero is buried in 'St Mary's Kirk' (Lyle, p. 215).

THE SANG
In SC galley proofs, Angus originally titled this poem 'The Seang', which she changed to 'The Song'; Charles Graves altered it to 'The Sang'. An earlier draft also included a fifth line in the final stanza that read 'the love that was nae love fur me' (NLS, MS 27479, folio 9).

An article titled 'Miss Marion Angus: An Appreciation' that evaluates Angus's legacy calls 'The Sang' a 'heart-moving poem', claiming that she 'felt the pathos of unrequited love, and the heart-breaks of life; she had an eye for lonely and forgotten people' (L., p. 6). Nan Shepherd concludes that 'The Sang' reveals 'the reluctance of a girl to be emotionally involved by a passion which she cannot share' ('Marion Angus', p. 40). Christopher Whyte takes this further by observing that the speaker's 'lover makes a song which has an independent life and will survive her. She has given in spite of refusing to give. One could even go so far as to say that a part of herself has been stolen' (p. 376).

THE PROOD LASS
'The Prood Lass', *Scots Magazine*, September 1926, p. 467.

In this poem, the speaker's taunts (particularly 'Gin winter wauk the tree / syne I'll keep tryst wi' ye', lines 14–15) suggest the kinds of riddles often found in Scottish ballads.

BARBARA
'The Sorrofu' Lass', *Scots Magazine*, August 1927, p. 338.

'Barbara' is one of the few poems for which there is a record of Angus's commentary. In a letter to Charles Graves, she explains some of the poem's emotional tensions:

> 'Barbara' is being addressed by her friend all the way thru; the friend of Barbara entreats her to meet her as she comes at morning from a night of dreams. *In her dreams* she had slain Barbara who had drawn away her lover's affections and she now repents ever having dreamt such a dream for she is torn between love for Barbara

and jealousy of her. In the last 3 verses she cries to her to wear the gown she had worn on a certain happy day before this tragedy had come between them before Barbara had taken her love from her with a 'lif' of her gowden heid'. I am afraid this is not very lucid but I thought the feeling was true to human nature of desiring to be once more happy and light-hearted with Barbara again as tho the eerie dream had never existed and she had not gone thro the horrors of hate and jealousy [...] P.S. The Barbara poem does not go straight on. The speaker breaks off after telling of the dream and bids Barbara come to meet her that she may see her not as she saw her in her dreams but in life and as she had seen her on an earlier day. (NLS, MS 27476, folios 25–7, c. 16 June [1927], her emphasis)

Along with 'Jealousy', this poem gives a fascinating portrait of tensions between women in love. Charles Graves in 'The Poetry of Marion Angus' singles out 'Barbara' in his discussion of Angus's evocation of the 'magic of the ballads'. He claims that 'Barbara'

> differs from the majority of modern vernacular poems both in language and rhythm; it appeals to a markedly different sense from that to which the forthright utterance of most verse in the doric appeals. It strikes a note which, in order to parallel, we have to go back to that miracle of the vernacular, Hogg's 'Kilmeny', and which perhaps it is impossible to sustain in any work of great compass. The poem, from its opening to its close, is 'all air and fire'. It achieves its atmosphere, without apparent effort, from its opening moments. (p. 97)

According to J. M. McPherson's *Primitive Beliefs in the North-East of Scotland*, 'fairy darts' were believed to be 'shot by the fairies'. Although 'outwardly they caused no visible hole or wound in the skin', they were believed to damage people and livestock (p. 105).

JEALOUSY
Janet Caird calls 'Jealousy' a 'powerful poem in ballad form, of hate and guilt and remorse for revenge taken on a girl who had stolen the speaker's lover' ('The Poetry of Marion

Angus', p. 45). Nan Shepherd suggests that 'Jealousy' reveals 'the cruelty in an unattractive woman, who watches her lover drawn away from her' ('Marion Angus', p. 39).

THE BLUE BOAT
The *Scots Observer* claims that 'The Blue Boat' is 'perhaps the most original poem' in SC ('Porpoise Press Poets', p. 15). In a letter to Helen Cruickshank, Angus's nephew W. S. Angus calls it 'among the half-dozen best of my aunt's poems' and laments that it was omitted from SPMA (AUSC, MS 2737, folio 35, c. 15 September 1950). Janet Caird notes that 'The Blue Boat' features one of Angus's repeated themes: 'the broken pledge' ('The Poetry of Marion Angus', p. 47).

THE WILD LASS
'The Wild Lass', *Scots Magazine*, March 1926, p. 430. The *Scots Magazine* version features a shorter first stanza written in the past tense.

In 'Feminine Quartet', Marion Lochhead refers to Angus's 'genius for telling a story in a few verses, of almost unbearable poignancy, as in "The Wild Lass", which is full of tender compassion' (p. 25). Janet Caird suggests that 'The Wild Lass' features 'the outsider, who haunts so many of [Angus's] poems' ('The Poetry of Marion Angus', p. 47).

'IN THE STREETS THEREOF'
Janet Caird observes that ' "In the Streets Thereof" ' 'expresses the peace of death and the hope of heaven very movingly' ('The Poetry of Marion Angus', p. 47). The title is a biblical quotation describing the prophet Zechariah's vision of a restored Jerusalem:

> There shall yet old men and old women dwell in the streets of Jerusalem, and every man with his staff in his hand for very age. And the streets of the city shall be full of boys and girls playing in the streets thereof. (Zechariah 8:4–5)

In 'Green Beads: The Story of a Lost Love', Angus also refers to this passage. One character, musing upon a minister's disapproval of dance and music, quotes this passage to himself as a rejoinder to the minister's dour remarks

(p. 559). The specificity of the game the children play in '"In the Streets Thereof"' recalls other poems which firmly situate biblical episodes in familiar Scottish environments (cf. 'Naomi', 'Martha's House', 'Nicht o' Nichts').

MEMORY
Primitive Beliefs in the North-East of Scotland, a favourite book of Angus's, describes a rock formation called 'Clach-na-Bhan' in the North-East which is associated with fertility rituals for women:

> By natural action, a hollow had been scooped out of the rock forming what looked like an arm chair. Women about to become mothers climbed the hill, and seated themselves in the hollow, believing that this chairing ensured an easy delivery [...] Single women also made pilgrimages in the assurance that by contact with the blessed stone, they would secure husbands. (McPherson, p. 79)

Although it is not clear whether this formation is the same one Angus mentions in 'Memory', it is interesting to consider the poem in the light of this information as many of Angus's poems depict women who long for a lover and/or a child (cf. 'Waater o' Dye', 'Ann Gilchrist', 'The Ghost' and 'Welcome'). The narrative behind 'Memory' is elusive but the place is associated with a recollection of 'bonnier company' (line 8).

THE TREE
Janet Caird reflects upon the 'oddly jaunty rhythm' of 'The Tree' in 'The Poetry of Marion Angus', wondering whether the tree represents 'guilt, conscience, God?' (p. 47). *Primitive Beliefs in the North-East of Scotland* cites examples of 'supernatural qualities or powers' believed to belong to individual trees, including some that were believed to follow a guilty person as a reminder of his sin (McPherson, p. 77). Trees hold tremendous symbolic value in Angus's poetry. (Cf. 'Trees'; 'Huntlie Hill', where the speaker imagines becoming a 'bonnie birkin tree' (line 20); and 'Lost Country' which features at its centre 'one aged solitary tree / swept by the stormy drift' (lines 11–12).)

THE SILVER CITY
Angus's comments in 'The Silver City' reflect her ambivalent feelings about Aberdeen: it is 'kindly yet cold, respectable and wise' (line 2). After Angus moved from Aberdeen, she admitted: 'I did not care for Aberdeen with any deep affection [...] but I had friends and a knowledge of the place and its folk and without doubt it was a wrench leaving it but one must go on one's way without regret' (NLS, MS 19328, folio 70, no year).

THE MOURNERS
'The Mourners' references Isaiah 40:6–8 and I Peter 1:24–5. The mourners' words in the second stanza also recall Genesis 42:38 ('then shall ye bring down my grey hairs with sorrow to the grave'). Angus suggests that even though 'all flesh is grass' (line 7), the grass is part of the larger 'magical' beauty of the natural world that the mourners overlook (line 14).

WITHY WANDS
'Wind and I', *Glasgow Herald*, 27 February 1926, p. 8.

COWSLIPS SOON WILL DANCE
'Cowslips Soon Will Dance' underwent several title changes, as poem drafts in NLS reveal. Originally titled 'Soon', it was revised to 'March 21' and finally to 'Cowslips Soon Will Dance'. In later proofs someone – presumably Angus – added 'March 21' at the bottom of the page (MS 27479, folio 24). Angus usually did not date her poems but the date was perhaps significant: 21 March is usually considered the first day of spring and it was also her father's birthday.

THE CAPTIVE
An earlier draft of 'The Captive' is titled 'Release' and features four extra lines at the end of the poem. These offer a radically different message than in the book version:

> Yet quick the order's coming—
> Release from prison bars
> The right-of-way through forests,
> The freedom of the stars. (NLS, MS 27479, folio 25)

HERITAGE

In an earlier draft of 'Heritage', the penultimate line reads 'Till Time's last snow' rather than 'Till life's last snow' (NLS, MS 27479, folio 27). This poem, like 'Huntlie Hill', 'Penchrise' and 'The Fox's Skin', suggests that older pre-Christian presences in the Scottish landscape – the 'ancient folk' – are visible to those who consider the land as 'friends' (lines 5, 2). As in 'The Fox's Skin', Angus here redefines Scottish heritage in terms of its prehistoric peoples and the 'lost and gone and forgotten' marks they have left on the landscape ('Heritage', line 13).

WINTER

The playfulness of 'Winter' suggests some of Emily Dickinson's lighter verse. Some of Dickinson's work was available in the early twentieth century, but Angus makes no mention of her poetry in her essays.

COTTON GRASSES

In an earlier draft of SC, the volume finished with 'Trees'; 'Cotton Grasses' came between 'The Tree' and 'The Silver City'. Ending the volume with a description of the 'burden of a song / too sorrowful for singing' (lines 7–8) suggests Angus may have wished to emphasise the expression of what is negated in stanza three of 'Cotton Grasses': the 'tears unwept', the 'tenderness unwist', the 'lips unkissed' and the 'trysts unkept' (lines 9–12).

THE SINGIN' LASS (1929)

The galley proofs of SL are preserved in the NLS in MS 27483; there one can trace the last-minute changes to the book's contents that Angus and Charles Graves made. Angus's interest in time, memory and desire are still at the forefront of the poetry in SL, especially in enigmatic poems such as 'The Eerie Hoose' and 'Huntlie Hill'. Visitations by mysterious strangers, many of them female – including the title 'lass' – figure prominently as in SC (cf. 'The Wee Sma' Glen', 'Welcome', 'Hogmanay', 'Arrival' and 'A Traveller').

Many reviews of SL highlight the poems' supernatural aspects. The *TLS* review focuses upon Angus's evocation of haunted places and her use of Scots, claiming 'the vernacular best suits her genius for the eerie' (p. 798):

> Her gramayre is not the naïve supernaturalism of the Scottish ballads; but her imagination moves most freely among unknown modes of being, in a region where partitions between seen and unseen, present and past, melt away, where the living lover is more ghostly than the dead, and the blind old crone is one with the blythe girl who hastes to join the young lads casting at the peat. Miss Angus is in love with all free, wild things, gipsies and gangrel bodies and untamed hearts: her compassion goes out to the faded harebell and the forsaken bird's nest. (pp. 798–9)

The *Scotsman* review of *SL* praises Angus as 'probably the most individual poet writing to-day in Scots' and, like the *TLS* review, comments upon her evocation of the supernatural. The *Scotsman* review notes that *SL* marks not a departure from her previous themes but rather reveals 'a tendency [...] to run in one channel. That channel is both "still and deep" [...] To adopt her own phrase, it is "the wind an' a' puir traivellin' craturs" you hear in Miss Angus's verse.'

THE GHAIST
In 'Feminine Quartet', Marion Lochhead suggests that 'The Ghaist' is one of Angus's many 'stories told hauntingly, unforgettably, in a few lines of verse' (p. 26).

HEART-FREE
Writing to Charles Graves about the proofs for *SL*, Angus remarks: 'I think perhaps "Heart-Free" is not very good [as a title] and if you think not, the heading might simply be the beginning of the first line[:] "So noo we twa"' (NLS, MS 27476, folio 55, *c.* 10 April 1929). She kept 'Heart-Free' as the title in the published version.

Janet Caird, in 'The Poetry of Marion Angus', calls 'Heart-Free' a 'poem in the old tradition of the poet assigning gifts, or legacies, to the world' (p. 45). (Cf. 'The Place Where my Love Johnny Dwells' in Lyle's *Scottish Ballads*.) Nan Shepherd indicates that 'Heart-Free' illustrates the speaker's 'cold relief' at finding her 'passion is dead' ('Marion Angus', p. 40).

WINTER-TIME
Martinmas, a quarter day in the Scottish folk calendar, is celebrated on 11 November. Traditionally, it is the date when hired farm labourers could move to a new farm to begin another job; they also would receive their pay for the previous term's labour (Livingstone, passim). (Cf. Jacob's 'Charlewayn' and 'The Lowland Ploughman'.) In 'Winter-Time', Martinmas becomes an appropriately eerie threshold space in which to witness the strange events described in the poem. Angus's evocation of a mirror-based divination rite in stanza two recalls 'In A Mirror'.

HOGMANAY
'Hogmanay', like 'At Candlemas' and other similar poems, features a meeting of two selves: an older speaker who witnesses the arrival of her younger self. Hogmanay, celebrated on 31 December, is at the cusp between two years and thus is a space in which one can reflect upon previous events and plan future actions. In 'Hogmanay', the Scottish tradition of first-footing is subverted. Rather than the traditionally lucky first-footer – a dark-haired, handsome stranger – here the speaker finds her younger self at the door. The speaker urges her to come in, even though she recognises that she is 'deid lang syne' (line 4).

ANN GILCHRIST
Joy Hendry argues that 'Ann Gilchrist' 'powerfully evokes our sympathy on behalf of a woman ostracised as a witch' (p. 296). Janet Caird gives this precis of the poem:

> in four stanzas, [Angus] tells the tale of a woman, dubbed a witch by the community, feared by the narrator at the beginning, but at the end understood for what she is – a poor outcast crazed by the loss of a child. ('The Poetry of Marion Angus', p. 46)

WELCOME
'Welcome', like 'Ann Gilchrist', explores the life of a lonely woman who longs for a child, a common theme in Angus's poetry. In 'Welcome', the speaker addresses the 'auld man' (line 1) and the 'lass wi' the raggit shoon' (line 2), treating them with the compassion she dreams of showing a child.

THE EERIE HOOSE
'The Eerie Hoose', *Scots Magazine*, March 1929, p. 447.

W. H. Hamilton, in 'The Poetry of the Year', calls 'The Eerie Hoose' one of Angus's 'awesomely tender songs of the soul's borderland' (p. 12). Charles Graves claims: 'The Eerie Hoose' is 'one of the best examples of the power of atmosphere' in Angus's work, noting that it 'stands almost alone in its class in modern Scottish poetry' ('The Poetry of Marion Angus', p. 107). In 'The Eerie Hoose', Angus uses the phrase 'says she' to frame the narrative, recalling ballads such as 'Johnnie o' Braidiesleys' (Lyle, pp. 48–50). This device adds another level of mystery in the poem; the forbidden 'ae word' (line 9) is never revealed and the contents of the locked room are not divulged. The colour of the rooms and the presence of the locked door recall fairy tales (specifically Bluebeard stories) but Angus also calls upon a range of folk tales in which an unexplained curse or prophecy dictates a person's behaviour.

More extensive commentary on 'The Eerie Hoose' appears in my 'Liltin' in the "Eerie Hoose": Aspects of Self in the Poetry of Marion Angus'.

THE CAN'EL
Dorothy McMillan wonders about the 'incomprehension of the male speaker' in 'The Can'el', suggesting that 'his sense that something indefinable has happened to him provokes the reader to ponder the meaning of the woman's actions and motives'. She concludes:

> But one knows better than to insist on pinning down the suggestiveness of the candle or the heart, like a moth perhaps near the flame. It remains unclear whether the woman has used her sexuality or avoided it – she keeps her secret. (p. 50)

Although Dorothy McMillan assumes that the speaker is a man, it is entirely possible that the speaker is female as there are no gender-specific words indicating the speaker's identity. 'Breist' (line 5) is used in Scots without reference to gender; in Angus's poetry, however, 'breist' is associated specifically with female bodies. In poems such as 'Penchrise', 'The Fiddler', 'Barbara', 'Huntlie Hill', 'The Singin' Lass', 'The Eerie Hoose' and 'Joan the Maid', 'breist' refers only to women (and often, as in 'Barbara', to their eroticised bodies).

'The Can'el' is enigmatic; the act of holding the speaker's heart over a candle flame is metaphorical, but to what is this experience being compared? The ritual at the heart of the poem is not explained. The use of ballad language adds to the mystery by further distancing it from the actual world.

THIS WOMAN
As in 'Barbara' and 'Jealousy', 'This Woman' discusses the speaker's sorrow for the loss of a beloved and jealousy towards a rival.

JEAN CAM'BELL
Janet Caird observes that Angus's tendency to give proper names to the people in poems such as 'Jean Cam'bell' allies her with the ballad tradition and grants 'to the eeriest a disturbing suggestion of reality' ('The Poetry of Marion Angus', p. 47). In 'Jean Cam'bell', Angus uses external clues – the age of the woman's plaid – in contradistinction to the unchanging psychological state of the speaker as she ages. Memory, as in 'Hogmanay' and other poems, keeps the speaker's youth ever present.

THE SINGIN' LASS
Dorothy McMillan claims that in 'The Singin' Lass' the focus should be upon the speaker's 'commitment to his luve' and his 'fascination with the singin' lass' (p. 49) but in fact, 'interest is displaced from the speaker to the two women – it is not his feelings but their stories that we are moved to speculate about' (p. 50). In a tradition long used by male poets, Angus here writes about a distant woman whose song captivates the speaker (cf. William Wordsworth's 'The Solitary Reaper'). Here the speaker fixates upon the 'lucky penny' (line 1) that the 'singin' lass' (line 8) now carries close to her heart; the speaker recognises that the penny is physically closer than he (or she) ever will be to the alluring stranger.

MOONLIGHT MEETING
In her notes to Charles Graves about *SL*, Angus tells him

that 'there is just one improvement which I think might be made in the last verse of Moonlight Meeting [.] The repetition of cauld is not good'. She asks to replace 'the first cauld' with 'laigh' (NLS, MS 27476, folio 55, *c.* 10 April 1929).

Writing to Marion Lochhead in May 1930, Angus admits: 'it is curious that John Buchan wrote to me that "Moonlight Meeting" is one of his favourites and I was not sure if I should include it in the book so little does one know' (NLS, MS 26190, folio 232, *c.* 6 May 1930).

The poem's title perhaps references Robert Browning's love poem 'Meeting At Night'.

WINDS OF THE WORLD
The title 'Winds of the World' may refer to Rupert Brooke's poem 'The Great Lover' which appeared in various editions including several volumes during World War One:

> Oh, never a doubt but, somewhere, I shall wake,
> And give what's left of love again, and make
> New friends, now strangers...
> But the best I've known,
> Stays here, and changes, breaks, grows old, is blown
> About the winds of the world, and fades from brains
> Of living men, and dies.
> Nothing remains. (lines 64–9)

Angus's poem offers a different interpretation of the nature of romantic dreams; she suggests the physical manifestation of these possibilities may be lost to time and circumstances, but the 'thocht o' them' (line 11) will persist.

ARRIVAL
Like 'Nicht o' Nichts' and 'Welcome', 'Arrival' dramatises an encounter with a holy presence, one situated within the simple domestic setting of a 'darkened house' (line 1).

AMONG THORNS
In 'The Poetry of Marion Angus', Janet Caird observes that 'Among Thorns' is one of many in Angus's repertoire that makes overt biblical references (here Luke 8:4–21): 'Among Thorns' 'refers directly to the parable of the sower, but in

the poem the crop that springs up is "marigold on marigold" – marigolds are in an earlier poem symbols of love and passion' (p. 47). The biblical parable suggests that seeds thrown in the thorns do not flourish; these seeds represent those who are too concerned with worldly needs to hear God's word. In Angus's poem, the 'starving soil' (line 13), although filled with thorns, still yields poppies and marigolds; the poem celebrates the 'miracle of barrenness' (line 12) – the ability to produce vibrant art in difficult circumstances.

CAMBUS WOODS
In 'Cambus Woods' Angus associates the appearance of orchids in the spring with 'a lover long asleep' with 'some unforgotten tryst to keep' (lines 6–7). The speaker in 'Cambus Woods' calls upon a dead acquaintance to return in the spring when the orchids begin to bloom. In folklore, orchids are often associated with fertility: 'witches were supposed to use the tubers in their philtres' while in ancient myth they were 'believed to be the food of the Satyrs, and to have incited them to excesses' (M. Grieve, II, pp. 603, 604). According to *The Silver Bough: A Study of the National and Local Festivals of Scotland*, the purple orchis is called 'the Enticing Plant'; F. Marian McNeill cites another writer who reports many believe that 'if you take the proper half of the root of the orchis and get anyone of the opposite sex to eat it, it will produce a strong affection for you, while the other half will produce as strong an aversion' (I, p. 83). Cambus o' May wood is near Ballater, in Deeside.

OF SORROWFUL THINGS
A letter Angus wrote to a friend sheds light upon the value she placed upon 'sorrowful things': 'Think what lighthearted creatures we should be if suffering in other people did not send us into depths of gloom. Life is a queer business and I think only worth while at all if one can look beyond it' (NLS, MS 19326, folio 29, c. February 1930). In another letter she admits to a friend that John Buchan had written her to say that 'Of Sorrowful Things' is 'in his opinion the finest' of her work (NLS, MS 26190, folio 232, c. 6 May, no year).

DAWN AND TWILIGHT

Janet Caird compares 'Dawn and Twilight' to the work of A. E. Housman, a poet whose work Angus admired, noting that in 'Dawn and Twilight' and in 'New Year's Morning' she 'strikes exactly his note of concise bleakness' ('The Poetry of Marion Angus', p. 47).

THE TURN OF THE DAY (1931)

TD is a collection of new poetry and several poems from previous volumes, much to Angus's dismay. She wrote scathingly of the volume: 'there is not much new in it [...] My only hope is that it may go off well enough to permit the publisher to bring out a collected edition some time hence' (NLS, MS 19328, folio 34, *c.* 19 March [1930]). At the time Angus was distracted from literary affairs by her sister Ethel's illness. In a letter to a friend, she frets:

> I am dreadfully embarrassed about the book coming out this week. [...] it is almost all old stuff and you at least are quite familiar with the most of the poems. The publisher seemed to want old poems republished along with what new ones I *had*. This year all my emotions which should otherwise have gone into verse have been used up [...] on my sister and all the troubles. (NLS, MS 19328, folio 124, *c.* 23 March [1931], her emphasis)

Writing later in the year, she admits: 'Of late I have hardly read any reviews of my book. When I do I wonder why nothing any one says seems to matter and I should have been so proud could my poor[,] poor dear have shared my pleasure' (NLS, MS 19328, folio 142, *c.* 6 June [1931]).

Nevertheless, despite Angus's concerns about the book's success, it was well received. The *TLS* review claims: 'for beyond time's treason and the weakness and pathos of men she has a vision of the abiding hills of the North, and it is their staunchness and mystery which sound as an undertone even in her lightest and gayest verses' (p. 635). The review in *Modern Scot* suggests that Angus has, 'like Housman, an almost unbearably acute sensitiveness to "the heartbreak in the heart of things", to the disparity between the potentialities and the realities of life'; the writer draws attention to the 'shorter poems' in the collection, calling them 'technically [...] more perfect' than the longer ones (Kennedy, p. 87). The *Scotsman* notes the inclusion of older material in the volume, but argues that this is helpful because her earlier work is difficult to obtain. It concludes that the volume 'confirms the impression that Miss Angus is, perhaps, the most important woman poet in the vernacular tongue Scotland has produced' ('Two Scots Poets').

The poems in *TD* feature a range of themes; sorrow and loss figure noticeably. Important too is the continued presence of mysterious or enigmatic women: Joan of Arc, 'The Stranger', Jenny in 'The Doors of Sleep' and others.

SPRING
By beginning on a note of rejuvenation, Angus takes a step away from the sorrowful 'Anemones' that concluded the previous volume.

A BRETON WOMAN SINGS
'A Breton Woman Sings' originally was supposed to appear in SC but later was rejected. The draft version in NLS has some modifications: line one reads, 'on that clear morning's dawning' instead of 'on resurrection morning'; the draft of stanza two reads:

> At Easter, in the Chapel,
> When waxen candles burn,
> 'Tis for your arm about me,
> And a bonny boat's return.

She also changes the penultimate line from 'We will keep close to Mary's feet' to the version appearing in this volume (NLS, MS 27479, folio 26). The poem is not one of Angus's better works but it does give one an insight into her revision practice. The immediate physicality of the stanza reproduced above is distilled and made more impressionistic in the *TD* version.

THE BROKEN BRIG
'The Broken Brig', *Scots Magazine*, July 1930, p. 307.

Writing to a friend in 1930, Angus offers a rare commentary on her poetry. She asks: 'Will you understand I wonder the meaning of the "Broken Brig" [?] To me it is quite clear and I shall not *explain* it to you. "Simply faith without sight"' (NLS, MS 19328, folio 72, c. 2 July [1930], her emphasis).

Joy Hendry contends that 'The Broken Brig' and others in Angus's work 'combine feyness and archetypal imagery, drawing on the elemental power of "Lyke-Wake Dirge" to create a profoundly disturbing picture of the helplessness of humanity against the blows of fate' (p. 296). 'This ae nicht' (line 1) recurs in many ballads, particularly 'The Lyke-Wake Dirge'.

THE LISSOME LEDDY
'The Lissome Leddy', *Scots Magazine*, January 1930, p. 283.

Scottish composer Isobel Dunlop composed a piece called 'The Fairy Spinner' which is based on 'The Lissome Leddy' (NLS, Acc. 9121, number 112, c. December 1938).

THE STRANGER
'The Stranger', *Modern Scot*, 1 (1930), p. 6.

Dorothy McMillan argues that 'The Stranger', like many of Angus's poems, has an ambiguous narrative that 'refuse[s]' to 'tell us all we want to know'. She writes:

> Angus makes us feel that women have secret stories that cannot be simply brought to the surface without falsifying their distinctive lives. More than that she makes us feel that they should not be ferreted out, that women are entitled to hug their secret selves. The drive to detect the covert narratives along with the sense that such a desire is tactless is what makes some of the poems truly disturbing. (p. 50)

In many of her poems, Angus associates bright eyes with an interaction with the supernatural (cf. 'Waater o' Dye', 'Singin' Waater', among others).

JOAN THE MAID
Angus was asked by fellow writer Ronald Campbell Macfie to contribute a poem for a volume on Joan of Arc. Angus was diffident about her poem; she wrote to Patrick Geddes, who was involved with the project: 'in all probability [the poem] may not be in the least suitable for your purpose. It is merely some one associating a Scots working maid in

her mind with the French girl heroine as a kind of prototype'. She explains to Geddes that she had read an account of Joan of Arc in the work of Frederic Mistral but she did not feel knowledgeable enough 'to attempt anything with the poet as subject' (NLS, MS 10551, folio 163, c. 25 May 1930). Angus also refers to Joan of Arc in CD when Christabel calls her 'Joan, the maid! noblest, bravest, best of women!'; she comments upon her 'terrible, tragic, piteous tale', noting the involvement of Scots in the fight against Joan of Arc's enemies, the English (p. 18).

CURIOS
To stay on 'Queer Street' is a euphemism for having 'financial difficulties' (Evans, p. 884). In 'Curios', Angus imagines the landscape of 'Queer Street' with its pawn shops full of junk and its keys not for tangible items but rather for ephemeral 'Memories' (line 12).

THE BLUE JACKET
Maurice Lindsay expresses his hesitation at including 'The Blue Jacket' in SPMA in a letter to Helen Cruickshank; he remarks: 'a baby in a cradle *doesn't* resemble a nut in a shell' (AUSC, MS 2737, folio 39, c. 6 November 1949, his emphasis). Presumably because Helen Cruickshank or others insisted, the poem appears in SPMA.

Dorothy McMillan notes that 'The Blue Jacket' 'excludes the male world', stating 'it seems regressive, privileging infantilism and asexual motherhood'. She wonders:

> Does Annie use her little sister so that she may project her own fantasies on to her? Does she look for an excuse to avoid the full sexual experience, or, having been stung by it, does she dream of an irrecoverable innocence? (p. 50)

The answers, of course, are not given by the poem. In 'The Blue Jacket', Angus creates an eerie world in which the female speaker expresses her own fears in contrast to the innocence of her younger sister, who dreams of childbearing, as children do, as an abstract rather than a physical process.

LOST COUNTRY AND OTHER VERSES (1937)

Angus's final volume, LC, differs from her previous two. Its contents are more haunted by loss than are previous volumes: loss of her home, loss of the 'country' of the North-East itself, and loss of that landscape's emotional, internal correlative in memory. Writing to Nan Shepherd in the 1930s, Angus remarks: 'I have been housebound so long that I have forgotten the "feel" of sun and wind – and "werena my hairt licht I wad dee" for longing for the old places and roads' (AUSC, MS 3036, folio 4, no date). Angus's 'longing for the old places' suffuses the poems in LC.

Overall, LC is not as strong a volume as her previous two volumes. The eerie quality of the best verse in the previous volumes is tempered by a recognition that 'the sands o' Time rin doon – doon' ('Links o' Lunan', line 13). Angus herself was not satisfied with LC's contents. In a letter to Nan Shepherd, she writes:

> When my little book does appear[,] my dear Nan[,] it will be a disappointment to you if you are looking for anything 'wild and strange' which poetry ought to be. My muse is not a bird with a broken wing but more like a domestic hen with a crippled leg. Furthermore as [William] Power bid me I might as well have, 'put it in the back of the fire' as given it to Gowans & Grey who he says are mere *book binders* and it will fall as flat [...] as a half baked scone. I really let them have it because they wanted to do a collected edition. (AUSC, MS 3036, folio 2, undated, her emphasis)

Angus's frustration with her failed attempts to get a collected volume published during the 1930s is evident in her letters.

When LC did appear, it was reviewed positively. The *TLS* review called her poems 'at once romantic and homely, romantic in their evocation of that "Lost Country" of hill and moorland and mountain streams which she describes as the "country of my dreams"' (p. 45). The *Scotsman* review suggests that while LC lacks some of the 'magical' quality of SC and SL, it is still accomplished: 'the peculiar art by which she calls up figures of the past – fiddlers, spaewives, or perhaps more ordinary mortals – as if they were projections of her personality is still here, in a degree'.

LOST COUNTRY
'Lost Land', *Glasgow Herald*, 7 November 1935, p. 10. The *Glasgow Herald* version is subtly different from the book version. A side-by-side comparison of stanzas one and four illuminates Angus's revision process (the *Glasgow Herald* version is on the left):

A singing burn—tho' many such Run among hilly lands, No other had that friendly touch Slipping through my hands.	Two mountain streams that pass Thro' dark and hilly lands, By secret names I named you, as You slipped between my hands.
[...]	[...]
Cold moorland, vext by winds' alarms, Small stream and lonely tree, To you I'm stretching out my arms, Lost Country!	Cold moorland, vext by winds' alarms Lost footpath, naked streams, To you I'm stretching out my arms, Country of my dreams.

The alterations appear minor, but a closer look reveals some of the key distinctions. In general, Angus moves from a lament for a specific space to a more open-ended vision of how an internal landscape can be 'lost' (line 14) due to age and emotional isolation. In the book version, the past tense in the first stanza ('slipped') suggests that the loss is irreparable.

One can discern this meaning shift through an examination of the treatment of the landscape in each version's imagery. In the first stanza, Angus changes 'singing burn' (line 1) to 'two mountain streams' (line 1), one of the recurrent geographical features in her poetry. In the contemporaneous 'News' the speaker describes observing 'the warld and a' / that's haud therein, / at the back o' yon hill / whaur twa burns rin' (lines 17–20). In 'Invitation', the speaker tells her lover to 'come kiss me / whaur the twa burns rin' (lines 1–2). In 'George Gordon, Lord Byron', Angus describes the 'toon / atween the rivers twa' (lines 10–11). The relative specificity of 'two mountain streams' makes it possible to suggest a correlative in the North-Eastern landscape; one could imagine either the Dee and the Don rivers outside

Aberdeen or the North and South Esk outside of Arbroath could be the rivers represented here.

CHANCE ACQUAINTANCE
'Chance Acquaintance', *Glasgow Herald*, 8 May 1934, p. 10.
  The *TLS* refers to 'Chance Acquaintance' in its review of *LC*, noting that Angus 'give[s] homely veracity' to her poems, including 'the young man's regret at turning his back on a fair face' (p. 45).

WHEN AT FAMILIAR DOORS
'Tide-Borne', *Glasgow Herald*, 23 February 1931, p. 10. In the *Glasgow Herald* version, Angus uses the past tense in the last two lines: 'Strangers have lit our evening fire, / strange hands have made our bed' (lines 11–12).

TWO IS COMPANY
An undated draft of 'Two is Company' titled 'Auld Wives' Tales' is preserved in AUSC in MS 3017, folder 8/1/1. It is written on the reverse side of a piece of stationery from the West Kirk of Greenock. (Angus's brother-in-law was a minister at Greenock's West Kirk – now called St Luke's – from 1904 until the early 1940s.) The poem is significantly different from 'Two is Company':

  We ga'ed and we ga'ed to the auld thorn tree,
  That hings by the Wishin' Well,
  Me, and Nelly o' Little Stanehive,
  And her that bides hersel'.

  Quoth I, 'That silken goon o' mine
  Hed ye seen when it was new,
  Ere the flitterin' moth won until the kist
  And riddled it thro' and thro'!

  Says Nelly, 'My locks was like the corn
  In the bonnie hairst fields o hame,
  The tides of sorra gaed ower ma heid
  And turned them white as faem.'

  'I hed a lover in Logie Pert'
  Quo' she that bides hersel'

> 'And whiles we keep a ghaistly tryst
> By the thorn at the Wishin' Well.'

Changing the characters to 'Jean and Nelly o' Upper Stanehive / and the third ane was mysel'' (lines 3–4) from 'Me, and Nelly o' Little Stanehive, / and her that bides hersel'' (lines 3–4) is interesting; in the draft version the unnamed 'her that bides hersel'' keeps a 'ghaistly tryst' (lines 15–16) while in the book version there is no lover mentioned – just a general reference to 'the braws' the speaker 'had lang syne' (lines 15, 16). The eerie tenor of the draft version recalls other of Angus's ghostly love poems. Christopher Whyte suggests that a 'rueful yet eloquent silence' marks the poem (p. 380).

CORRICHIE
'The Queen of Scots Rode', *The Listener*, 20 May 1931, p. 863. Because the version in *The Listener* differs noticeably, it is reproduced below:

> By this burn side a queen rode light
> Through moor, and moss and saugh,
> To see her gay lords win a fight
>   In yon green haugh.
>
> Red berries on the rowans hung,
> The leaf began to turn
> It's strange that long ago she rode
>   By our wee burn.
>
> And strange that then the rowans high
> Swung on a golden tree
> Above the singing burn and I
>   Not here to see.

The battle of Corrichie was fought in 1562 between the troops of Mary, Queen of Scots and the Gordons in Aberdeen (Cannon, p. 249).

NAOMI
'Naomi', *Glasgow Herald*, 4 November 1933, p. 4. The epigraph published in the *Glasgow Herald* reads: 'And the city was moved because of her, and they said, "Is this Naomi?".'

'Naomi' refers to Ruth 1:19 which describes Naomi's return to Bethlehem after many years living in Moab. The *TLS* review of *LC* claims that Angus in 'Naomi' 'translate[s] a Biblical incident convincingly into her native idiom' (p. 45).

THE BURDEN
'The Burden', *Glasgow Herald*, 25 November 1933, p. 10. The *Glasgow Herald* version uses no personal references.

The *TLS* review of *LC* suggests that the 'old wife carries the burden of life' with 'wisdom' in 'The Burden' (p. 45).

THE WIDOW
'Husband and Wife', *Glasgow Herald*, 14 March 1932, p. 10. The final lines of the poem in the *Glasgow Herald* are: 'Ye daurna pit / sic only daftlike word / on Easter Drum's heid stane, / I hear ye say' (lines 12–15). Drum is between Banchory and Aberdeen.

DESIRES OF YOUTH
'Desire of Youth', *Outlook*, April 1936, p. 40.

GATHERING SHELLS
Janet Caird, in 'The Poetry of Marion Angus', addresses the character of the 'Grannie's sister' (line 1) in 'Gathering Shells'. She observes that this woman 'brushed away' questions about her life by the ocean but, 'when the wind was blowing in the trees she sang of the shells on the sea-shore' (p. 47). Janet Caird wonders whether 'Gathering Shells' 'could stand as a metaphor for the poetry of Marion Angus, eschewing the grand and lofty (and grandiloquent); finding her matter in a world of mysteries and wonder lying around her' (p. 47).

THE PLAID
'The Cloak', *Glasgow Herald*, 13 January 1932, p. 10. The *Glasgow Herald* version begins:

> Come see the bonnie cloak;
> 'Twas wrocht across the sea;
> As warm as milk as saft as silk
> And haps me to the knee.

This suggests that the speaker is eager to show others the cloak before it is 'cursed' (line 9); in the book version, the speaker seems more reticent to share the shame the cloak now symbolises.

A WOMAN SINGS
'A Woman Sings', Modern Scot, 3 (1933), p. 324.

THE MUSICIAN
'A Musician', Glasgow Herald, 24 September 1935, p. 8.

This poem appears in several forms but the only major change is to the place name associated with the fiddler. In the Glasgow Herald version, the location is given as Drumtochty. In an undated letter to Alexander Keith, Angus suggests another possible version: 'Fyfie'. As she notes in her letter, 'it really is not a matter of tremendous import' (AUSC, MS 3017, folder 8/1/1, c. 18 March, no year). In a later note she tells Keith: 'The name was first printed "Drumtochty" which could be retained [...] Just as you like as your judgment is probably better than mine and I have no preference particularly' (AUSC, MS 3017, folder 8/1/1, c. 22 July, no year). There is a Kilbirnie in Ayrshire, but the place intended here may be the Kilbirnie west of Banff.

NEWS
'News of the World', Glasgow Herald, 3 December 1931, p. 10. The Glasgow Herald version omits lines 13–16.

NICHT O' NICHTS
'Christmas Eve', Glasgow Herald, 23 December 1933, p. 4. The Glasgow Herald version makes more extensive use of personal pronouns in stanza two:

> My twa clear candles
> Bonnily they shine,
> My loaf is o' the wheaten meal,
> My cloth o' the linen fine. (lines 5–8)

Janet Caird indicates that 'Nicht o' Nichts', like many other poems by Angus, features an interaction between the speaker and mysterious strangers. The strangers in 'Nicht o'

Nichts', she argues, 'are surely meant to remind us of Mary and Joseph and the Christ-child' ('The Poetry of Marion Angus', p. 45).

THE SPAE-WIFE
'The Spey-Wife', *Glasgow Herald*, 17 November 1934, p. 4. In the *Glasgow Herald* version, the first stanza is in the past tense; the woman speaks directly to the speaker, not generally to 'fouks' (line 4) as in the book version.

Nan Shepherd in 'Marion Angus' suggests that 'The Spae-Wife' reveals that Angus 'knows that to have wronged is a sharper agony than to be wronged' (p. 39). The start of 'The Spae-Wife' resembles one of Angus's favourite childhood poems, 'The Brownie of Blednoch' by William Nicholson, which she references in 'Scottish Poetry Old and New' (p. 25).

NEW YEAR'S MORNING
'Year's End', *Glasgow Herald*, 31 December 1931, p. 8. The *Glasgow Herald* version concludes:

> And Someone in the shadow
> Keeps whispering in my ear,
> 'When little's left to hope for,
> The less will be to fear.' (lines 9–12)

The use of the capitalised letter in 'Someone' recalls a similar technique in earlier versions of 'In a Mirror' and 'The Seaward Toon'. (See the note for 'Dawn and Twilight'.)

MARTHA'S HOUSE
'Martha's House', *Glasgow Herald*, 18 August 1932, p. 8. The *Glasgow Herald* version refers to 'myrrh and balm and rue' (line 19) instead of 'mint and myrrh and rue' (line 16). The poem probably refers to Martha, sister of Mary, as described in the gospels of Luke and John. In Luke 10:41–2, Martha prepares food for Jesus and his followers.

FOXGLOVES AND SNOW
'Foxgloves and Snow', *Glasgow Herald*, 21 July 1934, p. 4.

MEMORY'S TRICK
'Memory's Trick', *Glasgow Herald*, 14 December 1935, p. 10. The *Glasgow Herald* version refers to 'my friend the best' as the person the speaker 'loved best' (line 14). The less intimate version in the book recalls other revisions in which Angus omits or limits personal references, expanding the distance between speaker and poet.

ONCE LONG AGO
'Once Long Ago', *Glasgow Herald*, 20 July 1935, p. 4.

THE FAITHFUL HEART
'The Faithful Thought', *Glasgow Herald*, 2 February 1934, p. 10. The *Glasgow Herald* version gives the origin of the man as 'Ernan-side' (line 1).

LINKS O' LUNAN
The *TLS* review of *LC* praises the 'wild magic which [Angus] personifies in the Annie Lizzie of "Links o' Lunan"' (p. 45). The Links of Lunan are at Lunan Bay, near Montrose.

AT PARTING
Dorothy McMillan suggests that in 'At Parting' Angus 'subverts the characteristic authority of the male parting poem'. She explains that the poem's 'male speaker [...] loses control of the situation' and 'the girl's involuntary reaction invades his presence of mind leaving him uncertain and the poem incomplete' (p. 49).

NOVEMBER IN EDINBURGH
It is useful to compare 'November in Edinburgh' to an article about Scottish writer George MacDonald which Angus wrote in 1930 for the *Scots Observer*. In it, she discusses the appeal of seeing places mentioned in the works of favourite writers. 'November in Edinburgh', with its reflections upon the lives of Thomas Carlyle, Robert Burns and Walter Scott, recalls Angus's interest in people who have described places so vividly that readers feel close to that writer just by being in these places. Angus's interest in place is discussed in the introduction.

Angus enjoyed her time in Edinburgh. In the early 1930s

she writes to Helen Cruickshank: 'Greatly I enjoyed my visit to Edinburgh. [...] Let no one speak to me of the "coldness" of Edinburgh. It is a calumny' (AUSC, MS 2737, folio 1, c. 29 March, no year).

ON A BIRTHDAY
'On A Birthday', *Glasgow Herald*, 29 September 1932, p. 8.

SELECTED POEMS OF MARION ANGUS (1950)

During her life Angus had wanted a collected edition of her poems but was not able to convince her publishers to take on the project. After her death, her work was collected into *SPMA* through the efforts of Maurice Lindsay and Helen Cruickshank. The project nearly failed, as letters preserved in AUSC reveal. Maurice Lindsay worried about the economic viability of the book because 'poetry is always the first artistic casualty whenever an economic blizzard blows up, particularly in Scotland' ('Introduction', p. x). Short of cash, the project finally was realised through the anonymous gift of £100. In a 1969 letter to Nan Shepherd, Helen Cruickshank reveals that fellow writer Dot Allan was the generous donor who made *SPMA* possible (AUSC, MS 2737, folio 53, c. 22 January 1969).

SPMA brings together a variety of Angus's work but there are notable omissions. Maurice Lindsay considered that 'the slope between Miss Angus's best work and her poorest was steeper' than he had expected ('Introduction', p. x). Poems such as 'Barbara' do not appear, along with others Lindsay may have considered to be 'trafficking with elves' ('Introduction', p. xii). The review of *SPMA* in the *Scotsman* questions some of the omissions from the volume, but praises it for making available her poetry to readers. It calls Angus a 'genuine poet', one of 'the many gifted women poets whom Scotland has produced' ('In Scots').

UNCOLLECTED POEMS

Angus published in a range of journals and periodicals and, as her letters suggest, she did not keep a record of all the publications; discovering new poems can be a matter of making a lucky find. Reproduced in this section are a handful of her uncollected works to give readers a sense of the other kinds of poems she wrote during her life but did not publish in book form.

UNSEEN
'Unseen', *Scots Observer*, 5 December 1929, p. 10.

WIZARDRY
'Wizardry', *Scots Observer*, 27 March 1930, p. 4.

THE KISS
'The Kiss', *Scots Magazine*, April 1931, p. 13.

THE DOVE
'The Dove', *Scots Pictorial*, 8 July 1922, p. 634. This poem has no author listed with it but it has the hallmarks of Angus's work – repetition, the language of the ballads (especially in line 1), and the address 'think ye' (line 17). It recalls 'The Wild Lass'.

AFTER THE STORM
'After the Storm', *Glasgow Herald*, 28 October 1927, p. 10. The author given for 'After the Storm' is M. E. A., Angus's initials. (*TL* was published as the work of M. E. Angus). The poem, like 'The Dove', is not a strong piece but it is interesting in its English-language treatment of a subject Angus explores so often in her poetry: the sea.

The Poems of Violet Jacob

VERSES (1905)

In the 1930s, when Jacob was asked to provide information about her writing career, she listed all her poetry volumes except *V* and *BM*, perhaps to distance herself from her earlier work (NLS, MS 9997, folios 37–8, c. 30 October 1932). *V* is not a strong volume; it is burdened with overly ornamented diction and in its subject matter can be derivative. It does give insight into her impressions of India and Egypt, however; usefully, it demonstrates how her poetics evolved between *V* and *SA*. It also highlights how the use of literary Scots emerging in *SA* seems to liberate her poetry from *V*'s overwrought imagery. Although *V* was not widely reviewed, the *Scotsman* review praises its 'picturesque impressions of India' and its 'many lyrical pieces of varied content', noting 'the work is always graceful and pleasing'.

AN IMMORTELLE

An immortelle, or everlasting, is the name for a flower that does not lose its colour when it is dried (*OED*). In 'An Immortelle', Jacob's speaker reinterprets a prelapsarian garden as filled not with life-giving plants but instead with deadly ones; the speaker's departure from the garden – brought about by the arrival of an angel who locks the gate – does not prevent her from reflecting upon her experiences there. This gothic interest in decay characterises many poems in *V*.

BEYOND THE WALLS

Jacob explores the lives of travellers in both her poetry and fiction. 'Beyond the Walls' paves the way for such later poems as 'Donald Maclane', 'The Last o' the Tinkler' and 'The Tinkler's Baloo'. (Cf. also 'The Deil'.)

'COME ON, COME UP, YE ROVERS'

It is useful to compare ' "Come On, Come Up, Ye Rovers" ' to 'An Immortelle'; although both are minor poems, the pairing reveals a theme that becomes more significant in Jacob's later poetry: the different freedoms accessible to men and women. The male context of ' "Come On, Come Up, Ye Rovers" ' speaks of the perceived freedom of sailors to explore the world beyond 'small men's limits' (line 20). The speaker suggests that the 'sons of morning' (line 25) have free entry to 'lands where dreams come true' where an angel will welcome them (lines 28–9). Although ' "Come on, Come Up, Ye Rovers" ' ends with the sailors' imagined deaths, it reinforces the freedom that men have to seek their fortune far from home. This poem serves as a direct contrast to the landscape and voice of 'An Immortelle' in which the speaker, who appears to be female, is denied the use of her garden by an angel who casts her out, leaving her only a flower commonly associated with mourning to remind her of the 'secret garden' (line 1) she has lost. As with Angus, however, one should be cautious when making assumptions regarding gender.

AIRLIE KIRK
'Airlie Kirk', like the contemporaneous 'The Lowland Ploughman', offers a good example of the kind of speaker appearing more regularly in Jacob's poetry after V: rural, identifiably Scottish, and often poor. Her evocation of the landscape in 'Airlie Kirk' also prefigures the prominent role of the natural world in her poetry after 1905.

IN LOWER EGYPT
Jacob lived in Egypt in 1903–4. Here Jacob imagines an interaction with Cleopatra, the 'Serpent, by a serpent slain at last' (line 19); the depiction of the 'shadow of a queen' (line 12) suggests a fascination with women's lives that underlies Jacob's work.

THE CALL
'The Call', like many poems in V and later volumes, concerns itself with the longing to travel 'out across the threshold' of a restrictive home (line 21).

THE VALLEY OF THE KINGS
The Valley of the Kings, in Upper Egypt, is the site of the great pyramids where many ancient Egyptian royals were buried. In her evocation of the 'sacrilegious hands' (line 33) violating the tombs she may refer to either the 1898 or the

1905 discoveries of royal mummies in the Valley of the Kings and the resulting international interest in archaeological work in Egypt.

Isis and Osiris are two ancient Egyptian deities. Osiris is associated with judging the dead in the afterlife and often is depicted on sarcophagi.

THE LOWLAND PLOUGHMAN
In 'The Lowland Ploughman', Jacob explores a scenario that appears in many later poems, including 'Tam i' the Kirk' and 'Bonnie Joann': a poor labourer wooing his beloved. (For information on Martinmas, see the note for Angus's 'Winter-Time'.)

Selections from POEMS OF INDIA
Jacob lived in India from 1895 until 1900 while her husband was stationed in Mhow, now in India's Madhya Pradesh state. In her diary in 1897, Jacob writes: 'I never can make out what [the atmosphere] is. Sacrifice, fate, perhaps death itself; something that is always close, everywhere. I suppose it is death, of which there is so much. But there is an exhilaration in it, I don't know why' (*DLI*, p. 92). The language of 'Poems of India' is influenced by impressions recorded in her letters and journals. Excerpts from *DLI* are provided with these poems to illustrate the connections between her non-fiction writing and her poetry.

II. NIGHT IN THE PLAINS
'Night in the Plains' reflects the intense heat and the ever-present threat of illness and death Jacob experienced while living in India. Writing to her mother in March 1896, Jacob tells her:

> We have had a smallpox epidemic and a cholera scare; everybody had to be vaccinated and we attended the hospital in batches. [...] A draft of infantry from Doolali brought cholera with them and some men died. They were quietly buried in the night, so I had not the benefit of their funerals. (*DLI*, p. 37)

She apologises that 'there's a good deal of illness and this letter seems to be all illnesses and insects. They're rather the principal topics just now' (*DLI*, p. 37). *DLI* also reveals the 'unendurable' heat of India; she writes of hearing 'the voices of the *bazaar*, that are never quiet, especially in hot weather nights, rising from the city' (*DLI*, p. 78). Kali is a Hindu goddess of destruction and creation and consort of the god Shiva.

III. THE RESTING-PLACE
'The Resting-Place' recalls an incident in *DLI* in which Jacob comes across a tomb outside Mandu, now in India's Madhya Pradesh state. She writes:

> To reach one of the most beautiful tombs I had to cut my way [through the foliage] with my Norwegian knife; the arched portal was filled by a stone door, or rather, a half door, immovable and firmly built into the jamb, thickly carved in intricate patterns, and through the empty side of the arch you could see a stone sarcophagus. I would give much to know the names and histories of all these great people who lie hidden away in the vegetation of this lonely place. (*DLI*, p. 66)

In *V*, 'bhai' is translated as 'brother'.

IV. EVENING IN THE OPIUM FIELDS
'Evening in the Opium Fields' recalls an experience Jacob describes in a letter from February 1896: 'I came out into a field of opium poppies, mainly rose pink with fringed petals, and growing among what looked like young barley; intersecting this, ran little irrigating channels that caught the evening light' (*DLI*, p. 33). Later, Jacob describes another trip to the opium fields:

> Rode in the evening to the opium fields, now in their glory, a carpet stretching for acres and acres in a mass of colour, crimson, purple, rose-pink and white mixed with the greyish green of the leaves, and paddy birds, dead white, wandering among them. Central India is the land of poppies. (*DLI*, p. 56)

V. 'GOD IS GREAT'
'"God is Great"' reflects upon Jacob's interaction with Muslims while in India. Her letter to her mother in Septem-

ber 1898 describes watching evening prayers in a Muslim temple in Bhopal, India:

> We got out at the Jamma Musjid, a large mosque, just as the sun was setting and it was the prayer hour. [...] We went up and looked through a door into a court where, with their faces turned to Mecca, knelt or stood or lay about four hundred men. On the tower above them the tall minarets were topped with gilded balls; the sun struck on them and on the warm stone and the white pigeons flew about like flashes; just in front of us, inside the door through which we looked, a young man in a ragged shirt and trousers lifted his hands to his head and cried in a voice that rang over the sounds of the city outside. 'Allah! illah Allah!' We stood as near the door as we dared and listened to his high wild voice. The kneeling men prostrated themselves. (*DLI*, p. 138)

VII. CHERRY-BLOSSOM AT DAGSHAI
Dagshai is located in northern India in the present-day state of Himachal Pradesh.

SONGS OF ANGUS (1915)

SA marks a shift away from the ornamented poetry of V to simpler poems featuring greater use of personae, frequently of rural men and women. Jacob's poems of exile feature strongly in this volume, including 'Craigo Woods' and 'The Gean-Trees'. Many poems in SA appeared first in *Country Life*. Three poems – 'The Tod', 'Logie Kirk' and 'The Jacobite Lass' – first appeared in Jacob's 1911 novel *Flemington*.

John Buchan, in his preface to SA, contends that 'its chief note is longing, like all the poetry of exiles, a chastened melancholy which finds comfort in the memory of old unhappy things as well as of the beatitudes of youth' (p. ix). SA met with acclaim and was particularly popular among expatriates. The review in the *Scotsman* suggests that 'there is no weak number in the book', claiming, 'small though it be, the volume has in it a charming vitality of its own'.

An unpublished comic poem by Jacob to John Murray,

SA's publisher, sheds light upon her impatience to get the volume published. She writes:

> Dear Maister Murray,
> I'll thank ye to hurry,
> Or I shall say scurri-
> Lous things aboot you;
> For folks here amang us
> Think your conduct is wrangous
> And ma poems o' Angus
> Are lang ower-due.
>
> It's twa years, 'tis a fact,
> Syne ye signed the contract,
> So I'll thank ye to act
> In a proper-like way.
> I've ma living to gain,
> Get yon buikie in train,
> And I'll aye remain,
> Yours sincerely V. J. (NLS, MS 27413, folio 51, no year)

TAM I' THE KIRK

'Tam i' the Kirk', *Country Life*, 12 November 1910, p. 668.

Colin Milton in 'Modern Poetry in Scots before MacDiarmid' suggests that 'much' of the 'appeal' of 'Tam i' the Kirk' lies in 'the way in which it communicates erotic excitement'. He notes:

> The association between the rose and female sexuality is a very old one in the European literary tradition, of course, and the connection between them is made in the third stanza, where the speaker reflects that 'nane but the reid rose kens what my lassie gied him— / It and us twa'. It was this teasing frankness about sex, so familiar in the folk tradition, together with the fact that the poet celebrates the erotic in opposition to a religious tradition which is made to seem selfish and repressive in comparison, which made it appeal to [C. M.] Grieve. (p. 32)

One of many Scottish ballads associating roses and sexuality is 'Sweet Willie and Fair Annie', in which Willie puts a rose 'in Annie's lap', telling her 'the bonniest to the bonniest fa's, / hae, wear it for my sake' (Hay, p. 113).

In 'Tam i' the Kirk', in addition to the tension between Tam's desire and the teachings of the church, one also can see what Dorothy McMillan calls 'the weight of earlier stories of love' in Jacob's work. She concludes: 'the cry with which the poem ends is the voice of a male lover, but it is also the expression of a woman's repressed desire' (p. 49).

'The Baltic Brigs': Jacob often refers to the Baltic in her poetry. The North-East of Scotland has many trade connections to countries around the Baltic.

THE HOWE O' THE MEARNS
'Howe o' the Mearns', *Cornhill*, February 1910, p. 210 and 'Howe o' the Mearns', *Living Age*, 9 April 1910, p. 66.

Janet Caird notes that the 'subject' of 'The Howe o' the Mearns' 'is banal enough [...] but the banality is redeemed by the Scots, used with great skill, and the haunting melody of the last line of each verse' ('The Poetry of Violet Jacob and Helen B. Cruickshank', p. 32).

In one letter, Jacob tells her friend of a note she received from 'a man who gives lectures at the Young Men's Guild of St Columba', a church in London. She relates with some pride:

> He was speaking on the Scottish Vernacular and said how well worth preserving it is and a young man called out that that was quite true, if only to enable people to read 'The Howe of the Mearns'. Wasn't that nice? (NLS, Acc. 11214, *c.* 22 January, no year)

THE LANG ROAD
'Lang Road', *Current Literature*, 41 (1906), 496–7 and 'Lang Road', *Living Age*, 15 December 1906, p. 642.

As the publication dates suggest, Jacob wrote 'The Lang Road' *before* she lost her son in World War One. The line 'the een o' love can pierce the mools that hide a sodger's grave' (line 25) eerily prefigures elements of her poems from MSA.

THE BEADLE O' DRUMLEE
'The Beadle of Drumlee', *Country Life*, 18 January 1913, p. 76.

Marion Lochhead calls 'The Beadle o' Drumlee' 'pure comedy without too bitter a satire' ('Violet Jacob', p. 132). She also suggests that the poem 'would have delighted Burns' ('Feminine Quartet', p. 23).

THE WATER-HEN
'The Muirhen', *Country Life*, 21 September 1912, p. 375.

According to *Notes on the Folk-Lore of the North-East of Scotland*, the water-hen's call 'is interpreted as "Come hame – come hame"' (Gregor). In 'The Water-Hen' the speaker hears in the call of the water-hen his own thoughts; 'come hame' becomes an ironic, silent refrain in the poem for the speaker who recognises he has lost everything that 'hame' entails: his beloved, his landscape, his sense of hope.

Janet Caird calls 'The Water-Hen' a 'finely constructed poem of a lover's quarrel' ('The Poetry of Violet Jacob and Helen B. Cruickshank', p. 33). Carol Anderson observes that 'this deceptively simple poem gains power from its unobtrusive "echo" effects, created through repetition with variation in the structure, and subtle use of alliteration and assonance' ('Tales of Her Own Countries', p. 354).

The reference to the 'twa mill dams' (line 1) in the poem recalls two real dams near the House of Dun. One of Jacob's friends wrote to her in 1920, referring to the poem by its earlier title:

> I was so enchanted to hear about 'the twa mill dams'. Not that I had ever questioned them for a moment – because, like everything you write, they just were [...] But what makes it lovely to hear about the poem's connection with your old home is that 'The Muir Hen' is my supreme favourite. (NLS, MS 27416, folio 73, c. 15 January 1920)

THE HEID HORSEMAN
'The Heid Horseman', *Country Life*, 17 January 1914, p. 84. Drafts of 'The Heid Horseman' held in the Montrose Library Archives reveal minor changes Jacob made to the poem.

THE GEAN-TREES
'The Gean-Trees', *Country Life*, 27 April 1912, p. 624.

In his preface to SA, John Buchan praises the 'haunting lilt of "The Gean-Trees"' (p. ix). The Sidlaw hills are in Angus. The Vale of Strathmore divides the Scottish Highlands from the Lowlands.

THE TOD
'The Tod' first appeared in Chapter 3 of Jacob's novel *Flemington* (1911), where it is presented as a song sung by the character Skirling Wattie. The fox recurs as a subject in Scottish folk-song: there is a song called 'The Tod' in David Herd's collection, *Ancient and Modern Scottish Songs* (1776).

THE BLIND SHEPHERD
Marion Lochhead claims 'The Blind Shepherd' is 'charged with a grave and measured sadness that never breaks down' ('Violet Jacob', p. 133). Janet Caird similarly argues that Jacob's use of literary Scots

> transforms what could have been a pietistic character study into a moving statement of loss, resignation and hope. 'The Blind Shepherd' is one of a handful of religious poems [...] which make simple statements of faith without mawkishness – no small achievement. They show the restraint which marks all of her poetry to an astonishing extent. ('The Poetry of Violet Jacob and Helen B. Cruickshank', p. 33)

THE DOO'COT UP THE BRAES
Ferryden is a small fishing village in Angus just south of Montrose. Helen Cook observes that Jacob 'recognised the wanderlust that took men in brigantine and schooner "oot-by Montrose" to the Baltic and "roon half the warld"' (p. 617).

LOGIE KIRK
Like 'The Tod' (see above), this first appeared as a song in Chapter 3 of *Flemington*, sung by Skirling Wattie.

THE PHILOSOPHY OF THE DITCH
The Montrose Library Archives hold an earlier draft of 'The Philosophy of the Ditch'. Published eleven years before Hugh MacDiarmid's ground-breaking *A Drunk Man*

Looks at the Thistle (1926), 'The Philosophy of the Ditch' also offers a look at the philosophical musings of a drunken man.

THE LOST LICHT
'The Lost Licht', *Cornhill*, September 1912, pp. 312–13. The *Cornhill* version omits stanza two and stanza six; it also includes several stanzas Jacob modified for publication in SA. The alternate stanzas are reproduced below:

> I sat me by the kirk to greet,   21
> Below the birken tree;
> And syne the fa' o' bairnies' feet
> Cam' through the graves to me.
>
> Oh, white were they! an' ilka wean   25
> That trod the kirkyaird land
> Bore through the darkness o' the streen
> A licht intil its hand.
>
> And aye the can'les flickered pale
> Below the darkened sky,   30
> But the licht was like a broken trail
> When the third wee bairn gae'd by;
>
> For whaur the can'le-flame should be
> Was neither blink nor shine—
> The bairnie turned its face to me   35
> An' I kent that it was mine!

Marion Lochhead calls 'The Lost Licht' 'one of [Jacob's] most moving poems' ('Feminine Quartet', p. 23). Helen Cook praises 'Jacob's ability to convey a sense of the uncanny and the eerie as found in the old Scots ballads', citing 'The Lost Licht' as an example (p. 618). 'The Lost Licht', in addition to poems such as 'The Cross-Road' and others, address a moment in which the living and dead communicate, however fleetingly.

THE LAD I' THE MUNE
'The Lad i' the Mune', *Country Life*, 4 October 1913, p. 439.

THE GOWK
'The Gowk', *Country Life*, 22 November 1913, p. 695.

'The Gowk' and other poems such as 'The Whustlin' Lad', 'Charlewayn' and 'A Widow' sympathetically record the 'wark' women do 'late an' airly at the farm' ('Charlewayn', lines 9–10). L. M. Cumming praises 'The Gowk' for the 'great economy' with which it conjures up 'the farm background, the bustling, harsh-tongued auntie, the niece and her love story in three stanzas' (pp. 40–1). Marion Angus, in 'Scottish Poetry Old and New', praises the 'delicious, sly pawkiness' of the poem that is 'very characteristic of East of Scotland folk' (p. 28).

Hearing the first call of the gowk or cuckoo for the season can bring one luck, according to Scottish folk belief:

> It is considered very lucky indeed to be moving about when the first cuckoo's notes reach the ear. This may perhaps account for the verse 'Gang and hear the gowk yell, Sit and see the swallow flee, See the foal before its mither's 'ee, Twill be a thriving year wi' thee'. (Simpson, p. 11)

THE JACOBITE LASS
The 'white white rose' (line 9) was a symbol of support for the Stuarts during the eighteenth-century Jacobite uprisings. Jacob provides another Jacobite voice in her late poem 'Cairneyside'. This poem first appears as an untitled song in Chapter 16 of *Flemington*, sung by Skirling Wattie.

THE WHUSTLIN' LAD
'The Whistling Lad', *Country Life*, 2 December 1911, p. 804.

An article in the *Saturday Review of Literature* declares that 'The Whustlin' Lad' contains 'many elements that should be a part of real poetry. It lives, breathes, entertains the mind, and moves the heart' (B., p. 224). The poem's irregular line lengths capture the speaker's cheery duplicity as she keeps both her mother and lover at bay.

CRAIGO WOODS
'Craigo Woods', *Cornhill*, November 1913, p. 699, and 'Craigo Woods', *Living Age*, 17 January 1914, p. 130.

'Craigo Woods' is one of Jacob's most popular exile

poems. It describes an area just outside of Dun which many now associate with Jacob herself. In *Octobiography*, Helen Cruickshank writes: 'I now feel Craigo Wood is sacred to Violet Jacob and I have never used the name in my own verse, although this was our nearest and dearest woodland Sunday walk' (p. 14). L. M. Cumming claims that 'the descriptive element is uppermost' in 'Craigo Woods', arguing 'that loving description can bring a Scottish wood in the transfiguring September light before any Scottish reader' (p. 42). This in part explains the poem's popularity. But as Carol Anderson points out: 'Craigo Woods' moves 'beyond mere nostalgia, to explore memory and loss' of the exile ('Tales of Her Own Countries', p. 354). The landscape, Jacob suggests, can be regained only in the exile's death. Janet Caird compares 'Craigo Woods' to Robert Louis Stevenson's 'Blows the Wind on the Moor', noting that both share that 'hope of return at the moment of death' ('The Poetry of Violet Jacob and Helen B. Cruickshank', p. 32). Janet Caird's evocation of Stevenson's poem points to the dark imagery Jacob includes in her otherwise nostalgic poem. Like Stevenson, Jacob, beneath a veneer of nostalgia, includes unexpectedly negative images of home: its 'wraith' (line 16) haunts the speaker, the clouds above are 'greetin'' (line 3), and the trees look like 'ghaists' (line 5).

THE WILD GEESE
'The Wild Geese', *Country Life*, 7 March 1914, p. 327.

L. M. Cumming claims that 'the fierce longing of the exile' in 'The Wild Geese' 'takes on an unbearable poignancy' (p. 44). Joy Hendry agrees, observing that Jacob's 'finest' work 'balances sentiment on a knife edge to create a statement of sometimes heart-rending poignancy'. She upholds 'The Wild Geese' as an example, noting: 'seldom has the longing for the country left been so well expressed' (p. 293).

Folk musician Jim Reid has set 'The Wild Geese' to music; it is available on *I Saw the Wild Geese Flee* (1984).

MORE SONGS OF ANGUS AND OTHERS (1918)

In MSA, Jacob continues to write in literary Scots, this time turning her attention to the subject of war. Stricken with grief at the loss of her son, she nevertheless produced a number of war-related poems for this volume. Some of these poems make for uncomfortable reading today; as Judith Kazantzis notes in *The Virago Book of Women's War Poetry and Verse*, the conjunction of 'sentimentality and patriotism [...] during the Great War years' (p. xxiii) does not always date well; in some poems from this period politics can overwhelm the poetics, making for far less lasting work.

The reviews of *MSA* in the *Scotsman* and the *TLS* largely avoid discussing Jacob's war poems. The *Scotsman* praises the 'neat and daintily humorous rhymes' and the 'pretty vignettes of scenery', noting that *MSA* also has 'many graceful, dreamy poems in a smoothly running standard English that is pleasant in spite of a constant tendency to sadness of feeling'. The *TLS* calls her Scottish poems in the volume 'delightful' (p. 587). Later critics, however, have been less captivated by her war poetry. L. M. Cummings, writing in *Scottish Bookman* in 1935, calls her war writing 'poignant with deep-felt sorrow and a tragic emphasis on the glory and sacrifice of war' but concludes:

> yet they make us faintly uncomfortable. The cry from the heart is still audible, but after twenty years we shrink from the old simplicity of vision and our tired disillusion alike, and are less moved by these poems than by some. (p. 39)

Carol Anderson summarises it best when she calls Jacob's war poems 'mixed in quality' ('Tales of Her Own Countries', p. 354). Certainly, several of Jacob's war poems — some of which do not appear here — are not as crafted as her later work; in many poems appearing in *MSA*, the patriotic message overwhelms the text. As Janet Caird suggests, in these poems, 'one feels the mask is slipping' ('The Poetry of Violet Jacob and Helen B. Cruickshank', p. 33). Nevertheless, in works such as 'The Brig' and 'The Field by the Lirk o' the Hill', she powerfully evokes the losses of war, particularly those sustained by the women left behind. The recognition that the occasional 'glimpse of peace / lies at the heart of pain' suffuses the poems in the volume ('Fringford Brook', lines 29–30).

TO A. H. J.

'A. H. J.' is Jacob's son, Arthur Henry Jacob ('Harry'), who died in World War One. Sarah Bing calls 'To A. H. J.' Jacob's 'most direct' poem about Harry's death: in it Jacob 'addresses him personally and in English, thus lowering the masks of language and narrative personae' (p. 107).

JOCK, TO THE FIRST ARMY

'Jock, to the First Army', *Country Life*, 5 February 1916, p. 163.

Marion Lochhead compares 'Jock, to the First Army' favourably with the work of Rupert Brooke, suggesting that his 'lovely' poem 'The Soldier' 'cannot surpass in force those words of the dead soldier in "Jock to the First Army"' (p. 133).

THE FIELD BY THE LIRK O' THE HILL

'The Field by the Lirk o' the Hill', *Country Life*, 13 May 1916, p. 579.

L. M. Cumming praises the 'touching beauty' of 'The Field by the Lirk o' the Hill' (p. 39). The phrase 'lirk o' the hill' appears in some ballads, particularly 'The Broom of Cowdenknows' (Lyle, pp. 151–5).

MONTROSE

'Montrose', *Country Life*, 23 June 1917, p. 644.

L. M. Cumming claims that 'Montrose' is 'a perfect description of Montrose that in its essence conjures up any Angus town to the exile' (p. 39).

THE ROAD TO MARYKIRK

'The Road to Marykirk', *Country Life*, 8 May 1915, p. 611.

THE BRIG

'The Brig', *Country Life*, 8 December 1917, p. 561.

In many of Jacob's poems, outstretched hands represent the human connection between life and death. In 'The Brig', as in other poems in MSA, the mother assumes the role of soldier in the son's absence; she contemplates the 'Brig o' Dreid' (line 31) between her and her son. The 'Brigg o' Dread' in 'The Lyke-Wake Dirge' spans the border between life and death; crossing it is a terrifying experience. In 'The

Brig', however, Jacob does not focus upon the experience of *crossing* the 'Brig o' Dreid' but rather shows the tremendous optimism of her speaker who is certain she will meet her son again in the 'fields o' life' (line 15).

Sarah Bing observes the speaker's insistence upon the son's presence parallels Jacob's own feelings for her son after his death. She cites one of Jacob's 1917 letters in which Jacob reveals:

> He is *so* near me often. Last night I was made so happy by feeling him beside me – I never know when it is going to happen and sometimes when I expect him to come I am disappointed and again, when I don't expect it, suddenly he is there tho' I cannot see him – but I feel it so strongly. (p. 109, Jacob's emphasis)

THE KIRK BESIDE THE SANDS
'The Kirk Beside the Sands', *Country Life*, 28 August 1915, p. 283.

GLORY
'Glory', *Country Life*, 9 December 1916, p. 694.

THE SHEPHERD TO HIS LOVE
'The Shepherd to His Love', *Country Life*, 15 January 1916, p. 67.

'The Shepherd to His Love' recalls in its title Christopher Marlowe's 'The Passionate Shepherd to His Love', although the tone of Jacob's poem differs: in hers, the speaker does not offer his beloved the material items listed as enticements in Marlowe's poem ('beds of roses / and a thousand fragrant posies') but instead tries to reassure her that 'there's nane to see' them if she will join him outside (line 5). Jacob's speaker concerns himself more with his own frustration, offering only a few lines of praise for his beloved in the final stanza of the poem.

Here Jacob is offering her own version of a pastoral lyric, perhaps reflecting upon the work of earlier poets such as Allan Ramsay (*The Gentle Shepherd*) and Edmund Spenser (*The Shepheardes Calendar*). In Jacob's poem, however, the speaker's boredom breaks to the surface in a flash of petulance at his beloved's 'pranks' (line 17).

A CHANGE O' DEILS
'A Change o' Deils', *Country Life*, 24 July 1915, p. 111.

The 1881 volume *Scottish Proverbs* lists the simplified 'changes are lightsome' among its collected proverbs (Henderson, p. 105); Jacob's version of the proverb is appropriately earthy for her speaker. Here the female speaker is, as L. M. Cumming describes her: 'red-cheeked, sonsy, [and] crudely provocative' (p. 40). Dorothy McMillan suggests that 'A Change o' Deils' in its few lines 'tells a long tale of female naturalness and male rigidity' (p. 49).

THE LAST O' THE TINKLER
'The Last of the Tinkler', *Country Life*, 7 August 1915, p. 183.

Marion Lochhead suggests that 'The Last o' the Tinkler' 'expresses that unbitter weariness of life that only maturity and wisdom can feel' ('Violet Jacob', p. 133). The use of rhyme in the poem adds to its elegiac quality. As in many of Jacob's poems, travellers are 'treated with sympathy' (Cumming, p. 38).

FRINGFORD BROOK
'Fringford Brook', *Country Life*, 25 December 1915, p. 860. Fringford and Hethe are two villages in Oxfordshire.

PRISON
Carol Anderson, in 'Tales of Her Own Countries: Violet Jacob', singles out 'Prison' as one of Jacob's more successful war poems, noting that it 'movingly express[es] a dry, controlled grief' (p. 354).

PRESAGE
'Presage', *Country Life*, 14 October 1916, p. 423.

'Presage' recalls her poems from *V* in its diction and imagery.

THE BIRD IN THE VALLEY
The *TLS* review of *MSA* notes that 'The Bird in the Valley' 'catches well a magical moment of the night' (p. 587).

BACK TO THE LAND
'Back to the Land', *Living Age*, 25 November 1925, p. 450.

In 'Back to the Land', Jacob describes the lives of her speaker's predecessors as:

> Men who have tilled the pasture
> > The writhen thorn beside,
> Women within grey vanished walls
> > Who bore and loved and died. (lines 17–20)

The gender division she relates is not accidental. Jacob links men to production; the land, crisscrossed with plough scars, records the men's labour even though they are no longer alive. In contrast, Jacob associates the women with forbearance, self-sacrificing love, and one inexorable fate: death. Unlike men, they leave no traces behind them. The children and the lives they 'bore' (line 20) are no longer visible. For Jacob, the absence of women in the written historical record must have been frustrating. Dorothy McMillan suggests that Jacob's incorporation of the 'secret narratives of woman' in *The Lairds of Dun* represents an attempt to redress the general omission of women from Scottish history (p. 49).

'Back to the Land', like many poems in MSA, is haunted by the apprehension of spectral figures in the landscape, the 'companies of buried folk' (line 11) the speaker hears all around her.

THE SCARLET LILIES
'The Scarlet Lilies', *Current Literature* 41 (1906), p. 465.
 Carol Anderson calls 'The Scarlet Lilies' 'almost Pre-Raphaelite', noting the way that it 'evoke[s] passion and sexuality' ('Tales of Her Own Countries', p. 354).

FROSTBOUND
'Frost-Bound', *Living Age*, 3 February 1906, p. 258.

'THE HAPPY WARRIOR'
Here Jacob offers her own interpretation of the persona William Wordsworth explored in his poem 'Character of the Happy Warrior'. Wordsworth's 'happy warrior' is self-abnegating, brave and constant; he calls him 'he / that every man in arms should wish to be' (lines 1–2). Wordsworth claims that the 'happy warrior' is one

> who, if he be called upon to face
> Some awful moment to which Heaven has joined
> Great issues, good or bad for human kind,
> Is happy as a Lover; and attired
> With sudden brightness, like a Man inspired;
> And, through the heat of conflict, keeps the law
> In calmness made, and sees what he foresaw;
> Or if an unexpected call succeed,
> Come when it will, is equal to the need. (lines 48–56)

By contrast, Jacob's speaker hardly can be called 'happy'; he is downtrodden and aware of his own insignificance. He does take pleasure, however, in the 'scars' he received in battle, reinterpreting them as 'stars' and a 'crown' (lines 27, 28). Jacob was no doubt acutely aware of the difference between the battles to which Wordsworth alludes in his poem and the mechanised horror of World War One battlefields.

BONNIE JOANN AND OTHER POEMS (1921)

Although *BJ* appeared only three years after *MSA*, the two volumes are quite different in character and content. With her war poems for the most part behind her, Jacob expands her subject matter in *BJ* to include more dramatic monologues, many of which explore the psychology of the outsider: the exile, the traveller, the poor labourer. The intensity of loss and the often raw emotional response to that loss in her 1918 poems diffuse in *BJ*, allowing for a wider emotional range. With frequent references to 'blurred' images ('A Winter Phantasy', line 18), the poems in this volume and those that follow emphasise the difficulty of seeing 'plain' ('Charlewayn', line 31).

Jacob's use of literary Scots in *BJ* continued to garner her praise. The *Scots Pictorial* review of *BJ* calls Jacob 'the last representative of Doric poetry', claiming that Jacob's poetry 'brings new life to the dying muse of the vernacular'; the reviewer writes that her work contains 'the spirit of true poetry' (p. 521). Although this review suggests that Scots as a language was 'dying', in the wider Scottish literary world, the debate over whether there was a 'Renaissance' in Scottish writing was beginning to simmer and the use of Scots was at the centre of that debate. The discussion would erupt more provocatively in the early 1920s through the efforts of C. M. Grieve's alter ego Hugh MacDiarmid. Jacob's involvement in the first volume of *Northern Numbers* (1920) in particular brought attention to her work as part of an existing tradition of poetry in the Scots language.

BONNIE JOANN
'Bonnie Joann', *Country Life*, 1 February 1919, p. 107.
   The *Scots Pictorial* review of *BJ* claims that 'Bonnie Joann' is 'one of the loveliest love lyrics written in any tongue' (p. 521).

THE WIND FRAE THE BALTIC
'The Baltic Brig', *Country Life*, 8 March 1919, p. 243.

THE TRAMP TO THE TATTIE-DULIE
'The Tramp tae the Tattie-Dulie', *Country Life*, 26 June 1920, p. 901.
   In a letter now in the Montrose Library Archives, Jacob sends a copy of 'The Tramp tae the Tattie-Dulie' to her friend James Christison, asking about the accuracy of the language in the poem. She writes:

> I *must* worry you again as I am away here without any reference books and want to send the enclosed to *Country Life*. Will you read this and just send me a line to say if there's anything you think not right in any part of it. Also, particularly – have I spelt the following words right? 'threets' (threats) (or is it *threits*?) 'gutsy' (greedy) – should it be *gutsie*? 'onchanchy' – is that right? – then is it 'neep' (turnip) or *neip*? (c. 4 June, no year, her emphasis)

HALLOWE'EN
'Hallowe'en', *Country Life*, 4 December 1920, p. 716. This version includes the footnote 'in Angus bothies the head horseman's locker stands on the right-hand side of the fire'.
   Hallowe'en in folk tradition is the time when the dead return home for the night, as described in ballads such as 'The Wife of Usher's Well'. According to F. Marian

McNeill's *The Silver Bough: A Study of the National and Local Festivals of Scotland*:

> it was not only the souls of the departed that were abroad on Hallowe'en. [...] The Other-world was temporarily upset; but at Hallowe'en there was more than an upsetting – there was a complete upheaval, and all the denizens of that world were released for the night, free to work weal or woe on those human beings they encountered. (III, p. 13)

With memories of World War One so firmly in the minds of her readers, Jacob here calls up what Helen Cook describes as the 'poignant contemporary sadness' of 'Hallowe'en' in the post-war years (p. 617). Jacob also refers to popular folk activities during Hallowe'en including carrying 'runts o' kail' (line 12) as torches and bobbing for apples (cf. McNeill, *The Silver Bough*, III, pp. 11–42).

THE DAFT BIRD
'The Daft Bird', *Country Life*, 19 July 1919, p. 67.

'KIRRIE'
'Kirrie', *Country Life*, 8 November 1919, p. 575.

The *Scots Pictorial* review of *BJ* calls 'Kirrie' a 'song with a haunting lilt' (p. 521). In 'Kirrie', Jacob gives a townsperson's exaggerated delight with Kirriemuir, although her own fondness for the 'braw, braw toon' (line 17) is evident in letters she wrote explaining her decision to move there at the end of her life.

In a letter now in the Montrose Library Archives, Jacob wrote to James Christison of the Montrose Library about 'Kirrie', asking for his advice. She tells him:

> I have just heard from Mr. Crombie who is working on the Scottish Nat[ional] Dictionary Association inquiring about the word 'bizzar' used by me in the poem 'Kirrie'. They want to incorporate it in the Dictionary, but apparently their correspondent in Angus, and they themselves, have never heard it. I heard it about fifteen years ago and used it because I liked it so much. 'For I doot the bizzar's leein', for it's fules would gang tae London when they kent o' Kirriemuir.' They also ask

whether it is obsolete, or obsolescent. I would not bother with them, were it not that I feel it would be a dreadful pity to have such a fine word left out, if it is authentic? Will you tell me whether you think it *is* authentic, or a corruption of 'besom' and whether, in that case, it is, in your opinion, obsolete? Or obsolescent? [...] My nieces and nephews originally reported the word to me, as used by one of the maids at Dun. (c. 27 June, no year, her emphasis)

Christison responds:

In reference to your interesting query about the word 'bizzar,' I see in the copy of your poem 'Kirrie' in 'Bonnie Joann' you put the meaning of this word as 'jade.' Now I think the form 'bizzar' is a Scottish form of the word 'buzzar' similar to what you hear sounding as a call to mill workers to return to their work. It is quite a suitable expression for a loud-tongued, boastful, or as we would say in Scotland, a person give to making a 'blaw.' I think this is quite a feasible theory about the word, but I do not think it is a corruption of the word 'Besom'. I would not say that the word is obsolete, but it is not in common use. If I get any more light upon it I shall let you know.

The *Dictionary of the Scots Language* references 'Kirrie' in its definition of 'bizzar'.

THE END O'T
'The End O't', *Country Life*, 3 January 1920, p. 9.
'The End O't' is one of Jacob's most powerful later poems. Dorothy McMillan offers this precis of 'The End O't':

The poem's speaker is a young woman, pregnant and abandoned; the seeding thistle is the metaphor for her sense of her life being over. But the metaphor is double-edged, for seed has been planted too. The growing evidence that she is no longer a maid suggests that that is by no [means] 'the end o't'. (p. 49)

Five years before Hugh MacDiarmid publishes *A Drunk Man Looks at the Thistle*, Jacob here uses the 'fine braw thistle' (line 1) to symbolise the sexual freedoms of men compared to the restrictive codes of sexual behaviour for women. The poem also functions as a response poem to Robert Burns's 'The Rantin Dog, the Daddy O't' which celebrates male sexual freedom and sees pregnancy not as a burden but as a cause for celebration. My 'Women "Wha' Lauched and Lo'ed and Sinned": Women's Voices in the Work of Violet Jacob and Marion Angus' explores 'The End O't' in more depth.

THE KELPIE
'The Kelpie', *Country Life*, 1 March 1919, p. 221.

As in 'Northern Lichts', Jacob here captures a child's sense of fear at the world around him using a mixture of Christian and pre-Christian references common in folk tales. According to the *Dictionary of Celtic Mythology*, a kelpie is a

> fairy water-creature of Scottish folklore, initially thought to inhabit lonely, fast-moving streams and later any body of water. Usually thought to be a horse, sometimes human, the kelpie is most often described as at least mischievous and more likely malevolent. The creature entices travellers on to its back and then rushes into deep pools to drown them. His tail strikes the water in thunder and he disappears in a flash of lightning. In human form the kelpie is a rough, shaggy man who leaps behind a solitary rider, gripping and crushing him. (Mackillop, p. 281)

BALTIC STREET
'Baltic Street', *Country Life*, 17 April 1920, p. 505.

Baltic Street runs roughly parallel to the High Street of Montrose. Scurdyness is a lighthouse outside Montrose.

BAILIE BRUCE
'Bailie Bruce', *Country Life*, 12 April 1919, p. 412.

L. M. Cumming in the *Scottish Bookman* comments upon the 'shrewdness' and 'local truth' of 'Bailie Bruce', explaining that 'the substitution of bags for plates brought about his downfall, and "His ae bawbee" was ignominiously revealed to a delighted congregation' (pp. 37–8).

CHARLEWAYN
'Chairlewain', *Country Life*, 15 February 1919, p. 161.

Charles's Wain is 'an old popular name for the seven bright stars of the Great Bear [...] The constellation forms the rough outline of a wheelbarrow or rustic wagon and the name is held to be a corruption of "Churl's Wain" (peasant's cart)' (Evans, p. 213). The song mentioned in the poem's epigraph refers, as does the speaker of 'The Lowland Ploughman', to the tradition of moving from one farm to another during Martinmas. In 'Charlewayn', the speaker's lament recalls the contemporaneous poem 'The End O't'.

THE GANGEREL
'The Gangerel', *Country Life*, 11 June 1921, p. 713.

THE TINKLER'S BALOO
'The Tinkler's Baloo', *Country Life*, 24 January 1920, p. 99.

THE BANKS O' THE ESK
'The Banks o' the Esk', *Country Life*, 22 February 1919, p. 187.

INVERQUHARITY
'Inverquharity', *Country Life*, 17 September 1921, p. 345.

FAUR-YE-WEEL
'Faur-Ye-Weel', *Country Life*, 2 April 1921, p. 390.

Carol Anderson calls 'Faur-Ye-Weel' a 'fine drinking-song' ('Tales of Her Own Countries', p. 354); it is one of several poems Jacob seems to have written with music in mind (cf. 'The Tinkler's Baloo').

THE SHADOWS
'The Shadows' explores the exile's longing for home, and unlike most of Jacob's exile poems, it is in English. The specific, named elements of Scots-language exile poems such as 'Craigo Woods' are replaced here by abstracted, formless 'shadows' (line 2). In 'The Shadows' Jacob disembodies the speaker so that he (or she) too is a 'shadow' (line 4); the speaker is referenced only through parts of the body (the 'heart', line 11) and the movement of that body ('footsteps', line 7). The speaker becomes more like the 'wraiths' (line

16) haunting the beloved landscape in 'Craigo Woods' than a figure of substance. The poem suggests that the exile will 'not return' even in death to that landscape (line 12).

A WINTER PHANTASY
'Moonstruck', *Country Life*, 8 January 1921, p. 48.

Comparing Hugh MacDiarmid's 1925 poem 'Au Clair de la Lune' and Jacob's 'A Winter Phantasy' (1921) yields interesting parallels. Although the poems differ in language and intent, the imagery of MacDiarmid's poem – in the third section in particular – recalls that of Jacob's earlier poem. Although clearly there are differences between 'Au Clair de la Lune' and 'Winter Phantasy' (which is not a strong work), one should not overlook the similarities: both consider earth from an extra-terrestrial perspective; both reflect upon the eerie light and movement of the planets; and both contemplate the relationship between memory and time.

TWO NEW POEMS (1924)

Porpoise Press published *TNP* – with its illustrations by A. Mason Trotter – as part of its broadsheet series. The *Scotsman* review called the series 'a courageous local literary undertaking, and one deserving of encouragement'. It noted that 'some work of genuine accomplishment has been presented in the course of the series, and it is worthily rounded off by two fine poems by Mrs. Violet Jacob'. The broadsheet included 'Rohallion' and 'The Little Dragon' (not reproduced here), a less successful poem that recalls Jacob's earliest work in its heavily embroidered imagery.

Jacob was excited to be involved with the broadsheet series but anxious about her ability to produce new work quickly. In a letter dated 8 October (no year), Jacob tells Roderick Watson Kerr of the Porpoise Press that she would 'so like' to appear in the 'print series' and promises him that she will send him more work (NLS, Acc. 5756, folder three). In another letter she tells him that she has 'nothing' in 'either Scots or English at the moment and [I] feel as if I never could write a verse again'. She concludes: 'But this feeling, which I often get, will go in time [...] when I can send you anything else I will. I'll manage it somehow in time

[...] I really will send you something in *time*' (NLS, Acc. 5756, folder three, c. 9 February, no year, her emphasis).

Marion Angus, when approached by Roderick Watson Kerr to contribute to their broadsheet series, wrote back with typical humility:

> The Broadsheet is beautifully got up in every way and Violet Jacob's work[,] it goes without saying[,] is almost too high a standard for me to have much hope of writing anything good enough to be published in the same periodical along with hers. (NLS, Acc. 5756, no date)

ROHALLION
Rohallion is in Perthshire. Jacob signs a 1932 letter written from Rohallion (NLS, MS 9997, folios 37–8, c. 30 October 1932).

'Rohallion' is one of Jacob's more sentimental depictions of an exile's longing for home and as such is less effective than 'Craigo Woods' or 'The Wild Geese'. 'Rohallion' was not without appreciative readers, however. The *Scotsman*, in its review of *TNP*, called 'Rohallion' an 'essay in the Doric', noting that it 'voices the reflections of a philosophic tramp [...] conscious of the pull which will draw him back again to the district which he loves'.

THE NORTHERN LIGHTS AND OTHER POEMS (1927)

NL is a book of extremes: it features some of Jacob's most accomplished poetry, including her finest dramatic monologues and dialogues; *NL* also includes some of her least successful verse. These few poems which are either overly sentimental or exhibit a false jollity do not appear here for they represent Jacob's least-crafted work. In *NL*, she continues to explore human psychology, considering in particular the motivations of frustrated women with few opportunities to improve their lives.

NL was well reviewed. In part, reviewers responded to Jacob's evocation of landscape and her depiction of the lives of people within the North-Eastern landscape. The review in the *TLS* argues: 'No one has a better right than Mrs. Jacob to sing the praise of the Howe of the Mearns and the Braes of Angus', adding that 'her notes never ring truer than when she is inspired by the genius of that delectable land which stretches along by the spurs of the Grampians, in sight at once of the mountains and the sea' (p. 843). The *Scotsman* review addressed Jacob's 'happy knack of concentrating in a few stanzas the whole life of a countryside, the whole past and future of the person she delineates' and emphasised 'her flair for seizing upon a characteristic phrase which will illuminate the existence of the people of her poems' ('Three Scottish Poets').

NL is also marked by a continuing interest in 'sic-like things' that are 'past the sicht o' muckle men' ('The Northern Lichts', lines 23, 24); the liminal state she calls in 'Hallowe'en' the place 'atween the dark an' caun'le licht' (line 25) reappears in several poems in NL. The *TLS* review of NL refers to these as 'her excursions into the eerie', noting:

> Scottish poetry has always been at its best in matter of gramayre; and in such poems as 'The Northern Lichts', 'The Rowan', 'The Cross-Roads', Mrs. Jacob displays a delicacy of insight and a subtlety of rhythm which recall the work of Miss Marion Angus. (p. 843)

Ultimately, Jacob's work in NL exhibits what the *Scots Observer* calls 'a lapidary touch' (p. 14): the careful depiction of places and the people within those places.

THE NORTHERN LICHTS
'The Northern Lights', *Country Life*, 13 August 1921, p. 183.

As in 'The Jaud' and 'The Cross-Roads', among others, Jacob here uses the dialogue format common in Scottish ballads. Using two voices enables Jacob to present the event from two perspectives. In 'The Northern Lichts', Jacob explores a child's awareness of a world that is 'past the sicht o' muckle men' (line 23); she presents two different responses to the eponymous northern lights: one by the father, who sees them only as a beautiful natural phenomenon, and one by his child who sees in the lights reminders of the 'ghaists o' deid men' haunting his imagination (line 15). Carol Anderson suggests that Jacob's use of the dialogue form is 'perhaps most touching and chilling when it is between child and adult' as in 'The Northern Lichts' ('Tales of Her Own Countries', p. 354). The imagery of 'The Northern Lichts' echoes some of her exile poems but with a marked difference: in 'The Northern Lichts' the landscape the child sees is haunted not by memory but by the fear of the 'ghaists' of those who have died (line 15).

THE NEEP-FIELDS BY THE SEA
'The Neep Fields by the Sea', *Country Life*, 2 June 1923, p. 772.

Helen Cook claims that Jacob wrote 'The Neep-Fields by the Sea' when she 'was on her way to India' (p. 618). While this poem is not among Jacob's most successful poems, Janet Caird argues that 'The Neep-Fields by the Sea' 'combines nostalgia, an evocation of landscape and humour with much skill' ('The Poetry of Violet Jacob and Helen B. Cruickshank', p. 32). In 'The Neep-Fields by the Sea' Jacob breaks the otherwise regular stanza length in the poem's final stanza by extending it by two extra lines. This emphasises the disruptive force of the speaker's whimsical (and macabre) desire to return home in death – not to be buried in a grave but rather to serve as a 'tattie-dulie for fleggin' craws' (line 25).

THE ROWAN
Traditionally, rowans were considered 'a potent charm against witchcraft and evil spells' and were 'commonly planted at the door of the homestead to "keep the witches away"' (McNeill, *The Silver Bough*, I, p. 77). Sarah Bing notes that 'throughout all Jacob's work there runs an element of the supernatural, of a world beyond that of the living' (p. 100). Even to contemporary readers, Jacob's evocation of the supernatural is effective; writing nearly seventy years after *NL* appeared, columnist James O'Hagan recalls 'sleepless childhood nights after reading the atmospheric Violet Jacob poem which finishes with the devastating "For the warlock's livin' yet—But the rowan's deid!"'

THE LICHT NICHTS
'The Licht Nichts', *Country Life*, 6 October 1923, p. 441.

THE JAUD
In 'The Jaud', Jacob refers to the practice of burying marginalised community members at the far edge – or even

outside the walls of – the church yard. The poem, like 'The Northern Lichts', uses a dialogue format. In 'Modern Poetry in Scots before MacDiarmid', Colin Milton points out that there is no 'interpretative commentary' in the poem; readers must decipher each speaker's identity. He claims this poem 'has the spare power of the best ballad work' (p. 32). Dorothy McMillan points out that the poem is 'less sanguine about female choice – it contains rather narratives of lost opportunity. [...] The unavailable alternative life of the 'jaud' teases the reader – it must have been unhappy, it may not have been dull' (p. 49). Colin Milton also observes that 'despite its traditional appearance, "The Jaud" reflects that questioning of traditional conceptions of women's social and sexual place and exploration of female identity which is a characteristically modern preoccupation' (p. 33).

My 'Women "Wha' Lauched and Lo'ed and Sinned": Women's Voices in the Work of Violet Jacob and Marion Angus' and Colin Milton's 'Modern Poetry in Scots before MacDiarmid' explore 'The Jaud' in more depth.

THE DEIL

The devil's claims about his life in 'The Deil' recall the romanticised portrayal of travellers in Jacob's earlier work (including 'Beyond the Walls'). Similarly, the speaker's disenchantment with her old life after she meets the devil echoes 'Charlewayn', where the speaker's sexual experiences make her impatient with her familiar domestic routine. In 'The Deil', the speaker's conclusions surprise readers: now that she's met the devil (literally or metaphorically), no other man will do.

THE HELPMATE

The dour speaker in 'The Helpmate' – loath to dance or sing for fear of 'pleasurin' the deil' (line 8) – serves as a foil for the speaker in 'The Deil'; she, unlike the speaker of 'The Deil', accepts her status as 'helpmate'. She claims to be 'wiselike' (line 12) and 'mild' (line 14) but she threatens her future husband with rough treatment if he misbehaves. The poem's structure reinforces her claims. The line lengths remain regular until the final stanza; here, where the speaker admonishes her fiancé not to come home drunk,

Jacob extends the lines to mimic the increased pitch and velocity of the speaker's words. Janet Caird attributes the poem's narrative quality to the 'novelist's approach to character', suggesting that the poem 'has a whole novel in twenty-five lines' ('The Poetry of Violet Jacob and Helen B. Cruickshank', p. 33).

STEENHIVE
The town described here is Stonehaven, also known locally as Steenhive, which is located in the Mearns. The final line of 'Steenhive', as in 'The Cross-Roads', reveals the identity of the speaker.

THE GUIDWIFE SPEAKS
In 'The Guidwife Speaks', as in many of Jacob's poems in women's voices, one finds a critique of the rigid gender roles that reduce both men and women to caricatures. Sarah Bing explains that in 'The Guidwife Speaks' 'the handsome man the guidwife married has become a surly and taciturn companion'; she notes that nevertheless, he is 'a companion all the same' (p. 106). The poem's title suggests that the speaker, like her husband, is frustrated into silence by their unhappy coexistence. The poem becomes her one speech, spoken after a long silence, about her feelings of loss and loyalty.

DONALD MACLANE
'The Tinkler Wife', *Country Life*, 2 December 1922, p. 700, and 'The Tinkler Wife', *Scottish Chapbook*, 1 (1923), p. 330.
  Jacob offers a dark vision of social restrictions upon women in 'Donald Maclane' by exploring the life of a woman who has left home for the 'road that has ne'er an end' (line 22). The poem shares many characteristics with 'The End O't': both are addressed to the male lover; both express regret commingled with acceptance; both explore the relationship between shame and self-expression. In 'Donald Maclane', Jacob pushes the dialogue further by relating the narrative of a woman who exists in the outermost peripheries of society. Lured away by a traveller, the speaker perhaps had imagined once she, as the speaker of Jacob's early poem 'The Call' states, would go 'out, out across the threshold' and 'into the night, the sighing, luring

night' (lines 21–2). Instead, she realises that 'fules think lichtly when fules are young / tae pu' the nettle and no be stung' ('Donald Maclane', lines 13–14). Janet Caird calls 'Donald Maclane' a 'bleak little tale of a girl seduced by a tinker', noting that it is 'told with no false sentiment' ('The Poetry of Violet Jacob and Helen B. Cruickshank', p. 33). Unlike 'The Tinkler's Baloo', 'Donald Maclane' suggests that the 'rovin' trade' (line 32) is marked by instability and serious deprivation rather than adventure.

THE CROSS-ROADS
'The Cross Roads', *Country Life*, 1 September 1923, p. 269.

As in 'The Northern Lichts' and 'The Jaud', Jacob uses the dialogue form in 'The Cross-Roads'. The poem's success lies in her decision to withhold critical information about the identity of one of the speakers until the poem's final lines. Janet Caird writes that 'The Cross-Roads' gives readers 'an authentic *frisson*'; she suggests that Jacob here 'is touching on a strain deep in Scottish poetry' ('The Poetry of Violet Jacob and Helen B. Cruickshank', p. 32).

THE SCOTTISH POEMS OF VIOLET JACOB (1944)

SPVJ collected much of Jacob's poetry in Scots in one volume. Dedicated to 'the comrade beyond', the volume is marked by war-time austerity with no introduction or preface; it includes nearly seventy of her poems, giving an interesting if one-sided introduction to her work. Notable omissions from the volume include 'Charlewayn', 'The Lost Licht', 'The Deil' and 'The Banks o' the Esk'.

The *TLS* review of *SPVJ* claims that Jacob 'needs no commendation as a vernacular poet', suggesting that 'in content her verse is as racy and homespun as is its idiom'; it adds: 'there is plenty' of 'straight speaking' and 'tenderness and humour too' (p. 191). The *Scotsman* also focused upon her use of Scots and observed that 'the title of her collected poems in Scots is a reminder that Mrs. Jacob has written in English as well, yet nothing that she has done in English, excellent as her technique in this medium is, has found the same favour as her Doric'. Noting that 'Jacob stands high in popular esteem', the *Scotsman* review concludes that 'above all, the national note, with its foundation in local patriotism, is strong' ('Poems in Scots').

CAIRNEYSIDE
'Cairneyside', *The Deeside Field*, 6 (1933), p. 1.
   Joy Hendry suggests that 'Cairneyside' 'achieve[s] a lyric expression indicative of high poetic achievement' (p. 293). The poem revisits Jacobite history, an object of interest in both her fiction (in particular her novel *Flemington*) and her poetry (cf. the less successful early poem 'The Jacobite Lass').

UNCOLLECTED POEMS

THE BARLEY
'The Barley', *Living Age*, 13 January 1906, p. 66.
   'The Barley' recalls Robert Burns's 'The Rigs o' Barley'; in Jacob's poem, however, the speaker's recollections of his lover are tempered by the presence of the 'low mound lying by a standing stone' (line 23).

BINDWEED
'Bindweed', *Country Life*, 25 January 1919, p. 81.
   Bindweed is a fast-spreading weed, but in 'Bindweed' Jacob describes it as a reminder of innocent childhood days.

Glossary

English glosses for selected Scots words and phrases used in Angus and Jacob's poems are provided here; in some cases, the writer originally provided glosses for particular words and these are incorporated here with additional information drawn from several Scots dictionaries: *Jamieson's Dictionary of the Scottish Language* (1895), the *Concise Scots Dictionary* (1985), and the *Dictionary of the Scots Language* (2004), an online source that unites the *Dictionary of the Older Scottish Tongue* and the *Scottish National Dictionary* (http://www.dsl.ac.uk/dsl/index.html).

A

abune: above, over
aiblins: perhaps, sometimes
aipple-ringie: southernwood
airt: direction, point of compass
arn-tree: alder
Auld Hornie: nickname for the devil

B

bairn: child
baith: both
baloo: lullabye
beck: curtsy or bow
ben: in, especially in the inner part of a house
bent: moor or open land
bield: protection, shelter
bien: pleasant, well-kept
bigg: to build
biggit: built or furnished
billie: good companion or comrade
birk: birch tree
birl: in music, a trill or whirring sound
bit: small piece or portion
bizzar: headstrong, obstinate woman
blink: beam
bodle: small coin

bogle: ghost or bugbear; also: scarecrow
brae: hillside; also the bank of a river or lake
braid: broad
braw: fine or beautiful
braws: finery
bree: brow
brig: bridge; also, a ship
brose: porridge mixture sometimes supplemented with butter, salt or broth
brunt: burned or destroyed by fire
bubbly-jock: turkey
burn/burnie: stream or brook
buss: bush or thicket of low-lying plants
but an' ben: two-room cottage
byre: shelter for cattle

C

caird: a traveller; used pejoratively to mean a rough person
callant: fellow, person, young man
caller: fresh
cankered: cross, cranky
cannie/canny: cautious, careful; also, clever
cantie: lively, pleasant, cheery
carle: fellow, old man
cauldrife: cold, chilly
causey: causeway, paved path
causey-croon: middle of the street
chaumer: room
cheughit: choked
chiel: young man or fellow; also, a child
chitter: to tremble or shiver with the cold or fear; to chatter
clachan: hamlet, small village
clock: beetle
clood: cloud
clour: to knock
corbie: raven
corp': corpse
couped/coupit: overturned, upset
couthie: pleasant, agreeable or sympathetic

craig: throat
cratur: creature
croodlin': cooing (of a dove)
croon: crown
crusie: oil lamp
curcuddoch: close together or side by side

D

daft: foolish, stupid, silly
daunder: to wander or walk aimlessly
deave: to deafen or annoy
dee: to die
deid: dead
deil: devil
ding: to strike heavily
div: do
doited: foolish or confused, muddled
doo: dove, rock pigeon
doo'cot: dovecote
douce: sweet or pleasant
dowie: dismal, dreary, melancholy
draigon: paper kite
dree: to endure, suffer, bear
drookit/droukit: drenched, soaked, sodden with moisture
drouthy: dry or thirsty
dune: said of people, sallow or dark-complexioned; dun; also, done, finished
dunt: heavy blow

E

ee (plural: **een**)**:** eye
eident: busy, industrious, diligent
eneuch: enough, sufficient

F

fare: to go on one's way
fash: trouble, bother or inconvenience
fatna: what (regional expression associated with Aberdeenshire)

feat: clever, graceful
fecht: a fight; also: to fight
fell: fierce, ruthless, or cruel
fit: foot
fleer: mocking look or sneer
fleggit: scared, frightened
flit: to move or shift from one place to another
floor/floorin: flower/flowering
foo: how
fou: drunk
foumart: ferret, weasel
freit: an omen or a superstition
fustle: to whistle; also fuss, commotion, rustling noise

G

gang: to walk
gangrel/gangerel: vagabond, tramp
gar: to make or cause
gean: wild cherry tree
girn: to grin in a grotesque manner
gled: kite, bird of prey
gloaming: twilight, dusk
golach: beetle
gowk: cuckoo
greet (past tense: grat): to weep, mourn, lament
groat: a small coin
guizard/guiser: a mummer or person in costume

H

haar: a cold mist, usually from the sea
haim: part of a horse's harness
hairst: harvest
hale: whole
happed/happit/hapt: covered, wrapped around, sheltered
harken: to listen or eavesdrop
haud: to hold
haud yer whisht: hush
haugh/hawe: low-lying ground, often by a river
haver: to speak nonsense
hech: to pant or breathe uneasily

herp: harp
het: hot
hindmaist: last, in the rear
hirplin': limping
hoolet/howlet: owl
howe: hollow
howff: haunt, meeting place
howm: flat ground by a river; haugh

I

ill-faured: unattractive, ugly, ill-favoured
ill-gittit: ill-natured
ingle: hearth

J

jaud: jade or hussy; obstinate woman
jimp: slender
jo/joe: a sweetheart or lover

K

keek: peep or glance
ken (past tense: kent)**:** to know or recognise
kep: to meet
kirn: to churn
kist: chest or large box
kistit: buried, coffined
knowe: knoll or hill
kye: cow

L

lair: grave
lane: alone, by himself/herself
lang syne: long ago
lauch: to laugh
lave: remainder or rest
laverock: skylark
leal: faithful or loyal
licht: light

lichtsome: light-hearted, cheerful
lift: sky
lilt: a tune or song
limmer: scoundrel; whore; generally, a term of abuse
ling: grasses, heather
link: to walk arm in arm or pass one's arm through another's; to move quickly or briskly
links: sandy ground near the sea
linn: the pool below a waterfall
lirk: a hollow or fold in a hill
loan: strip of common or waste land
loon: a boy; a rogue or wretch; can range in meaning from 'scamp' to 'worthless scoundrel'
loorin': threatening, overcast
lowe: glow or flame of a fire
lowse: to let go
loup: to jump or leap
lug: ear
lum: chimney

M

maist: most, almost
maun: must, should, be required to
mavis: song-thrush
merle: blackbird
mickle/muckle: great, much, large in bulk or size
mirk: darkness
mool: loose soil (especially after being cultivated)

N

neep: turnip
niffer: to barter or trade

O

old-farrand: old-fashioned, antiquated
onding: heavy downpour (of rain or snow)

P

pailing: fencing
pawmies: canings or beatings
pearie/peerie: child's spinning (sometimes whistling) top
pechin': panting
plack: small coin
plaid: a length of cloth, usually worn as a shawl by women
poke: pocket
pollis: police
pow: head
preen: metal pin
puddock-stule: toadstool

Q

quean/queyn: a woman, usually unmarried

R

rashes: rushes
rauch: rough
rax: to stretch (often after sleeping)
redd: to prepare or clean
reistle: to rustle or to move noisily through
rodden: the rowan berry
runkle: wrinkle or crease
runt: dried-up plant stalk

S

sain: to bless, protect
sark: shirt or shift
screich/skreich: shriek or screech
shaw: wood or thicket
sheilin': shelter, protection
sheltie: Shetland pony
shilpit: weak or feeble
shoon: shoes
sic: such, this
siller: silver
silly: helpless, weak or delicate
skail: to disperse or scatter

GLOSSARY

skelp: to strike or beat
skep: hive
skilly: skillful, adept
skirl: to shout or scream
sma'-bookit: of slight or small stature, small in bulk
smoor: to suffocate, smother
sna/snaw: snow
sneck: latch
snibbet: locked, latched
sough: to rustle, whisper, sigh
spae-wife: fortune-teller
spate: a flood or elevated water level
speel/speil: to climb or clamber up, to ascend
speer/speir: to ask information of
spunk: spark
steading: the site where farm buildings stand
steek: to shut or shut out
steekit: locked, shut
steen: small pebble
steer: bustle or disturbance
stirk: young cow
stookit (grain): cut and bundled sheaves of grain
stoop: support or post
stoun: sharp pang
strae: straw
straik: to stroke, touch or rub
strang: strong
strang-nieved: strong in the hands
straucht: straight
sweir: reluctant, loath

T

tattie-dulie: scarecrow
tattie-liftin': harvesting potatoes
tawse: leather strap or thong
tear-begrutten: tear-stained, marked from weeping
tent (as in 'tak' tent'): to notice, to pay attention to
teuchit: lapwing
the streen: yesterday, yesterday evening
theek: cover or roof; thatch
thole: to suffer or endure

thrawn: twisted or crooked; also, obstinate
timmer: timid, bashful
tocher: dowry
tod: fox
toom: empty
toon: town
toorie: topknot or pom-pom on a hat
traivel: to go by foot
twine: to separate (but it can also mean to join)
tyne (past tense 'tint'): to lose, forfeit

U

unchancy: unlucky, unfortunate

W

wae: woeful or wretched
wale: abundance or choice
wame: stomach or belly
wark: work
warslin': wrestling, grappling
waukenin': waking, arousing; can also indicate a reproof
waur: worse
wean: child
weepies: ragweed
weet: wet, damp, rainy
weird: fate
whaup: curlew
wheen: a small amount, a bit
wheep: a shrill cry or whistle
whinny: covered with gorse
whumml'd: overturned
windy-sneck: window latch
wrack: wreck, especially of a ship
wud: wild

Y

yett: gate
yont: beyond, across
yowe: ewe

Bibliography

Marion Angus

Selected Volumes

Angus, Marion, *Christabel's Diary* (Arbroath: Buncle, 1899)
—, *The Lilt and Other Verses* (Aberdeen: Wyllie, 1922)
—, *Lost Country and Other Verses* (Glasgow: Gowans and Gray, 1937)
—, 'Robert H. Corstorphine: 1874–1942' in *Robert H. Corstorphine: 1874–1942* (Arbroath: Buncle, c.1942), pp. 3–5
—, *Round About Geneva* (Arbroath: Buncle, 1899)
—, *Sheriff Watson of Aberdeen: The Story of His Life, and His Work for the Young* (Aberdeen: Daily Journal, 1915)
—, *The Singin' Lass* (Edinburgh: Porpoise Press, 1929)
—, 'Scottish Poetry Old and New', in *The Scottish Association for the Speaking of Verse: Its Work for the Year 1927–1928* (Edinburgh: Constable, 1928), pp. 18–29
—, *Sun and Candlelight* (Edinburgh: Porpoise Press, 1927)
—, *The Tinker's Road and Other Verses* (Glasgow: Gowans and Gray, 1924)
—, *The Turn of the Day* (Edinburgh: Porpoise Press, 1931)

Published Posthumously

Angus, Marion, *Selected Poems of Marion Angus*, ed. Maurice Lindsay (Edinburgh: Serif, 1950)

Selected Periodical Work

A[ngus], M[arion], 'The Ghost', *Glasgow Herald*, 5 November 1924, p. 8
Angus, Marion, 'Blanchland: Ancient Home of the White Canons', *SMT*, August 1936, pp. 34–6
—, 'The Broken Brig', *Scots Magazine*, July 1930, p. 307
—, 'The Burden', *Glasgow Herald*, 25 November 1933, p. 10
—, 'Chance Acquaintance', *Glasgow Herald*, 8 May 1934, p. 10
—, 'Christmas Eve' ['Nicht o' Nichts'], *Glasgow Herald*, 23 December 1933, p. 4
—, 'The Cloak' ['The Plaid'], *Glasgow Herald*, 13 January 1932, p. 10
—, 'Desire of Youth' ['Desires of Youth'], *Outlook*, April 1936, p. 40

—, 'The Eerie Hoose', *Scots Magazine*, March 1929, p. 447
—, 'The Faithful Thought' ['The Faithful Heart'], *Glasgow Herald*, 2 February 1934, p. 10
—, 'Foxgloves and Snow', *Glasgow Herald*, 21 July 1934, p. 4
—, 'Green Beads: The Story of a Lost Love', *Pearson's Magazine*, May 1906, pp. 558–62
—, 'Husband and Wife' ['The Widow'], *Glasgow Herald*, 14 March 1932, p. 10
—, 'In a Little Old Town', *Glasgow Herald*, 26 September 1936, p. 4
—, 'The Kiss', *Scots Magazine*, April 1931, p. 13
—, 'The Lilt', *Scottish Chapbook*, 1 (1922), p. 37
—, 'A Link with the Past: A Poet's Stories of Tennyson and Carlyle', *Scots Observer*, 23 January 1930, p. 18
—, 'The Lissome Leddy', *Scots Magazine*, January 1930, p. 283
—, 'The Little Grey Town', *Scots Observer*, 2 January 1930, p. 9
—, 'The Little One' ['In a Mirror'], *Scottish Chapbook*, 1 (1923), p. 257
—, 'Lost Land', *Glasgow Herald*, 7 November 1935, p. 10
—, 'Martha's House', *Glasgow Herald*, 18 August 1932, p. 8
—, 'Mary Coleridge: A Poet Who Casts a Spell', *Scots Observer*, 14 November 1929, p. 14
—, 'Memory's Trick', *Glasgow Herald*, 14 December 1935, p. 10
—, 'The Mother', *Scots Pictorial*, 15 October 1921, p. 342
—, 'A Musician', *Glasgow Herald*, 24 September 1935, p. 8
—, 'Naomi', *Glasgow Herald*, 4 November 1933, p. 4
—, 'News of the World' ['News'], *Glasgow Herald*, 3 December 1931, p. 10
—, 'On A Birthday', *Glasgow Herald*, 29 September 1932, p. 8
—, 'On the Sheep Track' ['The Drove Road'], *Scots Pictorial*, 16 July 1921, p. 30
—, 'Once Long Ago', *Glasgow Herald*, 20 July 1935, p. 4
—, 'Peter and the Churches', *Scots Observer*, 3 October 1929, p. 16
—, 'The Pirate's Wife', *Scots Observer*, 17 December 1931, p. 13
—, 'The Prood Lass', *Scots Magazine*, September 1926, p. 467
—, 'The Queen of Scots Rode' ['Corrichie'], *The Listener*, 20 May 1931, p. 863
—, 'Remembrance Day', *Scots Pictorial*, 12 November 1921, p. 438
—, 'The Same' [The Fox's Skin'], *Scots Pictorial*, 28 January 1922, p. 78
—, 'Singin' Waater', *Nineteenth Century and After*, 106 (1929), pp. 262–3
—, 'So Soft She Sings' ['Mary's Song'], *Scottish Chapbook*, 2 (1923), p. 16

—, 'Some Passages in the History of Letitia Roy', *Century Magazine*, April 1892, pp. 933–44
—, 'The Sorrofu' Lass' ['Barbara'], *Scots Magazine*, August 1927, p. 338
—, 'The Spey-Wife', *Glasgow Herald*, 17 November 1934, p. 4
—, 'The Stranger', *The Modern Scot*, 1 (1930), p. 6
—, 'Tide-Borne' ['When at Familiar Doors'], *Glasgow Herald*, 23 February 1931, p. 10
—, 'Treasure Trove', *Scots Pictorial*, 11 March 1922, p. 226
—, 'Unseen', *Scots Observer*, 5 December 1929, p. 10
—, 'The Wild Lass', *Scots Magazine*, March 1926, p. 430
—, 'Wind and I' ['Withy Wands'], *Glasgow Herald*, 27 February 1926, p. 8
—, 'Wizardry', *Scots Observer*, 27 March 1930, p. 4
—, 'A Woman Sings', *Modern Scot*, 3 (1933), p. 324
—, 'Year's End' [New Year's Morning'], *Glasgow Herald*, 31 December 1931, p. 8
Ogilvie, Arthur [Marion Angus], 'Diary', *Arbroath Guide*, 20 November 1897–12 November 1888, p. 2

Published Without an Author or With Indefinite Provenance

A., M. E., 'After the Storm', *Glasgow Herald*, 28 October 1927, p. 10
'The Dove', *Scots Pictorial*, 8 July 1922, p. 634
'The Lilt', *Scots Pictorial*, 12 August 1922, p. 102

Selected Resources on Angus's Work and Life

Arbroath Herald Annual 1889 (Arbroath: Buncle, 1889)
Cannon, J. A., 'Battle of Corrichie', in *The Oxford Companion to British History*, ed. John Cannon (Oxford: Oxford University Press, 2002), p. 249
Caird, Janet, 'The Poetry of Marion Angus', *Cencrastus*, 25 (1987), pp. 45–7
Christabel, column, *Scots Observer*, 21 January 1928, p. 12
Collecott, Diana, 'What is Not Said: A Study in Textual Inversion', in *Sexual Sameness: Textual Differences in Lesbian and Gay Writing*, ed. Joseph Bristow (London: Routledge, 1992), pp. 91–110
Cruickshank, Helen, 'A Personal Note', in *Selected Poems of Marion Angus*, ed. Maurice Lindsay (Edinburgh: Serif, 1950), pp. xv–xxi
'Death of Rev. Henry Angus, D.D.', *Arbroath Herald*, 22 May 1902, p. 5

Duke, Winifred, letter to the editor, *Scotsman*, 22 August 1946, p. 4, in Scotsman Digital Archive, http://archive.scotsman.com/article.cfm?id=TSC/1946/08/22/Ar00400 [accessed 31 December 2005]

Dunne, J. W., *An Experiment With Time* (London: Black, 1927)

'English Department Prizes for 1880', *Arbroath Herald*, 3 July 1880, p. 1

Gordon, Katherine, 'Liltin' in the "Eerie Hoose": Aspects of Self in the Poetry of Marion Angus', in *Terranglian Territories*, ed. Susanne Hagemann (Berlin: Lang, 2000), pp. 379–88

Graves, Charles, 'The Poetry of Marion Angus', *Chapbook*, 6 (1946), pp. 97, 107

—, 'Scottish Poets of To-Day: Modern Tendencies', *Scots Magazine*, May 1926, pp. 120–4

—, 'Scottish Poets of To-Day: The New Makars', *Scots Magazine*, June 1926, pp. 216–19

H., J., letter to the editor, 24 August 1946, p. 4, in Scotsman Digital Archive, http://archive.scotsman.com/article.cfm?id=TSC/1946/08/24/Ar00400 [accessed 31 December 2005]

H[amilton], [W.], letter to the editor, *Scotsman*, 22 August 1946, p. 4, in Scotsman Digital Archive, http://archive.scotsman.com/article.cfm?id=TSC/1946/08/22/Ar00400 [accessed 31 December 2005]

—, 'The Poetry of the Year', *Scots Observer*, 5 December 1929, p. 12

'In Memoriam: Marion Angus', *Glasgow Herald*, 23 August 1946, p. 3

'In Scots', review of *Selected Poems of Marion Angus*, *Scotsman*, 3 August 1950, p. 7, in Scotsman Digital Archive, http://archive.scotsman.com/article.cfm?id=TSC/1950/08/03/Ar00700 [accessed 31 December 2005]

Kennedy, Adam, review of *The Turn of the Day* by Marion Angus, *Modern Scot*, 2 (1931), pp. 87–9

L., P. W., 'Miss Marion Angus: An Appreciation', *Arbroath Guide*, 31 August 1946, p. 6

Lindsay, Maurice, 'Introduction', in *Selected Poems of Marion Angus*, ed. Maurice Lindsay (Edinburgh: Serif, 1950), pp. ix–xiv

MacDiarmid, Hugh, 'The New Movement in Vernacular Poetry: Lewis Spence, Marion Angus', in *Contemporary Scottish Studies* (London: Parsons, 1926; Edinburgh: Scottish Educational Journal, 1976), pp. 61–3

MacRitchie, John, 'Arbroath's Singin' Lass', in *Arbroath Herald Annual 1996* (Arbroath, 1996), n/p

'Marion Angus: Death of Distinguished Scots Poet', *Arbroath Guide*, 24 August 1946, p. 6

Marwick, William, *Handbook Containing Rules, Programme, etc. of The Reading Guild (Late Ruskin Reading Guild)* (London: Mathews, n/d; Arbroath: Brodie and Salmond, n/d)

McBain, J. M., *Bibliography of Arbroath Periodical Literature and Political Broadsides* (Arbroath: Brodie and Salmond, 1889)

McConnell, Frank D., 'Chronology', in *Byron's Poetry*, ed. Frank D. McConnell (New York: Norton, 1978), pp. 479–81

Milton, Colin, 'Angus, Marion Emily (1865–1946)', in *Oxford Dictionary of National Biography*, ed. H. C. G. Matthew and Brian Harrison (Oxford: Oxford University Press, 2004), http://www.oxforddnb.com/view/article/59069 [accessed 15 August 2005]

Morgan, Edwin, 'Introduction: Lewis Grassic Gibbon and Science Fiction', in *Gay Hunter*, by James Leslie Mitchell (London: Heinemann, 1934; Edinburgh: Polygon, 1989), pp. i–viii

Obituary of Marion Angus, *Glasgow Herald*, 20 August 1946, p. 4

Obituary of Henry Angus, *Aberdeen University Review*, 25 (1937–8), p. 188

'Poetry of 1925', *Scotsman*, 31 December 1925, p. 6, in Scotsman Digital Archive, http://archive.scotsman.com/article.cfm?id=TSC/1925/12/31/Ar00607 [accessed 31 December 2005]

'Porpoise Press Poets', *Scots Observer*, 10 December 1928, p. 15

'Radio Programmes', *Scotsman*, 18 September 1930, p. 14, in Scotsman Digital Archive, http://archive.scotsman.com/article.cfm?id=TSC/1930/09/18/Ar01405 [accessed 31 December 2005]

'Report of the Annual Meeting 1932', in *The Scottish Association for the Speaking of Verse: 1931–33* (Glasgow: Davidson, n/d), p. 33

Review of *The Lilt and Other Verses* by Marion Angus, *Scottish Chapbook*, 4 (1922), p. 116

Review of *Lost Country and Other Verses* by Marion Angus, *Scotsman*, 6 December 1937, p. 13 in Scotsman Digital Archive, http://archive.scotsman.com/article.cfm?id=TSC/1937/12/06/Ar01306 [accessed 31 December 2005]

Review of *Lost Country and Other Verses* by Marion Angus, *Times Literary Supplement*, 15 January 1938, p. 45

Review of *The Singin' Lass* by Marion Angus, *Scotsman*, 15 July 1929, p. 2, in Scotsman Digital Archive, http://archive.scotsman.com/article.cfm?id=TSC/1929/07/15/Ar00201 [accessed 31 December 2005]

Review of *The Singin' Lass* by Marion Angus, *Times Literary Supplement*, 10 October 1929, pp. 798–9

Review of *Sun and Candlelight* by Marion Angus, *Times Literary Supplement*, 2 November 1927, p. 795

Review of *The Tinker's Road and Other Verses* by Marion Angus, *Scotsman*, 12 March 1925, p. 2, in Scotsman Digital Archive, http://archive.scotsman.com/article.cfm?id=TSC/1925/03/12/Ar00206 [accessed 31 December 2005]

Review of *The Tinker's Road and Other Verses* by Marion Angus, *Times Literary Supplement*, 19 February 1925, p. 123

Review of *The Turn of the Day* by Marion Angus, *Times Literary Supplement*, 20 August 1931, p. 635

Roll of Graduates of the University of Aberdeen, 1860–1900 (Aberdeen: Aberdeen University Press, 1906)

S., W., 'The Poetry of Marion Angus', *The Free Man*, 7 (1934), p. 10

Sackville, Margaret, 'Scottish Poets', *Scots Observer*, 3 October 1929, p. 21

S[almond], J. B., 'An Appreciation', *Arbroath Guide*, 25 August 1946, p. 6

'A Scotsman's Log', *Scotsman*, 21 August 1946, p. 4, in Scotsman Digital Archive, http://archive.scotsman.com/article.cfm?id=TSC/1946/08/21/Ar00406 [accessed 31 December 2005]

Shepherd, Nan, 'Marion Angus', *Scots Magazine*, October 1946, pp. 37–42

—, 'Marion Angus as a Poet of Deeside', *Deeside Field Club*, 2 (1970), pp. 8–16

Sketch of Arbroath Literary Club (Arbroath: Brodie and Salmond, 1896)

Taylor, Silvie, 'A Passion for the Splendour of Life', *Scots Magazine*, March 2001, pp. 304–8

'Three Scottish Poets', review of *Sun and Candlelight* by Marion Angus, *Scotsman*, 19 December 1927, p. 2, in Scotsman Digital Archive, http://archive.scotsman.com/article.cfm?id=TSC/1927/12/19/Ar00202 [accessed 31 December 2005]

'Two Scots Poets', review of *The Turn of the Day* by Marion Angus, *Scotsman*, 26 March 1931, p. 2 in Scotsman Digital Archive, http://archive.scotsman.com/article.cfm?id=TSC/1931/03/26/Ar00204 [accessed 31 December 2005]

W., N. K., 'Modern Scotswomen III: Marion Angus', *Scottish Standard*, April 1935, p. 29

Wheeler, Leslie W., 'Marion Angus (1866–1946)', in *Ten Northeast Poets: An Anthology*, ed. Leslie W. Wheeler (Aberdeen: Aberdeen University Press, 1985), p. 1

Whyte, Christopher, 'Marion Angus and the Borders of Self', in *A History of Scottish Women's Writing*, ed. Douglas Gifford and Dorothy McMillan (Edinburgh: Edinburgh University Press, 1997), pp. 373–88

Violet Jacob

Selected Volumes

Kennedy-Erskine, Violet and William Douglas Campbell, *The Bailie MacPhee* (Edinburgh: Blackwood, 1891)
Jacob, Violet and Helena Carnegie, *The Infant Moralist* (Edinburgh: Grant, 1903)
Jacob, Violet, *Bonnie Joann and Other Poems* (London: Murray, 1921)
—, *Flemington* (London: Murray, 1911)
—, *Fortune Hunters and Other Stories* (London: Murray, 1910)
—, *The Golden Heart and Other Fairy Stories* (London: Heinemann, 1904)
—, *The Good Child's Year Book* (London: Foulis, 1927)
—, *The History of Aythan Waring* (London: Heinemann, 1908)
—, *The Interloper* (London: Heinemann, 1904)
—, *Irresolute Catherine* (London: Murray, 1908)
—, *The Lairds of Dun* (London: Murray, 1931)
—, *More Songs of Angus and Others* (London: Country Life, 1918)
—, *The Northern Lights and Other Poems* (London: Murray, 1927)
—, 'Preface', in *The True Story of My Life* by Hans Christian Anderson, trans. Mary Howitt (London: Longman, 1847; London: Routledge, 1926), pp. vii–x
—, *The Scottish Poems of Violet Jacob* (Edinburgh: Oliver and Boyd, 1944)
—, *The Sheepstealers* (London: Heinemann, 1902)
—, *Songs of Angus* (London: Murray, 1915)
—, *Stories Told By the Miller* (London: Murray, 1909)
—, *Tales of My Own Country* (London: Murray, 1922)
—, *Two New Poems*, Broadsheet No. 12 (Edinburgh: Porpoise Press, 1924)
—, *Verses* (London: Heinemann, 1905)

Published Posthumously

—, *Diaries and Letters from India, 1895–1900*, ed. Carol Anderson (Edinburgh: Canongate, 1990)
—, *Flemington*, ed. Carol Anderson (London: Murray, 1911; Aberdeen: ASLS, 1994)
—, *Flemington and Tales from Angus*, ed. Carol Anderson (Edinburgh: Canongate, 1999)
—, *The Lum Hat and Other Stories, Last Tales of Violet Jacob*, ed. Ronald Garden (Aberdeen: Aberdeen University Press, 1982)

Selected Periodical Work

Jacob, Violet, 'Adam', *Country Life*, 14 August 1920, p. 206
—, 'Back to the Land', *Living Age*, 25 November 1925, p. 450
—, 'Bailie Bruce', *Country Life*, 12 April 1919, p. 412
—, 'The Baltic Brig', *Country Life*, 8 March 1919, p. 243
—, 'Baltic Street', *Country Life*, 17 April 1920, p. 505
—, 'The Banks o' the Esk', *Country Life*, 22 February 1919, p. 187
—, 'The Barley', *Living Age*, 13 January 1906, p. 66
—, 'The Beadle o' Drumlee', *Country Life*, 18 January 1913, p. 76
—, 'Bindweed', *Country Life*, 25 January 1919, p. 81
—, 'Bonnie Joann', *Country Life*, 1 February 1919, p. 107
—, 'The Brig', *Country Life*, 8 December 1917, p. 561
—, 'Cairneyside', *Deeside Field*, 6 (1933), p. 1
—, 'Chairlewain' ['Charlewayn'], *Country Life*, 15 February 1919, p. 161
—, 'A Change o' Deils', *Country Life*, 24 July 1915, p. 111
—, 'The Church and the Country-Side', *Country Life*, 2 July 1910, pp. 14–16
—, 'Craigo Woods', *Cornhill*, November 1913, p. 699
—, 'Craigo Woods', *Living Age*, 17 January 1914, p. 130
—, 'The Cross Roads', *Country Life*, 1 September 1923, p. 269
—, 'The Daft Bird', *Country Life*, 19 July 1919, p. 67
—, 'Day Before Yesterday, Anne', *Country Life*, 28 August 1920, p. 282–3
—, 'Day Before Yesterday, Parish Legends from Llanigon', *Country Life*, 11 September 1920, p. 347–8
—, 'The Doo'cot Up the Braes', *Christian Science Monitor*, 1 January 1919, p. 15
—, 'The End O't', *Country Life*, 3 January 1920, p. 9
—, 'Faur-ye-weel', *Country Life*, 2 April 1921, p. 390
—, 'The Field by the Lirk o' the Hill', *Country Life*, 13 May 1916, p. 579
—, 'The Flowers of the National Gallery', *Country Life*, 3 December 1921, pp. 739–41
—, 'Fringford Brook', *Country Life*, 25 December 1915, p. 860
—, 'From the Corner Seat', *Country Life*, 14 May 1910, p. 718
—, 'Frost-Bound', *Living Age*, 3 February 1906, p. 258
—, 'The Gangerel', *Country Life*, 11 June 1921, p. 713
—, 'The Gean-Trees', *Country Life*, 27 April 1911, p. 624
—, 'Geordie's Lament', *Country Life*, 17 December 1924, p. 1030
—, 'Glory', *Country Life*, 9 December 1916, p. 694
—, 'The Gowk', *Country Life*, 22 November 1913, p. 695

—, 'Hallowe'en', *Country Life*, 4 December 1920, p. 716
—, 'The Heid Horseman', *Country Life*, 17 January 1914, p. 84
—, 'The Howe o' the Mearns', *Cornhill*, February 1910, p. 210
—, 'The Howe o' the Mearns', *Living Age*, 9 April 1910, p. 66
—, 'Inverquharity', *Country Life*, 17 September 1921, p. 345
—, 'James the Fourth and His Poet', *Scots Magazine*, January 1929, pp. 276–82
—, 'Jock, to the First Army', *Country Life*, 5 February 1916, p. 163
—, 'John Macfarlane', *Country Life*, 5 November 1921, p. 569
—, 'The Kelpie', *Country Life*, 1 March 1919, p. 221
—, 'The Kirk Beside the Sands', *Country Life*, 28 August 1915, p. 283
—, 'Kirrie', *Country Life*, 8 November 1919, p. 575
—, 'The Lad i' the Mune', *Country Life*, 4 October 1913, p. 439
—, 'Lang Road', *Current Literature*, 41 (1906), pp. 496–7
—, 'Lang Road', *Living Age*, 15 December 1906, p. 642
—, 'The Last o' the Tinkler', *Country Life*, 7 August 1915, p. 183
—, 'The Licht Nichts', *Country Life*, 6 October 1923, p. 441
—, 'The Lilacs', *Christian Science Monitor*, 15 December 1914, p. 21
—, 'The Lost Licht', *Cornhill*, September 1912, pp. 312–13
—, 'A Manor House in Brittany', *Country Life*, 22 May 1920, pp. 685–6
—, 'Marsey Town', *Country Life*, 3 August 1918, p. 86
—, 'Montrose', *Country Life*, 23 June 1917, p. 644
—, 'Moonstruck', *Country Life*, 8 January 1921, p. 48
—, 'The Muckle Mou'', *Country Life*, 9 October 1920, p. 457
—, 'The Muirhen' ['The Water-Hen'], *Country Life*, 21 September 1912, p. 375
—, 'The Neep Fields by the Sea', *Country Life*, 2 June 1923, p. 772
—, 'The Northern Lights' ['The Northern Lichts'], *Country Life*, 13 August 1921, p. 183
—, 'Presage', *Country Life*, 14 October 1916, p. 423
—, 'Pride', *Country Life*, 12 June 1920, p. 790
—, 'Rejected', *Cornhill*, August 1915, pp. 198–9
—, 'The Road to Marykirk', *Country Life*, 8 May 1915, p. 611
—, 'The Scarlet Lilies', *Current Literature* 41 (1906), p. 465
—, 'The Shepherd to His Love', *Country Life*, 15 January 1916, p. 67
—, 'Tales of Country Life: Gwendoline's Hat', *Country Life*, 28 May 1910, p. 767
—, 'Tam i' the Kirk', *Country Life*, 12 November 1910, p. 668
—, 'The Tinkler Wife', *Country Life*, 2 December 1922, p. 700
—, 'The Tinkler Wife', *Scottish Chapbook*, 1 (1923), p. 330

—, 'The Tinkler's Baloo', *Country Life*, 24 January 1920, p. 99
—, 'The Tramp tae the Tattie-Dulie', *Country Life*, 26 June 1920, p. 901
—, 'The Twa Weelums', *Country Life*, 3 June 1916, p. 665
—, 'The Watch-Tower', *Living Age*, 20 January 1906, pp. 165–70
—, 'The Whistling Lad' ['The Whustlin' Lad], *Country Life*, 2 December 1911, p. 804
—, 'Whustlin' Lad', *Saturday Review of Literature*, 17 October 1925, p. 224
—, 'The Wild Geese', *Country Life*, 7 March 1914, p. 327
—, 'William Dunbar', *Country Life*, 19 March 1921, p. 350
—, 'The Wise-like Chap', *Country Life*, 17 January 1920, p. 69
—, 'A Young Man's Song', *Country Life*, 17 April 1920, p. 503

Selected Resources on Jacob's Work and Life

Anderson, Carol, 'Introduction', in *Diaries and Letters from India, 1895–1900*, ed. Carol Anderson (Edinburgh: Canongate, 1990), pp. 1–17
—, 'Introduction' in *Flemington and Tales from Angus*, by Violet Jacob, ed. Carol Anderson (Edinburgh: Canongate, 1998), pp. xi–xvii, 257–75
—, 'Jacob, Violet Augusta Mary Frederica (1863–1946)', in *Oxford Dictionary of National Biography*, ed. H. C. G. Matthew and Brian Harrison (Oxford: Oxford University Press, 2004), http://www.oxforddnb.com/view/article/58422 [accessed 15 Dec. 2005]
—, 'Spirited Teller of Tales from a Beloved Country', *Glasgow Herald*, 9 May 1998, p. 12
—, 'Tales of Her Own Countries: Violet Jacob', in *A History of Scottish Women's Writing*, eds Douglas Gifford and Dorothy McMillan (Edinburgh: Edinburgh University Press, 1997), pp. 347–59
Announcement of Marriage, *Scotsman*, 5 October 1894, p. 4 in Scotsman Digital Archive, http://archive.scotsman.com/article.cfm?id=TSC/1894/10/05/Ar0040731 [accessed 31 December 2005]
B., C. M., 'A Glance at the Field of New Literature — What Authors are Saying and Doing', review of *The Sheep Stealers* by Violet Jacob, *Los Angeles Times*, 5 October 1902, p. D10, in ProQuest Historical Newspapers, http://hngraphical.proquest.com [accessed 15 December 2005]
B., W. R., 'Cursive/Discursive', *Saturday Review of Literature*, 17 October 1925, p. 224

Bing, Sarah, 'Autobiography in the Work of Violet Jacob', *Chapman*, 74–5 (1993), pp. 99–109
'Biographical Notes: Officers Killed', *Scotsman*, 21 July 1916, p. 6, in Scotsman Digital Archive, http://archive.scotsman.com/article.cfm?id=TSC/1915/07/21/Ar00503 [accessed 15 December 2005]
'Books Which Children Will Read,' review of *The Golden Heart* by Violet Jacob, *Chicago Daily Tribune*, 2 December 1905, p. 10 in ProQuest Historical Newspapers, http://hngraphical.proquest.com [accessed 15 December 2005]
Broom, John, 'Some Neglected Scottish Novelists', *Catalyst*, 2 (1969), pp. 24–6
Buchan, John, 'Preface', in *Songs of Angus* by Violet Jacob (London: Murray, 1915), pp. vii–x
Burns, Robert, 'The Rantin Dog, the Daddie O't', in *The Complete Illustrated Poems, Songs, and Ballads of Robert Burns* (Secaucus, NJ: Chartwell, 1990), p. 342
Caird, Janet, 'The Poetry of Violet Jacob and Helen B. Cruickshank', *Cencrastus*, 19 (1984), pp. 32–4
Cook, Helen, 'The Flower of Angus', *Scots Magazine*, June 1997, pp. 616–19
Cran, Angela, 'Forgotten Spy Story Comes In From the Cold', review of *Flemington* by Violet Jacob, *Scotland on Sunday*, 11 December 1994, p. 13, in Lexis-Nexis, http://www.lexisnexis.com [accessed 21 January 2006]
Cumming, L. M., 'A Singer of Angus', *Scottish Bookman*, December 1935, pp. 35–45
'Death of Violet Jacob: A Notable Scottish Poet', *Scotsman*, 11 September 1946, p. 4, in Scotsman Digital Archive, http://archive.scotsman.com/article.cfm?id=TSC/1946/09/11/Ar00407 [accessed 21 January 2006]
'Edinburgh Graduation', *Scotsman*, 4 July 1936, p. 20, in Scotsman Digital Archive, http://archive.scotsman.com/article.cfm?id=TSC/1946/07/04/Pc02003/ [accessed 21 January 2006]
Ford, Mary K., review of *The Interloper* by Violet Jacob, *Current Literature*, 37 (1904), pp. 471–2
Garden, Ronald, 'Introduction', in *The Lum Hat and Other Stories* by Violet Jacob, ed. Ronald Garden (Aberdeen: Aberdeen University Press, 1982), pp. xiii–xx
—, 'The Scottish Poetry of Violet Jacob' (unpublished M.Litt. thesis, University of Aberdeen, 1976)
—, 'Violet Jacob in India', *Scottish Literary Journal*, 13 (1986), pp. 48–64
'Honorary Degrees: Edinburgh University Awards, Scotswoman Poet,' *Scotsman*, 14 March 1936, p. 14, in Scotsman Digital

Archive, http://archive.scotsman.com/article.cfm?id=TSC/1936/03/14/Ar01406 [accessed 21 January 2006]

Kazantzis, Judith, 'Preface', in *The Virago Book of Women's War Poetry and Verse*, ed. Catherine Reilly (London: Virago, 1997), pp. xxi–xxx

Keith, Alexander, 'Mrs Violet Jacob', in *Mine Honourable Friends: Essays and Odd Papers* (Aberdeen: Wyllie, 1922), pp. 96–102

—, 'Violet Jacob, the Sweet Singer of the Howe', *Aberdeen Press and Journal*, 14 September 1946, p. 2

'The Late Mr Kennedy-Erskine of Dun', *Scotsman*, 27 February 1908, p. 7, in Scotsman Digital Archive, http://archive.scotsman.com/article.cfm?id=TSC/1908/02/27/Ar00707 [accessed 15 December 2005]

Lochhead, Marion, 'Violet Jacob', *Scots Magazine*, November 1925, pp. 130–4

MacDiarmid, Hugh, 'Violet Jacob', in *Contemporary Scottish Studies* (London: Parsons, 1926; Edinburgh: Scottish Educational Journal, 1976), p. 8

'Montrose Old Church: £6000 Scheme of Alterations Approved', *Scotsman*, 10 February 1937, p. 14, in Scotsman Digital Archive, http://archive.scotsman.com/article.cfm?id=TSC/1937/02/10/Ar01409 [accessed 15 December 2005]

Murray, Isobel, 'The Forgotten Violet Jacob', review of *The Lum Hat and Other Stories: Last Tales of Violet Jacob*, *Cencrastus*, 13 (1984), p. 54

Obituary of Violet Jacob, *Times*, 11 September 1946, p. 7

Obituary of Violet Jacob, *Times*, 26 September 1946, p. 7

O'Hagan, James, 'A Feathered Feeding Frenzy', *Scotsman*, 12 November 1994, p. W16

'People in the Foreground: Violet Jacob', *Current Literature*, 37 (1904), p. 417

'Poems in Scots', review of *The Scottish Poems of Violet Jacob*, *Scotsman*, 23 March 1944, p. 7, in Scotsman Digital Archive, http://archive.scotsman.com/article.cfm?id=TSC/1944/03/23/Ar00700 [accessed 21 January 2006]

Reid, Charlotte, letter to the editor, *Cencrastus* 21 (1985), p. 59

Review of *Aythan Waring* by Violet Jacob, *New York Times*, 22 February 1908, p. BR104, in ProQuest Historical Newspapers, http://hngraphical.proquest.com [accessed 15 December 2005]

Review of *Bonnie Joann and Other Poems* by Violet Jacob, *Country Life*, 29 October 1921, p. 551

Review of *Bonnie Joann and Other Poems* by Violet Jacob, *Scots Pictorial*, 3 December 1921, p. 521

Review of *Flemington* by Violet Jacob, *Times Literary Supplement*, 30 November 1911, p. 493

Review of *Irresolute Catherine* by Violet Jacob, *Los Angeles Times*, 11 April 1909, p. 16

Review of *More Songs of Angus and Others* by Violet Jacob, *Scotsman*, 18 November 1918, p. 2, in Scotsman Digital Archive, http://archive.scotsman.com/article.cfm?id=TSC/1918/11/18/Ar00215 [accessed 15 December 2005]

Review of *More Songs of Angus and Others* by Violet Jacob, *Times Literary Supplement*, 28 November 1918, p. 587

Review of *Northern Lights and Other Poems* by Violet Jacob, *Scots Observer*, 1 October 1927, p. 14

Review of *Northern Lights and Other Poems* by Violet Jacob, *Times Literary Supplement*, 17 November 1927, p. 843

Review of *The Scottish Poems of Violet Jacob*, *Times Literary Supplement*, 15 April 1944, p. 191

Review of *The Sheep Stealers* by Violet Jacob, *Scotsman*, 1 September 1902, p. 2, in Scotsman Digital Archive, http://archive.scotsman.com/article.cfm?id=TSC/1902/09/01/Ar00206 [accessed 15 December 2005]

Review of *Songs of Angus* by Violet Jacob, *Scotsman*, 18 February 1915, p. 2, in Scotsman Digital Archive, http://archive.scotsman.com/article.cfm?id=TSC/1915/02/18/Ar00201 [accessed 31 December 2005]

Review of *Tales of My Own Country* by Violet Jacob, *Scots Pictorial*, 21 October 1922, p. 350

Review of *Tales of My Own Country* by Violet Jacob, *Times Literary Supplement*, 5 October 1922, p. 630

Review of *Two New Poems* by Violet Jacob, *Glasgow Herald*, 18 December 1924, p. 4

Review of *Two New Poems* by Violet Jacob, *Scotsman*, 15 December 1924, p. 2, in Scotsman Digital Archive, http://archive.scotsman.com/article.cfm?id=TSC/1924/12/15/Ar00226 [accessed 31 December 2005]

Review of *Verses* by Violet Jacob, *Scotsman*, 17 April 1905, p. 3, in Scotsman Digital Archive, http://archive.scotsman.com/article.cfm?id=TSC/1905/04/17/Ar00314 [accessed 31 December 2005]

'Scotch Without Dialect', review of *The Interloper* by Violet Jacob, *New York Times*, 13 August 1904, BR552, in ProQuest Historical Newspapers, http://hngraphical.proquest.com [accessed 15 December 2005]

'Scotswoman's Death: Suicide Verdict at Inquest', *Scotsman*, 28 December 1934, p. 6, in Scotsman Digital Archive, http://archive.scotsman.com/article.cfm?id=TSC/1934/12/28/Ar00600 [accessed 21 January 2006]

Sherwood, Mary, *History of the Fairchild Family: Or, the Child's Manual: Being a Collection of Stories (the Importance and Effects of a Religious Education)* (London: Hatchard, 1818; Roehampton: University of Surrey Roehampton Digital Library). http://wordsworth.roehampton.ac.uk/digital/chlit/shehis/ind.asp [accessed 15 December 2005]

'Strong Story of Devon', review of *The Sheep Stealers* by Violet Jacob, *Chicago Daily Tribune*, 31 October 1902, p. 13, in ProQuest Historical ProQuest Historical Newspapers, http://hngraphical.proquest.com [accessed 15 December 2005]

'Three Scottish Poets', review of *The Northern Lights and Other Poems* by Violet Jacob, *Scotsman*, 19 December 1927, p. 2, in Scotsman Digital Archive, http://archive.scotsman.com/article.cfm?id=TSC/1927/12/19/Ar00202 [accessed 31 December 2005]

Tweedsmuir, Susan, *The Lilac and the Rose* (London: Duckworth, 1952)

Vere-Hodge, Barbara, letter to the editor, *Scotsman*, 16 September 1946, p. 4, in Scotsman Digital Archive, http://archive.scotsman.com/article.cfm?id=TSC/1946/09/16/Ar00400 [accessed 31 December 2005]

Wandor, Michelene, 'An Unblushing Violet', review of *Diaries and Letters from India, 1895–1900* by Violet Jacob, *Sunday Times*, 15 July 1990, in Lexis-Nexis Academic, http://www.lexisnexis.com [accessed 5 December 2005]

Wheeler, Leslie W., 'Violet Jacob (1863–1946)', in *Ten Northeast Poets: An Anthology*, ed. Leslie W. Wheeler (Aberdeen: Aberdeen University Press, 1985), pp. 73–4

Other Sources

Additional Secondary Source Materials

An Anthology of Scottish Women Poets, ed. Catherine Kerrigan (Edinburgh: Edinburgh University Press, 1991)

Angus-Butterworth, L. M., *The Angus Poetical Tradition* (Edinburgh: Edinburgh Angus Club, n/d)

Bold, Alan, *MacDiarmid: The Terrible Crystal* (London: Routledge and Kegan Paul, 1983)

—, *Modern Scottish Literature* (London: Longman, 1983)

Boos, Florence, 'Working-Class Poetry', in *Companion to Victorian Poetry*, eds Richard Cronin, Alison Chapman and Anthony Harrison (Malden, MA: Blackwell, 2002), pp. 204–28

Borges, Jorge Luis, 'Time and J. W. Dunne', in *Other Inquisitions: 1937–1952*, trans. Ruth L. C. Simms (New York: Clarion, 1965), pp. 18–21

Burness, Catriona, '"Kept Some Steps Behind Him": Women in Scotland 1780–1920', in *A History of Scottish Women's Writing*, eds Douglas Gifford and Dorothy McMillan (Edinburgh: Edinburgh University Press, 1997), pp. 103–18

Crawford, Robert, 'MacDiarmid in Montrose', in *Locations of Literary Modernism: Region and Nation in British and American Poetry*, eds Alex Davis and Lee M. Jenkins (Cambridge: Cambridge University Press, 2000), pp. 33–56

Cruickshank, Helen, *Octobiography* (Montrose: Standard Press, 1976)

Devine, T. M., *The Scottish Nation: A History, 1700–2000* (London: Lane, 1999)

Dunn, Douglas, 'Language and Liberty', in *The Faber Book of Twentieth-Century Scottish Poetry*, ed. Douglas Dunn (London: Faber and Faber, 1992), pp. xvii–xlvi

Gibson, Colin, 'They Sang of Angus', in *Arbroath Herald Christmas Number* (Arbroath: Arbroath Herald, 1984), n/p

Gifford, Douglas, 'Re-Mapping Renaissance in Modern Scottish Literature', in *Beyond Scotland: New Contexts for Twentieth-Century Scottish Literature*, eds Gerard Carruthers, David Goldie and Alastair Renfrew (New York: Rodopi, 2004), pp. 17–37

Gordon, Katherine, 'Voices from the "Cauld, East Countra": Representations of the Self in the Poetry of Violet Jacob and Marion Angus' (unpublished doctoral thesis, University of Glasgow, 2000)

—, 'Women "Wha' Lauched and Lo'ed and Sinned": Women's Voices in the Work of Violet Jacob and Marion Angus', *Études Écossaises*, 9 (2003–4), pp. 73–89

Gregor, Walter, *Notes on the Folk-Lore of the North-East of Scotland* (London: Folk Lore Society, 1881; Internet Sacred Text Archive, 2004) http://www.sacred-texts.com/neu/celt/nes/index.htm [accessed 15 March 2006]

Grieve, C. M., 'Causerie', *Scottish Chapbook*, 1 (1922), pp. 62–3, quoted in *Modernism and Nationalism: Literature and Society in Scotland, 1918–1939: Source Documents for the Scottish Renaissance*, ed. Margery Palmer McCulloch (Glasgow: ASLS, 2004), p. 24–5 (p. 24)

Grieve, M[argaret], *A Modern Herbal: The Medicinal, Culinary, Cosmetic and Economic Properties, Cultivation and Folk-Lore of Herbs, Grasses, Fungi, Shrubs, & Trees With Their Modern Scientific Uses*, 2 vols (New York: Harcourt, 1931; Mineola, NY: Dover, 1971)

Hay, George, ed., *Round About the Round O With Its Poets* (Arbroath: Buncle, 1885), p. 113

Henderson, Andrew, *Scottish Proverbs*, rev. by James Donald (Glasgow: Morison, 1881; Detroit: Gale, 1969)

Hendry, Joy, 'Twentieth-Century Women's Writing: The Nest of Singing Birds', in *The History of Scottish Literature*, IV, ed. Cairns Craig (Aberdeen: Aberdeen University Press, 1987), pp. 291–310

Lehner, Ernst and Johanna, *Folkore and Symbolism of Flowers, Plants and Trees* (New York: Tudor, 1960; Mineola, NY: Dover, 2003)

Livingstone, Sheila, *Scottish Festivals* (Edinburgh: Birlinn, 1997)

Lochhead, Marion, 'Feminine Quartet', *Chapman* 27–8 (1980), pp. 21–31

'The Lyke-Wake Dirge', in *Border Ballads*, ed. William Beattie (London: Penguin 1952; repr. 1965), pp. 176–7.

MacDiarmid, Hugh, *Selected Poems*, eds Alan Riach and Michael Grieve (London: Penguin, 1992)

Mackie, Alastair, 'Change and Continuity in Modern Scots Poetry', *Akros*, 11 (1977), pp. 13–40

McCleery, Alastair, *The Porpoise Press: 1922–1939* (Edinburgh: Merchiston, 1988), p. 68

McClure, J. Derrick, 'The Language of Modern Scots Poetry', in *The Edinburgh Companion to Scots*, eds John Corbett, J. Derrick McClure and Jane Stuart-Smith (Edinburgh: Edinburgh University Press, 2003), pp. 210–32

—, *Language, Poetry, and Nationhood: Scots as a Poetic Language from 1878 to the Present* (East Lothian, Scotland: Tuckwell Press, 2000)

McCulloch, Margery Palmer, 'Fictions of Development 1920–1970', in *A History of Scottish Women's Writing*, eds Douglas Gifford and Dorothy McMillan (Edinburgh: Edinburgh University Press, 1997), pp. 360–72

McDowell, Lesley, 'Truth Is, The Lasses Have Had Little To Say', *Glasgow Herald*, 20 January 2000, p. 17, in Lexis-Nexis, http://www.lexisnexis.com [accessed 31 December 2005]

McMillan, Dorothy: see Porter

McNeill, F. Marian, *Hallowe'en: Its Origin, Rites, and Ceremonies in the Scottish Tradition* (Edinburgh: Albyn, 1970)

—, *The Silver Bough: A Study of the National and Local Festivals of Scotland*, 4 vols (Glasgow: MacLellan, 1957–1968; Edinburgh: Canongate, 1989)

McPherson, J. M., *Primitive Beliefs in the North-East of Scotland* (London: Longmans, 1929; New York: Arno, 1977)

Mellis, D. B. M. and W. J. Sinclair, 'The Parish of Dun', in *The Third Statistical Account of Scotland: The County of Angus*, ed. William Allen Illsley (Arbroath: Arbroath Herald Press, 1977), pp. 257–63

Milton, Colin, 'From Charles Murray to Hugh MacDiarmid', in *Literature of the North*, eds David Hewitt and Michael Spiller (Aberdeen: Aberdeen University Press, 1983), pp. 82–108

—, 'Modern Poetry in Scots Before MacDiarmid', in *The History of Scottish Literature*, IV, ed. Cairns Craig (Aberdeen: Aberdeen University Press, 1987), pp. 11–36

Modern Scottish Women Poets, eds Dorothy McMillan and Michel Byrne (Edinburgh: Canongate, 2003)

Modernism and Nationalism: Literature and Society in Scotland 1918–1939: Source Documents for the Scottish Renaissance, ed. Margery Palmer McCulloch (Glasgow: ASLS, 2004)

Norquay, Glenda and Gerry Smyth, 'Introduction: Crossing the Margins', in *Across the Margins: Cultural Identity and Change in the Atlantic Archipelago* (Manchester: Manchester University Press, 2002), pp. 1–10

Northern Numbers: Being Representative Selections from Certain Living Scottish Poets, ed. C. M. Grieve (Edinburgh: Foulis, 1920)

Northern Numbers: Being Representative Selections from Certain Living Scottish Poets, Second Series, ed. C. M. Grieve (Edinburgh: Foulis, 1921)

Porter [McMillan], Dorothy, 'Scotland's Songstresses', *Cencrastus*, 25 (1987), pp. 48–52

Radford, E. and M.A., *Encyclopedia of Superstitions*, ed. and rev. by Christina Hole (London: Hutchison, 1961)

Review of *Modern Scottish Poetry: An Anthology of the Scottish Renaissance, 1920–1945*, ed. Maurice Lindsay, *Times Literary Supplement*, 7 September 1946, p. 429

'Scotland as a Terra Incognita', *Glasgow Herald*, 14 July 1906, p. 9

'Scotland's Muse in Modern Dress', review of *Modern Scottish Poetry: An Anthology of the Scottish Renaissance, 1920–1945*, ed. Maurice Lindsay, *Scotsman*, 22 August 1946, p. 7, in Scotsman Digital Archive, http://archive.scotsman.com/article.cfm?id=TSC/1946/08/22/Ar00703 [accessed 31 December 2005]

Scottish Ballads, ed. Emily Lyle (Edinburgh: Canongate, 1994)

Scottish Literature, eds Douglas Gifford, Sarah Dunnigan and Lana MacGillivray (Edinburgh: Edinburgh University Press, 2002)

Simpson, A. Nicol, *From Sketches in Angus: Being a Series of Papers on the Natural History of Forfarshire* (Arbroath: Arbroath Herald, 1894)

Skoblow, Jeffrey, 'Scottish Poetry', in *A Companion to Twentieth-Century Poetry*, ed. Neil Roberts (Oxford: Blackwell, 2001), pp. 318–28

Smout, T. C., *A History of the Scottish People, 1560–1830* (New York: Scribner, 1969)

Spence, Lewis, 'Enchanted Scotland: Interaction of Racial Forces', *Scotsman*, 25 November 1940, p. 7, in Scotsman Digital Archive, http://archive.scotsman.com/article.cfm?id=TSC/1940/11/25/Ar00700 [accessed 31 December 2005]

—, 'Scots Poetry To-Day', *Nineteenth Century and After*, August 1929, pp. 253–68

Stevenson, Randall, *Modernist Fiction: An Introduction* (London: Longman, 1998)

Ten Northeast Poets: An Anthology, ed. Leslie W. Wheeler (Aberdeen: Aberdeen University Press, 1985)

The Virago Book of Women's War Poetry and Verse, ed. Catherine Reilly (London: Virago, 1997)

Wittig, Kurt, *The Scottish Tradition in Literature* (Philadelphia: Dufour, 1958)

Dictionaries

Concise Scots Dictionary, ed. Mairi Robinson (Edinburgh: Polygon, 1985)

Dictionary of Celtic Mythology, ed. James Mackillop (Oxford: Oxford University Press, 1998)

Dictionary of the Scots Language, ed. Susan Rennie (Dundee: Dictionary of the Scots Language Project, 2004), http://www.dsl.ac.uk/dsl/index.html

Jamieson's Dictionary of the Scottish Language, ed. John Longmuir (Edinburgh: Nimmo, Hay & Mitchell, 1895)

Oxford English Dictionary, various editions

Wordsworth Dictionary of Phrase and Fable: Based on the Original Book of Ebenezer Cobham Brewer, ed. and rev. by Ivor H. Evans (London: Wordsworth, 1993)

Archival Material and Illustrations

Birth Certificate, Esther Angus, Family Resource Centre, Islington, London

Census Returns, Arbroath, Scotland for 1881, 1891, Arbroath Public Library

Census Returns, Sunderland, England for 1871, Family Resource Centre, Islington, London

Drafts of poems by Violet Jacob, Montrose Library Archives

Violet Jacob's copy of *The Interloper* with insertions, Montrose Library Archives

Papers of James Christison, Montrose Library Archives

Papers of Helen Cruickshank, AUSC, MS 2737

Papers of Helen Cruickshank, Stirling University Library
Papers of Sir Patrick Geddes, NLS, MSS 10551, 10572
Papers of Charles Graves, NLS, MSS 27476, 27477, 27479, 27483
Papers of Neil Gunn, NLS, Dep. 209, Box 17, Folder 1
Papers of Mairi Campbell Ireland, NLS, MSS 19326, 19327, 19328
Papers and Journal of Harry Jacob, NLS, Acc. 11110, folios 1–5 (microfilm)
Personal Papers of Violet Jacob, NLS, MSS 27411-16, accession 11214
Papers of Alexander Keith, Porpoise Press, AUSC, MS 3017, folder 8/1/1
Papers of Roderick Watson Kerr, NLS, Acc. 5756
Papers of Marion Cleland Lochhead, NLS, MS 26109
Papers of Robert Macleod, NLS, MS 9997
Papers of Nan Shepherd, AUSC, MS 3036
Papers of Nan Shepherd, NLS, MS 27438
Papers of Mr and Mrs Waterson, Montrose Library Archives
Personal interviews, Nancy Cant, Arbroath, Scotland, c.1998–9
Photograph of Arbroath Literary Society, c.1893, Arbroath Public Library
Photograph of Marion Angus, no date, personal papers of Katherine Gordon
Photograph of the House of Dun, no date, used with permission from the National Trust for Scotland
Photograph of Marion Angus's childhood home, c.1998, personal papers of Katherine Gordon
Photograph of Violet Jacob, c.1936, used with permission from Angus Archives
Photograph of Zoar, c.2004, personal papers of Katherine Gordon
Private correspondence from Nancy Cant, Alistair Tough, Ian Johnson and Duncan Glen
W. S. Matthew's copy of *Selected Poems of Marion Angus*, with marginalia, Arbroath Public Library

Copyright Acknowledgements

The editor and publisher are extremely grateful to the following individuals and institutions for providing permission to reproduce copyright material in this volume:

Historic Collections, University of Aberdeen; Angus Archives, Angus Council Cultural Services; Alan J. Byatt; Dairmid Gunn; Malcolm U. L. Hutton; the Trustees of the National Library of Scotland; the National Trust for Scotland; Stirling University Special Collections.

THE ASSOCIATION FOR SCOTTISH LITERARY STUDIES

ANNUAL VOLUMES

Volumes marked * are, at the time of publication, still available from booksellers or from the address given opposite the title page of this book.

1971	James Hogg, *The Three Perils of Man*, ed. Douglas Gifford
1972	*The Poems of John Davidson*, vol. I, ed. Andrew Turnbull
1973	*The Poems of John Davidson*, vol. II, ed. Andrew Turnbull
1974	Allan Ramsay and Robert Fergusson, *Poems*, ed. Alexander M. Kinghorn and Alexander Law
1975	John Galt, *The Member*, ed. Ian A. Gordon
1976	William Drummond of Hawthornden, *Poems and Prose*, ed. Robert H. MacDonald
1977	John G. Lockhart, *Peter's Letters to his Kinsfolk*, ed. William Ruddick
1978	John Galt, *Selected Short Stories*, ed. Ian A. Gordon
1979	Andrew Fletcher of Saltoun, *Selected Political Writings and Speeches*, ed. David Daiches
1980	*Scott on Himself*, ed. David Hewitt
1981	*The Party-Coloured Mind*, ed. David Reid
1982	James Hogg, *Selected Stories and Sketches*, ed. Douglas S. Mack
1983	Sir Thomas Urquhart of Cromarty, *The Jewel*, ed. R.D.S. Jack and R.J. Lyall
1984	John Galt, *Ringan Gilhaize*, ed. Patricia J. Wilson
1985	Margaret Oliphant, *Selected Short Stories of the Supernatural*, ed. Margaret K. Gray
1986	James Hogg, *Selected Poems and Songs*, ed. David Groves
1987	Hugh MacDiarmid, *A Drunk Man Looks at the Thistle*, ed. Kenneth Buthlay
1988	*The Book of Sandy Stewart*, ed. Roger Leitch
1989*	*The Comic Poems of William Tennant*, ed. Maurice Lindsay and Alexander Scott
1990*	Thomas Hamilton, *The Youth and Manhood of Cyril Thornton*, ed. Maurice Lindsay
1991*	*The Complete Poems of Edwin Muir*, ed. Peter Butter

1992*   *The Tavern Sages: Selections from the 'Noctes Ambrosianae'*, ed. J. H. Alexander
1993*   *Gaelic Poetry in the Eighteenth Century*, ed. Derick S. Thomson
1994*   Violet Jacob, *Flemington*, ed. Carol Anderson
1995*   *'Scotland's Ruine': Lockhart of Carnwath's Memoirs of the Union*, ed. Daniel Szechi, with a foreword by Paul Scott
1996*   *The Christis Kirk Tradition: Scots Poems of Folk Festivity*, ed. Allan H. MacLaine
1997–8* *The Poems of William Dunbar* (two vols), ed. Priscilla Bawcutt
1999*   *The Scotswoman at Home and Abroad*, ed. Dorothy McMillan
2000*   Sir David Lyndsay, *Selected Poems*, ed. Janet Hadley Williams
2001*   Sorley MacLean, *Dàin do Eimhir*, ed. Christopher Whyte
2002*   Christian Isobel Johnstone, *Clan-Albin*, ed. Andrew Monnickendam
2003*   *Modernism and Nationalism: Literature and Society in Scotland 1918–1939*, ed. Margery Palmer McCulloch
2004*   *Serving Twa Maisters: five classic plays in Scots translation*, ed. John Corbett and Bill Findlay
2005*   *The Devil to Stage: five plays by James Bridie*, ed. Gerard Carruthers